A Structured Approach to Programming

second edition

JOAN K. HUGHES

President, Execudata

GLEN C. MICHTOM

Tandem Computers, Inc.

JAY I. MICHTOM

IBM I/S Management Institute

PRENTICE-HALL, INC., Englewood Cliffs, New Jersey 07632

Library of Congress Cataloging-in-Publication Data

Hughes, Joan Kirkby. (date)
   A structured approach to programming.

   Bibliography: p.
   Includes index.
   1. Structured programming.   I. Michtom, Jay I.,
1930-   . II. Michtom, Glen C.   III. Title.
QA76.6.H83 1987   005.1'13   86-30621
ISBN   0-13-854159-0

Editorial/production supervison and
   interior design: **Lisa Schulz Garboski**
Cover design: **Wanda Lubelska Design**
Manufacturing buyer: **S. Gordon Osbourne**

Printed in the United States of America

10 9 8 7 6 5 4 3 2 1

ISBN 0-13-854159-0   025

Prentice-Hall International (UK) Limited, *London*
Prentice-Hall of Australia Pty. Limited, *Sydney*
Prentice-Hall of Canada Inc., *Toronto*
Prentice-Hall Hispanoamericana, S.A., *Mexico*
Prentice-Hall of India Private Limited, *New Delhi*
Prentice-Hall of Japan, Inc., *Tokyo*
Prentice-Hall of Southeast Asia Pte. Ltd., *Singapore*
Editora Prentice-Hall do Brasil, Ltda., *Rio de Janeiro*

To Jill and Bill

"We'll never find another you."

Contents

Preface

Structured programming: some call it a *revolution*; others say it is the *way of the future.* Still others think it is a *fad* that will pass with time. Whichever it is, one thing is certain: after learning structured programming and its related technologies, you will undoubtedly change the way in which you solve problems using the computer. This book extends the concept of structuring from the program itself to the entire programming process.

The title, *A Structured Approach to Programming,* was selected to suggest that a total approach to programming is needed—a method requiring discipline in the specification, design, coding, and testing phases of a programming project. It is hoped that with a more formalized method of producing programs, programming will become more of a science.

The purpose of this book is to convey sound ideas and effective techniques needed for a structured approach. If you are a programmer, there is enough practical information for you to implement the techniques presented. If you are a manager, after reading this text you should be able to confidently manage or supervise others who are using structured programming methods.

This book is designed for anyone who is familiar with the basic concepts of programming. Because it is not an introduction to programming in general or to programming in a specific language, it would be appropriate to use this text in a course for which the prerequisites are one or more courses in programming. Professionals in the data processing field at any level would also benefit from the use of the techniques presented. Programmers and analysts could use these new ideas in their daily work. Project leaders and managers could, by understanding the concepts presented, promote the use of these technologies as well as supervise those who implement them.

A detailed knowledge of programming is not required; it is rather the understanding of the programming *process* that is important. Because the topics of program design, top-down development, structured programming, and testing are all presented in a language-independent manner, you do not need to be knowledgable in a specific programming language. However, if you are conversant with a specific programming language, you will find Chapters 8–11 of value.

A basic data processing terminology is presumed, but a glossary is included to ensure that you, the reader, and we, the authors, are using terms in the same way. New terms—those that have evolved as a result of this new discipline—are defined where first introduced in the text. If you are a manager, you will find the material in the "Management Implications" section of relevant chapters specifically oriented to the problems of management. If you are not a manager, you could skip these sections without loss of continuity; however, you may find them interesting as these will give you an insight into *the other side*.

Chapter 1 introduces the subject and presents an overview of the direction and organization of the book. Chapter 2 discusses program design where a *top-down development* approach is used, and Chapter 3 covers the planning and implementation phases of the top-down approach. Chapter 4 presents the basic constructs—sequence, choice, and repetition—as well as several optional structures in a language-independent manner. Chapter 5 explains how to develop a structured program where the technique used is called *stepwise refinement*. Chapter 6 presents a technique for helping to ensure valid, reliable programs—the *structured walk-through*, as well as information on inspections. Chapter 7 discusses some disciplined techniques for planning and running program tests. Chapters 8, 9, 10, and 11 are written in parallel fashion, each describing the application of structured programming principles to a particular language. The appropriate chapter(s) of these should be selected if you need to know structured programming at a detailed level. At the end of each chapter there is a summary and a set of review questions and exercises.

When the first edition was written, structured programming was relatively new. In the intervening years it has become a way of life. However, the basic principles still hold true. Some refinements have taken place, and the intent of this second edition is to include those that can make a significant difference in the quality of programs.

Two new language chapters have been added, Pascal and C. (Our thanks to Ross Nelson for his help with these chapters.) Chapter 9 on COBOL has been changed to address the changes that have taken place in the COBOL language and especially those useful for structured programming. Chapter 2 on top-down design has been greatly expanded to include both data flow diagrams and more on module characteristics to help design better programs, and Chapter 7 on testing incorporates a number of additions.

JOAN K. HUGHES
GLEN C. MICHTOM
JAY I. MICHTOM

1

A Programming Discipline

"Finding the deep simplicities in a complicated collection of things to be done is the creativity in programming."

H.D. Mills[1]

PROLOGUE

Not all the events in the following story took place on one program development effort. Rather, the story (or fable, if you will) is a composite of a number of actual circumstances taken from data processing projects as conducted in some installations today.

THE STORY OF THE DUPLICATE RECORD

Dan, a data processing analyst, meets with a potential user of a computing system installation to discuss the user's needs. As the user describes his information processing requirements in general terms, Dan thinks of clever ways in which to plan the programming of the solution to the problem. He even mentally writes some code. He breaks off the conversation as soon as it is polite to do so and hurries back to his desk to start work.

The design is completed in as short a time as possible and the coding is begun by two programmers—Marcia and Vern. They work on the most detailed parts first. Although they share an office, rarely do they review each other's work. They know, from programming school experience, that debugging will take a lot of time. So, in order to have sufficient time for debugging, they code the problem as fast as possible. Each routine is *designed* as it is programmed. As a routine is completed, Vern enters some test data as well as the *driver program* he has written to test the routine. The program *specifications* are interpreted independently by Vern and Marcia with some slight (but crucial as it is found out later) variations made. In addition, Dan makes a

[1]"New Discipline Wins Programmer Approval," *THINK*, IBM Corp., March 1973. Reprinted by permission from THINK Magazine, published by IBM, Copyright 1973 by International Business Machines Corporation.

minor change which he communicates to Marcia but not to Vern, who wasn't in the office when he stopped by to chat.

Marcia and Vern continue to code and test, finding as many bugs as they can. When asked about the status of a routine, they reply, "Just a few more bugs." After most of the routines are written, their response to the question of overall progress is, "It's about 90 percent complete." That response remains the same, week after week.

Toward the end of the coding phase, it is discovered that an extra three-character field is needed in the master record. The total record length has already been fixed, so Vern studies the record in detail and discovers three unused single characters at separate locations within the record; he decides to use them in his program to assemble the needed three-character field. The complete program is too large for main storage, so it is subdivided by arbitrarily placing special instructions in the program to cause portions of the program to *overlay* at execution time.

All parts are completed and *integrated* for final systems test. One week was scheduled for this purpose. The project is now five weeks late; overtime, including third shift and weekend time, is scheduled. Additional manpower is assigned to help in any way possible. For some inexplicable reason, certain records are being written out twice in succession into the file. A patch is made to the output routine to keep the last record and compare it with the current record and branch around the WRITE statement if a match is found. Confidence in the validity of the output is so low that another addition is made to sequence check the output records as they are written into the file.

Two major design flaws are uncovered. For one of them, it is decided to rewrite some of the routines. The other problem is too large a change to be incorporated into the program, so the limited documentation is updated with a restriction to the specifications.

As soon as the system goes into production, the user is upset because the system does not do what he had in mind. What's more, the environment has changed, necessitating further modifications to the programs. Due to the pressure of the schedule, the documentation was never completed, and the flowcharts that did exist at one time were not updated when the programs were debugged. Despite numerous patches—even some patches on patches—Vern and Marcia are proud of their system because it is full of tricky code which shows their real brilliance for programming.

A vast amount of time is spent maintaining and modifying the system. Finally it is decided to rewrite the application, and the process starts all over again.

The Moral of the Story   Inadequate planning and little use of disciplined, well-defined techniques lead to huge expenses in program development, maintenance, and modification.

WHAT IS STRUCTURED PROGRAMMING?

Is structured programming simply programming to a rigid set of rules? Is it writing subroutines or modules and combining them into one program? Is it more a science than an art? Is it the way some DP professionals have always written programs? Is it just new names for old ideas and procedures? Is it GOTOless programming? Is *unstructured* programming necessarily bad? In fact, what is *programming*?

A definition of *programming* might be "the design, writing, and testing of a program." By adding the word "structured," we could say that *structured programming* is "the design, writing, and testing of a program *in a prescribed pattern of organiza-tion.*"

In structured programming our attention is directed to *form* and *organization*. Just as a poet follows various forms of meter and rhyme when creating a poem, so a programmer follows basic logic structures when developing a program. These structures are defined later in this chapter, but they are mentioned here because some people think of structured programming as *programming in which only these basic logic structures are used.*

WHY THIS DISCIPLINE?

In the past, good programmers were thought to be those who wrote clever, tricky code that took the least amount of main storage and ran in the shortest possible time. This was justified because in the "old days" main storage was more expensive (therefore limited in size) and computers were much slower than they are today. The result of clever and tricky code was programs that were difficult, if not impossible, for someone else to read and maintain. In fact, programmers themselves often admitted having difficulty reading their own code six months later or even a month later. Virtually every program written is subsequently modified to meet changing specifications or eliminate bugs. Changes to intricate programs would further complicate reading them later. These programs have been referred to as *BS programs* because trying to unravel them reminds one of a Bowl of Spaghetti as in Figure 1-1.

With personnel costs rising faster than the increase in human productivity, most installation managers are concerned with how to increase productivity. Some modest gains have been made in this area, but greater improvements are needed. The majority of a programmer's time is spent finding and correcting errors in logic or modifying existing programs due to changes in specifications. A significant increase in program-ming productivity requires major improvements in program quality and ease of modi-fication.

One goal of structured programming is to avoid bad program structure. Another goal is to produce programs that can be read, maintained, and modified easily by other programmers. Many installation managers report that the costs of maintaining and modifying a program are greater than the costs of producing it, typically by a factor of three to five times. While that factor may not apply to all installations, the trend is that maintenance costs are high and rising. The result of making programs more readable, easier to debug, and easier to maintain is that the data processing operation is more efficient. This could reduce the percent of the DP budget devoted to software and personnel.

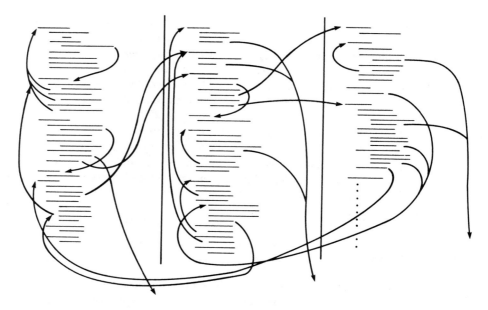

Figure 1-1. The spaghetti bowl

One of the initial spokespersons for structured programming was Professor Edsger W. Dijkstra. In its early days he stated, ". . . I think that we have learned so much that within a few years programming can be an activity vastly different from what it has been up till now—so different that we had better prepare ourselves for the shock." He believed that "well before the seventies have run to completion we shall be able to design and implement the kind of systems that are now straining our programming ability at the expense of only a few percent in man-years of what they cost us now, and that besides that, these systems will be virtually free of bugs."[2] Much of what he predicted has now come to pass.

Another early leader, Dr. Harlan D. Mills, an IBM manager of programming studies, draws an analogy between some present-day programming practices and that of a golfer who never considers his score. "We would probably laugh at a golfer who congratulates himself on completing 18 holes—but never counts his strokes. But that is exactly the attitude people have taken toward programming in the past. They may never ask themselves how many debugging runs they have made while developing their programs. Or, if their programs took up too much space in the computer's memory."[3]

---

[2]Edsger W. Dijkstra, "The Humble Programmer," 1972 A.M. Turing Award Lecture, *Communications of the ACM*, Vol. 15, No. 10, October 1972, p. 863. Copyright 1972, Association for Computing Machinery, Inc., reprinted by permission.

[3]H.D. Mills, "New Discipline Wins Programmer Approval," *THINK*, IBM Corp., March 1973. Reprinted by permission from THINK Magazine, published by IBM. Copyright 1973 by International Business Machines Corporation.

WHAT IS A STRUCTURED APPROACH?

As a result of criticisms like those of Dijkstra and of observations like those of Mills, we propose a three-part solution which we call a *structured approach to programming*:

- Top-down development
- Structured programming
- Structured walk-throughs

Actually, by combining the key words here, we could say that this book deals with *top-down structured programming*. The three techniques that make up the structured approach are briefly presented here to introduce the terminology. Each topic will be covered more thoroughly in separate chapters.

Top-Down Development

Traditionally, the design of an application is done from the top down, but the programming is done from the bottom up. How this might work is illustrated in Figure 1-2, an inventory control application. Each block could represent one program module or routine in the application. In a *bottom-up approach*, the lowest level routines are coded first. Thus, the program PREPARE STOCK STATUS REPORT might be assigned to one programmer for coding. Perhaps another programmer will code and debug the WRITE PURCHASE ORDERS module, while yet another programmer handles the PREPARE SHIPPING INSTRUCTIONS module.

When the lowest level routines are coded before higher level routines, it may be necessary to write driver routines to test these modules. Typically, driver routines send data to a module and receive output from a module. These driver programs may then examine and/or print the results so that the programmer may inspect intermediate results. For example, to test the WRITE PURCHASE ORDERS module, a driver must be written to send *data records* to that module. This driver routine must simulate to some degree the environment in which the finished program will be running; it must do some of the things the ANALYZE REORDER program (not yet written) is supposed to do. While driver routines are relatively simple, it does take time to write them. For the most part, they represent *throw-away code*. Since drivers are not part of the final program, resources are wasted in producing them.

In the traditional bottom-up approach we have been discussing, the lowest level routines are completed and tested. Then the next level routines are written and perhaps combined with the already written lower level modules for testing. Each higher level serves to test the assumptions made in the lower routines and points out inconsistencies or omissions made in them. Then higher and higher modules are tested until the entire program is completed. A problem with the bottom-up approach is that each module may work correctly with its driver, leading the programmer to think there are no more problems. Then when it is time to execute all the modules together, nothing works! How could this happen? There are a number of possible explanations. Some drivers

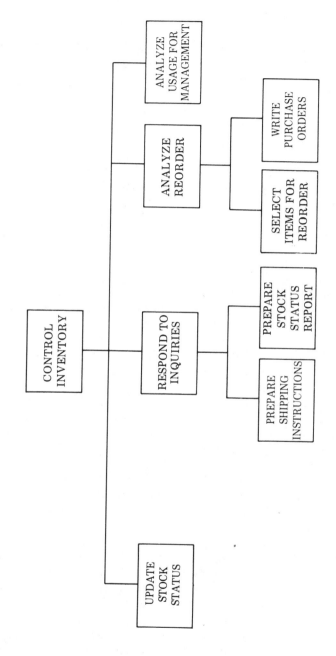

Figure 1-2 An inventory-control application

could have been written relatively early in the program development, but the specifications for the rest of the program could have changed in the interim. Or the specifications may have been interpreted differently by different people writing modules for the same program. Or, some aspects of the completed program may have been difficult or even impossible to simulate by driver routines.

Another problem with the bottom-up approach and the tendency to rush into coding is that there is often an accumulation of problems near the end of the development cycle. For example, in the ANALYZE REORDER section of Figure 1-2, it was discovered that simply including a *back-ordered-amount* in the inventory record wasn't enough. It was also desirable to include the date the purchase order was written so there could be subsequent follow-up should an item be back ordered for too long a period. This design change had impact on the PREPARE STOCK STATUS REPORT program (already coded and tested). Also, there was some question as to whether the PREPARE SHIPPING INSTRUCTIONS module belonged here or with the application that handled customer invoicing. At this point, in order to correct design errors, some of the alternatives are to patch the existing code to make the corrected design work, recode the whole problem, or modify the design to fit the existing code. This so-called *integration phase* of a project could become *redesign*, *recode*, *retest*, and *branch back to redesign*. It could end when a decision is made to put the program into production because the overrun of schedules is as much as the user will allow.

In *top-down development* both the design and programming are done from the top down. In this approach the functional specifications of a system and the program code are verified as being correct before going to a lower level of specification. Top-down development helps to eliminate problems associated with the bottom-up approach. It focuses on the partially completed program running throughout its development because there is continual integration and testing as program modules are developed.

Because modules are developed from the top down, *program stubs* standing in for routines to be developed in the next level down (Figure 1-3) must be used. A program stub consists of whatever minimal coding is required to allow the routine invoking it to be executed and tested. It may consist of nothing more than entry and exit statements and a message to the effect that this routine was executed. Optionally, it might also include coding to generate data required by higher modules. Stubs have some throw-away code, but the discarded amount is less than that of driver routines; stubs typically have simpler logic than do driver routines.

The higher level modules usually contain the overall logic and control of flow. Since these are coded first, the main logic of the module is validated first. The lower level modules usually contain exception routines or details which can well be deferred. In this way by doing the top first, you are virtually creating a *prototype* of the module. The stubs can later be expanded for the details. For further discussion of stubs, see Chapter 3.

In using the top-down-development technique, program designing in detail, coding, testing, and documenting can be done concurrently. Using this approach, it is possible in some cases to obtain computer output the first day these activities begin.

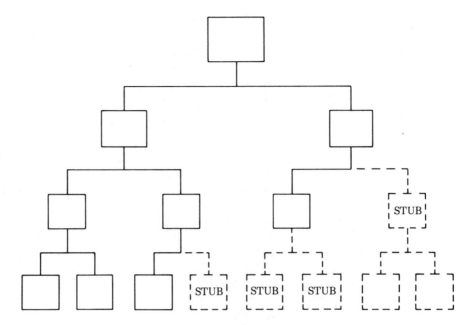

Figure 1-3. Top-down development using stubs

Note, however, that *detailed coding* is deferred. How to develop and implement a program using the top-down approach is discussed in Chapters 2 and 3.

Structured Programming

The Bowl of Spaghetti programs mentioned earlier are hard to follow primarily because of their complex flow of control. Structured programming, on the other hand, avoids this problem by:

1. limiting the number of control structures possible
2. allowing only those control structures that are simple and easy to follow

It has been proven that programmers can get by with only three structures. (For discussion of this proof, see the beginning of Chapter 4). Some people have opted to allow an additional structure or two, or permit slight variations in the three basic ones.

The three basic structures will be introduced here to give a brief overview before they are described in detail in Chapter 4. In these diagrams a *rectangle* represents an operation or function (e.g., a READ operation, a square root subprogram), a *diamond* represents a test, and a circle represents a merge point of two or more logic paths.

Sequence   This structure is the most fundamental of the structures; it provides for two functions to be executed in the order they appear.

These boxes might represent a single statement such as a READ or PUT or many statements such as those required to carry out a complex computation.

Choice or Selection   This structure is also called "IF THEN ELSE", usually written without the blanks. IFTHENELSE provides a choice between two alternatives. A test is made (via an IF statement), and then one of two paths is taken.

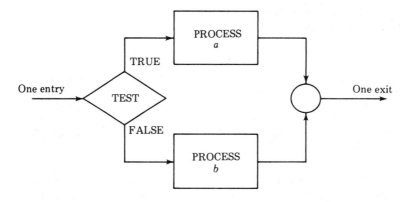

Each of the paths, the TRUE (or THEN) and the FALSE (or ELSE), leads to a common merge point so that processing continues in a forward direction regardless of which path is taken. Thus the structure has a single entry and a single exit. The decision paths may be labeled true/false, yes/no, on/off, etc.

It may be that for one of the results of the test there is no action to be performed. In that case only one of the process blocks would be included.

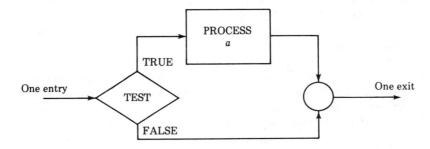

Or, the process box for which there is no action may be shown but labeled *null*.

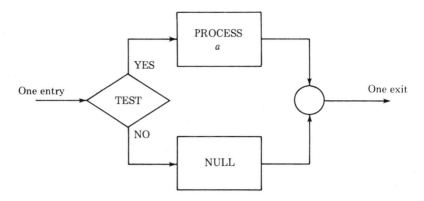

Loop or Repetition This structure provides for the repetitive execution or loop operation required by most computer programs. It is drawn as follows:

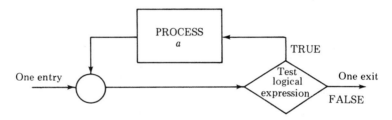

The flow passes through the merge point to the decision symbol. Here a *logical expression* is evaluated: if it is *true*, the *process* represented is executed and the expression is evaluated again. This iterative operation continues as long as the expression tested is true. When it becomes *false*, there is an exit from the structure. Because the expression controlling the loop is tested *first* (before the process is ever executed) it is possible that a false condition may initially exist—in which case the process statements are never executed. The statements represented by the *process* box must modify the control variable affecting the test—otherwise, the program would be in an endless loop. This repetition structure could encompass many statements—perhaps the bulk of the program. It is called a DOWHILE, meaning, "*do* (i.e., execute statements in the process box) *while* the logical expression specified is true."

These three structures are all you need. In later chapters optional structures are discussed, including a CASE structure (a generalization of the IFTHENELSE), and the DOUNTIL (a variation of the DOWHILE).

These structures may be combined with each other as required by the logic of the program. That is, whenever a single process box appears in the diagrams, it may be replaced by any of the allowed structures. In the diagram on the next page, the top box of the IFTHENELSE has been replaced by a DOWHILE.

In this way these building blocks can be combined in endless variations to solve all types of program logic requirements. Although the flow is pictured as left to right, these structures may be drawn so that flow is top to bottom.

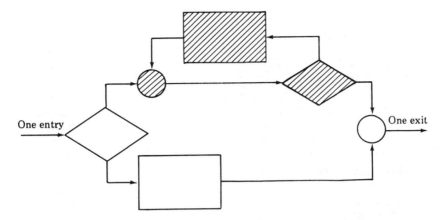

Using the basic structures just defined, it is possible (depending on the programming language used) to write programs that have *no GOTO statements*. For this reason, structured programming is sometimes referred to as *GOTOless programming*. However, this is too narrow a definition and impossible in some programming languages. The point is that the elimination of the GOTO is a by-product of expressing program logic by using only these structures.

Of course, the uncontrolled use of the GOTO as illustrated in Figure 1-1 must be avoided. There has been a debate as to whether or not the GOTO can or should be completely eliminated. Dijkstra was instrumental in challenging thinking in this area. In his classic letter to the editor of *Communications of the ACM*,[4] he wrote:

> For a number of years I have been familiar with the observation that the quality of programmers is a decreasing function of the density of **go to** statements in the programs they produce. More recently I discovered why the use of the **go to** statement has such disastrous effects, and I became convinced that the **go to** statement should be abolished from all "higher level'" programming languages (i.e., everything except, perhaps, plain machine code).

Knuth, however, has identified some specific areas where the GOTO may be justified.[5] One situation would be where the programming language being used does not have the necessary structure. In that case the structure can be simulated by a very defined and controlled use of the GOTO. This would be satisfactory as long as you preserved the principle of one entry and one exit, and defined flow of control.

Structured programming is not merely GOTOless programming. It is a disciplined approach that encompasses a number of technologies in an effort to produce clear,

[4]Edsger W. Dijkstra, "GO TO Statement Considered Harmful," *Communications of the ACM*, Vol. 11, No.3, March 1968, p. 147. Copyright 1968, Association for Computing Machinery, Inc., reprinted by permission.

[5]See Donald E. Knuth, "Structured Programming with **go to** Statements," *Computing Surveys*, Vol. 6, No. 4, December 1974. Copyright 1974, Association for Computing Machinery, Inc.

readable code. It is possible to write structured programs that contain GOTOs as well as unstructured programs that have no GOTOs.

Another by-product of using only the basic structures is that the logic flow of a program will be from *top to bottom*. That is, specified program statements will be executed in the order in which they appear in the source program listing. Of course, some blocks of code will be *skipped over* (as in the case of the IFTHENELSE), and some will be repeated (as in the case of the DOWHILE), but the branching will always be in a forward manner. This forward direction of program logic makes a program easier to read when it must be modified.

Structured Walk-throughs

A structured walk-through is a generic name coined by IBM for a series of reviews, each with different objectives and each occurring at a different time in the application development cycle. The basic plan is to have every part of the development effort carefully examined by people who are technically competent to do so and who have a vested interest in the success of the effort. Walk-throughs are used to review specifications with the user, to review the design to ensure that specifications are being met, and to review the test plan and test data. Programmers walk through each other's code together *before* their programs are compiled.

To understand the mechanics of a structured walk-through, assume that a programmer is working on part of a large program's detailed design.

1. When the programmer is ready, a walk-through session is arranged. Several colleagues are invited to review how the data interfaces between this module and the rest of the system are being handled.

2. When the meeting is scheduled, participants are informed of the purpose of the walk-through. They also receive material (e.g., spec sheets, assumptions, logic flow) to review before they come to the session. They are expected to be familiar with this material by the time of the meeting. *Thus, the walk-through is structured in the sense that all participants know what is to be accomplished and what role they are to play.*

3. The review session is conducted by a moderator. This could be the programmer or one of the other participants. It is not the *manager* of the programmer: management does not attend the walk-through, nor is a walk-through used as a basis for employee evaluation.

4. During the session, errors are detected and recorded but not corrected. One of the attendees serves as recorder and develops a *list of exposures* (i.e., errors or omissions). This list could be distributed to all reviewers for their reference.

5. Depending on the number and type of exposures found, this walk-through process may be repeated until no more *exposures* are detected. Then the program moves into the next stage of the development effort.

Thus, a structured walk-through is a tool for analyzing the design of a system and uncovering logic errors early in the design of a program. It is a method for reducing the number of coding errors that may enter a system. Reviews can be positive motivators for the project team as well as learning experiences for the team. All technical members of the project team, from most senior to most junior, are participants in this review process.

In summary, a structured walk-through is a productive working session which not only tracks progress but makes a positive contribution to that progress. The mechanics and psychology of a structured walk-through are described in Chapter 6.

IMPLICATIONS FOR MANAGEMENT

Top-Down Development

When systems design and programming are done top-down, managers have more control over the progress of program development. In the traditional approach, where the coding and testing were done from the bottom up, managers never knew just where the project stood. While they could determine which modules were apparently checked out, they could not predict the new errors that would undoubtedly show up in the final integration of the program.

Frequently the final integration of program modules into one *system* is begun near the end of the project. When new bugs are found at this point, the project deadline slips. The point is that, when using the bottom-up approach, a manager can review programmers' work weekly but not know for months just how near completion a programming task is. In the top-down development approach, it is possible to obtain valid and verifiable output at the beginning of the project as well as throughout the project development cycle. In other words, a system can be operational and can be continually tested while it is being built.

Structured Programming

When a programmer designs and codes a program using the basic structures introduced in this chapter, the benefits are threefold: improved source program *readability*, improved program *reliability*, and improved program *maintainability*. Once the structured approach is mastered, it is possible to produce code that has few or no errors. The need for detailed flowcharts to explain a program will be reduced or eliminated. Documentation time will be reduced because the programs themselves will be self-documenting. Programmer productivity is increased, thereby reducing personnel costs.

The structured approach incorporates a philosophy which emphasizes planning by encouraging or even forcing programmers to defer the details. Each stage of a development effort should be carefully done—avoiding specifics in the early stages. Too often, in the realm of programming, there is a tendency to get down to the coding level as quickly as possible for three reasons:

1. To many programmers, it is the most interesting and exciting part of their work.

2. To some managers or project leaders, no *work* is being done unless lines of code are being written.

3. The steps for coding a problem (such as generating the PREPARE STOCK STATUS REPORT) are well defined, whereas there are no precise methods or rules for thinking through overall logic and design.

However, for the success of a development effort, it is important—in the words of Harlan Mills—to "resist the urge to code."

Structured Walk-throughs

A structured walk-through is designed to detect and correct errors as early as possible in the development cycle, when the cost of correcting errors is lowest and their impact smallest. It is not a *project review* in the traditional sense because management is not directly involved in the review session. Management, of course, can be advised of the progress by the team leader. From a *personnel development* point of view, participants in structured walk-throughs have the opportunity to learn new techniques or refine their skills through the process of reviewing each other's work.

EPILOGUE

In contrast with the story at the beginning of this chapter, let us relate a development effort of a clothing manufacturer in North Carolina that used the structured approach. Unlike the earlier story, which was a composite of many incidents occurring on different projects, the following events occurred on a single project at one installation.

A data processing team of three people was assigned to the project. One of the members served as *team leader*. Part of the leader's work assignment included reviewing the work of the other two members and advising management as the project progressed. All three members had experience in both analysis and programming, and during the life of the project they worked in both capacities.

After initial meetings with the user for whom the program was to be written, the team met to discuss the problem, clarify the requirements, and uncover omissions in the specifications. Then they met again with the user, presenting in detail their understanding of the requirements. In this *walk-through* session, the specifications were discussed and mutually agreed upon. The team was ready to begin designing the program.

Designing the program was an iterative procedure. The highest level modules were defined first and reviewed carefully. Then, proceeding in a top-down fashion, lower modules were identified. When walk-throughs revealed deficiencies or omissions from the specifications, the design was revised. When it was felt that the design was firm, the highest level modules were coded and tested in a top-down fashion. Stubs were created as needed. Initially, the overall design was tested when these high-level controlling modules were executed. The detailed design of the lower modules was completed and coding proceeded downward, with previously coded stubs being expanded into modules. Each module was coded by using the basic structures introduced in this chapter. This necessitated the programmers' carefully planning each module before coding it. The team members were open and nondefensive about their work when they read each other's code to detect errors in design or logic.

As each module was completed, it was integrated into the expanding program by testing it with the other modules. Each module executed correctly the first time it was run! There were no logic errors in the entire program, which consisted of ten modules and a total of 7200 lines of code. The final test consisted of a single run during which the program executed correctly as a unit. There were no interface errors.

The project was completed 5 percent ahead of schedule—without overtime work. (Previous projects at this installation had used traditional techniques, and the allotted time schedules had typically been exceeded.) Thus, the extra efforts to produce correct code did not lengthen the project.

Computed over the length of the project, the number of debugged lines of high-level-language code per programmer per day was 99. Computed over the programming phase only, the number of lines of code per programmer per day was 212. Their productivity was approximately four times the rate attained on previous similar projects at that installation. The resulting program was modular in design and had clear, easy-to-read code. Additional benefits are anticipated as a result of simplified maintenance. Similar results are being attained at other installations where the top-down structured approach is being used.

SUMMARY

A threefold approach to the handling of errors is proposed: (1) minimize errors by using only allowable structures (sequence, choice, repetition) (2) uncover errors as early as possible, and (3) take steps to make the finding and correcting of later errors as simple and inexpensive as possible. Obviously, the fewer the errors, the better. Some results have been compiled on the relative cost of finding and correcting errors based on when they are found. Early detection means less cost, and the magnitude of difference runs to factors of ten, 20, and even 30!

Structured programming "could revolutionize programming in several ways. The most obvious benefits are increased productivity and reduced error rates. Programming is perhaps on the verge of becoming a science instead of a craft. The analogy has been made that the hardware people have known for years that any logic circuit can be made up from a few basic primitives, such as the 'AND' and 'OR' operations. Programming is now approaching something of the same maturity."[6]

[6]Daniel D. McCracken, "Revolution in Programming," *Datamation*, December 1973, pp. 50-52. Reprinted with the permission of DATAMATION® Copyright 1973 by Technical Publishing Company, Greenwich, Connecticut 06830.

"If structured programming is adopted as standard, then it may become necessary to write all programs to meet this standard. Even if such a standard is not adopted, programmers should know the concepts underlying structured programming, as part of their continuing effort to produce more effective, clearly written programs."[7]

REVIEW QUESTIONS AND EXERCISES

1. Define structured programming.
2. List the two main goals of structured programming.
3. Is structured programming GOTOless programming? Why or why not?
4. What are the characteristics of the top-down approach?
5. What kinds of problems do you see in implementing a structured walk-through technique in an installation where programmers have never had their work reviewed by colleagues or project leaders?
6. Name as many characteristics of a structured program as you can recall.
7. Take a copy of a program that you have written and report on its readability and clarity of logic. How would you improve the program if given a second chance at "reworking" it?

[7]John M. Morris, "Structured Programming," Pattern Analysis & Recognition Corp., Rome, N.Y., Tech Memo #73-20, 1973, p. 2.

2

Top-down Development:
Program Design

MURPHY'S LAWS · *Things are more complex than they seem to be.*
· *Things take longer than expected.*
· *Things cost more than expected.*
· *If something can go wrong, it will.*

CALLAHAN'S COROLLARY TO MURPHY'S LAW
· *Murphy was an optimist.*

MODULARITY

The intense interest in structured programming may be a manifestation of a growing awareness that "Murphy was right" as well as a coming maturation of computing. Structured programming is an outgrowth of the fact that "things are complex," and that "things take longer and cost more than expected." Top-down development should reduce the program's complexity and enable the program to be completed on time. If "something does go wrong," it provides the means to find problems earlier in the development process—thereby allowing time to correct them.

Top-down development can be applied to the *design phase* of a *system*, including the design of programs within a given system and the design of modules within a given program. It can also be adapted for design of the logic within a module. This is called *stepwise refinement* and is covered in Chapter 5. Since this book deals specifically with programming, we will not be getting into the other aspects of system design, notably data definition and structure. Should you be writing a program using data that already exists, you will need to take the structure of the data into account early. It may affect the design of your program significantly.

Figure 2-1 shows a payroll system which includes a weekly payroll program, a payroll register program, a check-writing program, a file-maintenance program for additions (employees hired), deletions (employees terminated), and changes (pay rate change, payroll deduction change, etc.), state and local government quarterly report programs, and a W-2 form-preparation program. In this figure the top box, payroll system, does not represent code, but is simply the name of the system and could be thought of as representing run instructions and all documentation.

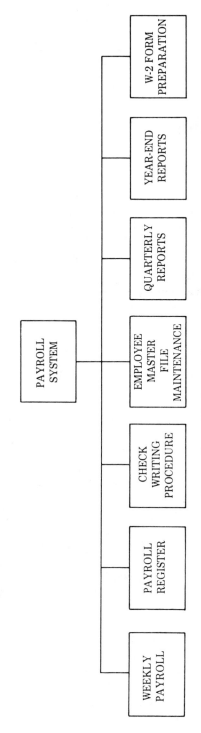

Figure 2-1. Programs in a payroll system

Each of the programs in this payroll system accomplishes a major task. Some of these programs are complex, in that they must perform a variety of operations. For example, the weekly payroll program does, among other things, the following:

- Gets employee time information and edits for validity
- Prepares control information for audit purposes
- Computes current pay
- Updates employee master
- Computes year-to-date pay fields and updates appropriate file(s)

Programs such as weekly payroll are easier to design and implement if they are further divided into modules. A *program,* then, accomplishes a major task, consists of one or more modules, and may be part of a system. A *module* is a collection of logically related code that is part of a program.

The concept of modularity is not new. Since the early 1960s, modular programming has been stressed. It offers the following advantages:

1. It allows a large program to be written by several people, thus providing the possibility of earlier completion.
2. It encourages the creation of commonly used routines to be placed in a library.
3. It simplifies the overlay procedure of loading a large program into main storage.
4. It provides more checkpoints on which to measure progress.
5. It provides a framework that should allow for more complete testing.
6. It simplifies design, making the program easier to modify.

Of these six advantages, the last three are particularly significant to installations that have had difficulties in producing well-tested programs on schedule. They have a major impact on the cost of developing, testing, debugging, and maintaining programs. The last item has increased in importance as the cost of maintaining and modifying programs has assumed a larger portion of data processing expenses.

Weighed against these advantages are some liabilities, which occasionally result in increased costs:

1. Execution time may be, but isn't necessarily, longer.
2. Storage size may be, but isn't necessarily, increased.
3. Compile and load time may be longer.

With current compilers and operating systems, these disadvantages are small and are usually offset by reduced development and *maintenance* costs.

Characteristics of a Module

This chapter deals with how to design a program—that is, *decompose* a program into its component modules—in a top-down fashion. Before we can discuss top-down development, it is important that you have a clear understanding of a module. Let us begin by listing some desirable characteristics of a module.

1. A module is a separate compilation unit (or part of a *batch compile*). This characteristic, while highly desirable, is not always possible. Some compilers, especially on small systems, don't allow separately compiled modules.

2. The statements are collectively referred to by a descriptive name, called the module name.

3. A module could be invoked by the operating system or by another module. When completing its action it returns to the routine that invoked it.

4. A module may call or invoke other modules.

5. A module should have a single *entry* and *exit*. There are cases where writing a subroutine with multiple entry points could save some redundant coding as well as minimize main storage requirements. However, in a study of companies using modular programming, it was found that users elected to have near duplicate modules rather than allow several entry and exit points in one module. The reasons given were that single-entry and single-exit modules ensure that the modules are closed and simplify program maintenance.[1]

6. A module is relatively small in size. Rarely should a module exceed several hundred lines of source code. Typically, they are 50 to 100 lines, just one or two pages of executable source statements. "Using small modules has certain advantages. Installations found that small modules allowed for more easily amended programs, modules were more likely to be reused, estimating and project control were more accurate, exhaustive testing was easier, and trainee and inexperienced programmers could be better utilized. Conversely, small modules do demand more initial design time, more linkages are required, run-time could be longer, more source lines must be written, more documentation is needed, and writing them may be less satisfying for the programmer."[2]

7. The module itself should not keep a history of what has occurred on previous invocations for the purposes of modifying its action or logic path. For example, a count of how many times a module has been called should be kept by the caller, not the module itself.

---

[1]John Rhodes, "Tackle Software with Modular Programming," reprinted from COMPUTER DECISIONS, July 1975. Copyright 1975, Hayden Publishing Company.
[2]Ibid.

8. A module has a single function: *the transformation of input to output that occurs when the module is executed.* It is the change that takes place from the time the module is entered until it completes its action. Ideally, each module should perform exactly *one* function and perform *all* of that function. The concept of *one module, one function* is the key to a well-designed program. In other words, a module is a program entity that does its own thing and whose function can be described in one sentence. Here are some examples of one-sentence functions:

- Edit transaction
- Load master file
- Compute weekly pay
- Compute nine-month moving average
- Invert matrix
- Print stock status report

Modules which perform a single function are most likely to be reusable by other programs. In time, a number of these modules can be collected in a library to simplify later programming. Using an analogy to manufacturing, these become "subassemblies" to be incorporated into various "products."

In designing a program, then, the functions that need to be performed become the program's modules. For example, the UPDATE MASTER FILE program in the payroll system we have been illustrating might basically contain the following modules:

1. A module to *read* a transaction.

2. A module to *modify* an existing record in a master file (change in pay rate, deductions, etc.).

3. A module to *add* a record to the master file (employee hired).

4. A module to *move* a record from the active master file to an inactive file (employee terminated).

Figure 2-2 shows each module's function as well as a relationship between the modules. In this example, the top module—which is described by the overall function of the program—invokes the other modules as needed.

It is important to realize that at this point of program design, nothing has been stated about *how* each module carries out its function. We are not concerned with program implementation yet. What is important is that the *invoking* module (e.g., the top module in Figure 2-2) regard the *invoked* module (e.g., ADDITIONS) as the proverbial "black box." A *black box* is known by its name and the results it produces. A user of the black box should not have to know anything about the box's internal operation.

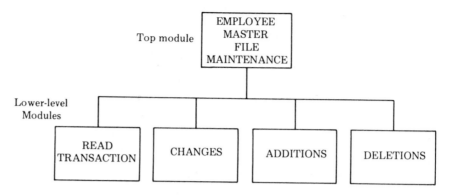

Figure 2-2. Program subdivided into modules

Module Definition

Modules can be defined in various ways; some much better than others. You must ask of each module you create, "What does it do?" "What is its purpose?" A module is a collection of code, but what holds it together? There are different kinds of modules, based on the principle that is used to define what they do. This factor is referred to as the *binding* or *cohesion* of a module in a classic paper by Stevens, Myers, and Constantine.[3]

The best principle for a module's definition is that it performs a single function, as do those shown in Figure 2-2. For example, the top module produces updated records. Of course, this module will have to call on other modules to help it carry out its function.

An advantage of modularizing based on function is that it enhances the possibility of modules being used elsewhere. For example, the READ TRANSACTIONS module might be used by a PERSONNEL FILE UPDATE program because the same type of record formats are also processed by that application. Another advantage of modularizing based on function is that a module can be easily tested. Since the function is the transformation of input to output, the input and expected output are known at the time a module is defined. Then the module can be tested to verify that, given a defined set of input, the desired output is, in fact, produced.

Less desirable are modules written to perform more than one function. There is a tendency to do this if the two functions are closely related, particularly if they use the same data. It is especially tempting to define a module in terms of two functions if in addition to using the same data, the output of one is the input of the other. An example of this is a module that first reads and then edits a record. However, as tempting as it is, you should resist combining the two functions into one module. The savings, if any,

[3]W. P. Stevens, G. J. Myers, L. L. Constantine, "Structured Design," *IBM Systems Journal*, Vol. 13, No. 2, 1974. Form No. G320-5323.

will be small, and the ability to reuse this multiple-function module will be compromised.

Be careful not to embrace modularity in name only. That is, don't create "modules" that are so poorly defined, they negate the advantages of modularity. Some programmers create modules that are really only a collection of small, unrelated actions, grouped together merely for convenience. Such a rationale might seem acceptable if the actions are all simple, such as the assignment of initial values at the beginning of a program, but even here see if these can be grouped together in some meaningful way to simplify later modification.

Possibly the worst type of module is what Stevens[4] called a *logical* module. In spite of its positive sounding name it has probably caused more programming problems and wasted more time than any other programming practice.

The practice is to combine into one general module a group of functions that perform similar operations—for example, a module to edit any one of various types of records or to perform one of a set of different calculations. In our previous example (Figure 2-2), had we combined CHANGES, ADDITIONS, and DELETIONS into a single module, it would have been a "logical" module.

A programmer's intent is generally to minimize code because some parts of the functions to be combined are the same. Thus some of the code they need could be common, and shared. Usually, the module is sent an indicator telling it which function it is to perform. Then it executes the common code and, where necessary, tests the indicator to determine which of alternative paths to follow.

The problem here is that the various functions get entangled with each other. Some of the common code may be common to only a subset of the functions, and soon the module contains many tests and branches. Correcting errors, and subsequently making changes to the module, becomes very difficult. Usually the changes pertain to one of the functions but not the others, and that's where the real trouble begins.

A better approach is to define each function as a separate module. Then, to avoid duplicate code, the common parts are removed and made into additional modules. These can then be invoked from each of the separate modules. This permits each of the functions to be tested, debugged and modified easily.

Module Interactions

Another important consideration in program design is the way in which your modules interact with each other. The goal is to make each module as independent of the others as possible. You will find this isolation very helpful in debugging. An error in one module has limited effect on the others and can more easily be traced and corrected.

There are three factors which determine how closely two modules are coupled together:

[4]Wayne P. Stevens, *Using Structured Design* (New York: John Wiley, 1981).

1. How much data is shared between them

2. How the sharing of data occurs

3. How much one module "knows" about the internals of the other and depends on that knowledge

This third point is also known as *information hiding*. In designing and writing modules, keep the details of how one module works a secret from other modules. The internal actions of one module should not affect the others. No module should ever be aware of data such as counters or indicators that are intended for the internal use of another.

The more data modules need to share, the more closely associated they are, which probably indicates that they are not really separate functions as described in the preceding section. They may be just groups of code, or perhaps a single function has been scattered among several modules.

A good way to test for modules with well-separated functions is, after defining the modules in your program, to list the data that needs to be shared between pairs of modules. If the number of data items is more than a few, you should reexamine the definition of your modules to see if they can be improved.

The second coupling factor is how the sharing of data takes place. If modules have been compiled together (necessary in some systems), then it is possible for a module to "reach into" another module and access or change its data. It woiuld therefore be closely-coupled with that module, and any change in the second module could have unexpected and dramatic effects on the first. This problem can usually be avoided if the modules can be compiled separately. Otherwise it simply requires discipline to identify all data that is to be used only from within a module, and avoid all references to it from outside the module.

Another way of sharing data is to have separately compiled modules reference a common pooled collection of data. This has been widely done with features such as PL/I's EXTERNAL, FORTRAN's COMMON, or COBOL's linkage section. Although this is sometimes convenient, the practice frequently gets out of hand. Many modules may reference the same data. If they change the data it soon becomes difficult to find out who changed what data. Again, debugging and modifying the program become harder. Therefore, the use of this type of data sharing, called *global variables*, should be minimized. The best way to share data is by explicitly passing named data elements. Here it is immediately obvious which data items are shared among which modules. The modules remain independent of each other.

The data items sent by a higher level module are known as *arguments*. The data received by a lower level module are known as *parameters*. (In some languages, such as Pascal, *parameters* are referred to as *formal* parameters, and *arguments* as *actual* parameters.) The parameters often become a definition of the module's function. In addition to simplifying the structure, passing data by parameter frequently leads to the creation of modules that can be used in other programs.

There are times when arguments are passed to a module but the calling routine does not want their values changed. For that situation, many compilers allow data to be passed in several ways. One way is to send to the called routine a *copy* of the data items, but protect the items themselves. This is usually termed call *by value*, since it is the value of the variable that is being passed. If the calling routine wants the variable to be updated, it can pass the argument *by name* or *by reference*. Then the called routine has the ability to alter it.

The third coupling consideration is how much a module depends on the inner workings of another module. If it relies on some internals, or worse yet, it controls the operation of the other module, the two are very closely coupled. If modules are compiled together, one might set a switch or an address in the other so that when it is invoked it performs a desired operation. Or it might branch to some internal location in the other module. All these practices lead to poor design and are to be avoided.

If two modules are compiled separately one can still attempt to control the other by sending it some special data, knowing how it will process it. For example, a Read module might close a file when it encounters a record whose key is all 9's. (A somewhat archaic practice.) A second module may wish to have a file closed, and might invoke the Read module, sending it a dummy record with a key of 9's. Sending artificial data, knowing what the Read module will do with it is an example of control coupling. Should the Read module subsequently be changed to handle end-of-file differently (a good idea), the second module would suddenly fail to operate correctly.

Control coupling, where one module knows and depends on how another module operates, needs to be distinguished from passing of *indicators*. It is quite acceptable, and in fact desirable, for a module to pass an indicator to another module. This indicator usually has only two states, such as ON/OFF or YES/NO. This could be an indication of whether or not the module was able to successfully complete its function. For example, an Edit module returns an indicator stating whether or not the data is valid. The distinction is that, in this case, the module sending the indicator does not know what the other module is going to do with the information being sent. It is merely informing the other module without relying on any specific action to be performed, or explaining the cause of its actions.

Limiting Module Complexity

Complexity grows as the logic for solving certain functions becomes more intricate. One of the purposes of designing programs in terms of modules is to limit complexity. Of course, having a module solve one function is the first step in limiting complexity. Other methods for limiting complexity include:

1. Set a maximum for the number of source statements in a module.
2. Set a maximum for the number of decision statements.
3. Set a maximum for the possible number of paths through a module.
4. Set a maximum development time for the module.

One or more of these methods may be used to limit module complexity. Limiting complexity by limiting size alone does not differentiate between long but simple portions of straight-line coding and short but difficult portions of code.

DATA FLOW DIAGRAMS

Now that we have seen what constitutes good modules in your program, let's examine how the overall structure of the program is determined. How do you go from a problem statement to a program design?

The first step is to think through the problem and give it some structure. The best way to do this is carefully to examine the data that is processed and produce what is called a *data flow diagram*. This is a general picture of the data that is needed, what is done with it, and the outputs that are produced. It depicts the natural flow of information and describes the operation as it is currently being performed manually. In fact, data flow diagrams really have nothing to do with computers and are often used to define manual operations. Producing a data flow diagram serves to clarify the problem and often shows up its vague or undefined aspects.

Data flow diagrams consist primarily of two parts:

1. The major *processes* that are performed

2. The data used and created by each of these processes

The processes are usually depicted in a circle or box, and lines are drawn between them to show the sequence of the processes. The data names are written along these lines showing how they flow from one process to the next. Figure 2-3 shows how a data flow diagram can help with program design.

Here the processes are shown in the circles, and the data along the lines. (*Hierarchy chart* is covered in the next section.)

These diagrams resemble *system flowcharts*. They differ from what may come later, *procedural flowcharts*, in that they don't show how the program operates. There is no logic or control included. They show *what* is to be done, but not *how* it is to be done.

Data flow diagrams start out at a very general level and are usually expanded once or twice. However, they never get down to a detailed level. Therefore they show all major inputs and outputs, but not minor ones. For example, normal error messages are not shown as output.

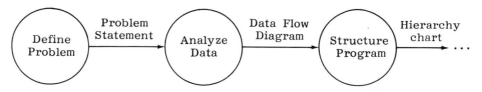

Figure 2-3. Example of a Data Flow Diagram for doing program design.

It is important to show clearly the major inputs and outputs and name them accurately. Similarly all the processes that are shown should be carefully named. A good procedure is to name all processes using a verb-object format. This helps define what is being done, and with what data. Thus processes would have names like "Edit Transaction," or "Calculate Federal Taxes."

Consider an on-line banking application in which inquiries can be made via a terminal about the status of a depositor's account. Current balance, high and low balances for the month, and amount of last deposit are some of the allowed inquiries. Here, there would be more than one major input. The transaction from the customer at the terminal is one, and the customer's account record is the other. It is also necessary to have another process to check the validity of the inquiry and the authorization code before issuing any information. The output is to send the response to the terminal. Figure 2-4 shows the data flow diagram for this inquiry.

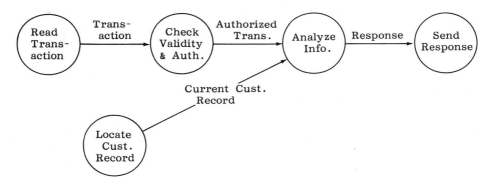

Figure 2-4. Data Flow Diagram for on-line banking inquiry.

TOP-DOWN PROGRAM DESIGN

Top-down program design is based on the idea of levels of abstraction becoming levels of modules in a program. Frost defines *abstracting* as a "generalizing process in which one concentrates on similarities between things and gathers them into a group based on those similarities, thus making up the abstraction."[5] For example, the abstraction *accounts receivable* is useful for those who wish to communicate generally without having to separately reference invoicing, cash receipts, paid transactions, or customer statements. These latter terms are lower levels of abstraction.

---

[5]David Frost, "Psychology and Program Design," *Datamation*, May 1975, p. 137. Reprinted with permission of DATAMATION®. Copyright 1975 by Technical Publishing Company, Greenwich, Connecticut 06830.

Hierarchy Charts

Levels of abstraction become the levels of modules in a program. In the design stage a *hierarchy chart* is constructed to represent these levels. The chart is similar in appearance to an organization chart. In addition, it is logically analogous because it is functionally oriented and shows *flow of control*. Each box in a program hierarchy chart represents a function or module.

Hierarchy charts are part of a documentation tool known as HIPO. The H stands for the Hierarchy charts, and IPO stands for the Input-Process-Output charts that describe each individual module. (See HIPO Design Aid and Documentation Technique Form GC20-1851, IBM.)

A hierarchy chart differs from a flowchart in that it does not show decision-making logic or flow of execution. For example, the flowchart in Figure 2-5 depicts a

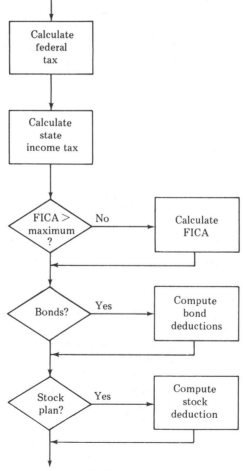

Figure 2-5. Flowchart of payroll deductions

portion of a payroll program. Here the logic for determining which deductions are to be computed and the sequence in which they will be computed is shown. This contrasts with the hierarchy chart in Figure 2-6, where only the functions and their relationship to other functions in the program are depicted. We see the grouping of functions which was missing in the flowchart. Each of the individual deductions is separate, but all are seen to be an expansion of the more general heading, CALCULATE DEDUCTIONS. The flowchart shows *procedure*; the hierarchy chart shows *function*. The hierarchy chart allows the programmer to concentrate on defining *what* needs to be done in the program before deciding *how* it is to be done. It also groups related functions together, which is a key to good program design.

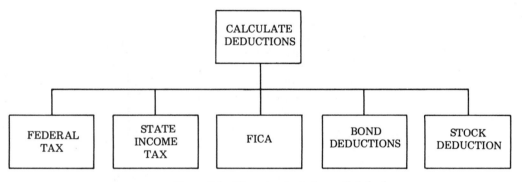

Figure 2-6. Hierarchy chart of payroll deductions

Developing a Hierarchy Chart

To create a hierarchy chart, begin with the data flow diagram. First draw a very simple hierarchy chart and then refine it to more detail. As you do this you are adding points of control, changing from a sequential flow to a structured hierarchy.

Refer back to the on-line banking example in the previous section. The data flow diagram for this application was shown in Figure 2-4. The top box of the hierarchy chart should be a statement of the entire application. In this case you could call it PROCESS INQUIRY REQUEST.

```
PROCESS
INQUIRY
REQUEST
```

The next step is to subdivide the top box into the main parts that make it up. Typically an application takes input data, processes it, and produces some output. The input data might come from more than one source and may have to be edited. The processing may also be complex and the output may require formatting or may consist of more than one form. However, for a first cut at subdividing, just look for the three main operations (Input, Process, Output) of the overall function.

To do this, scan along the data flow diagram from the left, looking for the last point where the data can still be considered as coming into the program. This can sometimes be a matter of judgment. In the case of our banking example, it probably is at the point where both an authorized transaction and a current record are obtained. This is shown by the line marked "Input" in Figure 2-7.

Next do the same for output. Start at the right and scan to the left, looking for the point where output data is first recognizable. Again, in the banking example, it is probably where the "response" is first seen (e.g., just before the process that sends the response to the terminal). This is shown in Figure 2-7 by the line marked "Output."

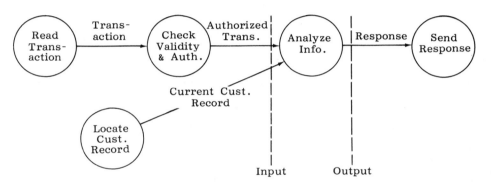

Figure 2-7. Data Flow Diagram for an on-line banking inquiry with Input and Output lines added.

Now that you have identified the input and output parts, whatever is left in the center is the main process. Sometimes there will be no *central process* (also called the *central transform*). The input and output lines may be the same as in a program that merely edits data and writes it to a file. In our banking example the Process ANALYZE INFORMATION becomes our central transform. The two inputs are shown separately, and there is just one output. Now the hierarchy chart looks as follows:

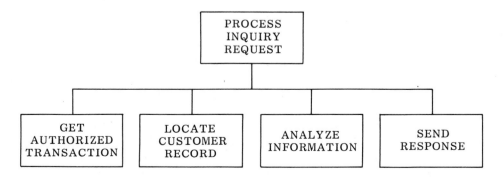

Here the modules *report* to the master controlling routine, PROCESS INQUIRY REQUEST. The controlling routine invokes the lower level modules, checks on their results, makes major decisions, and maintains control.

The approach of a single control module is adequate for small or simple programs. However, as the complexity of the program increases, so does the complexity of the main or top module. In a program with one routine controlling and making decisions for 100 other modules, the main module would be so complex that it would be difficult to debug and modify after it was completed. The solution is found in the analogy of a company president. If the company grew to 100 employees, it would be cumbersome to have all of the employees reporting directly to the president. Rather, vice-presidents would be given some of the control and decision-making activities. Similarly, a program will have second-level routines under the main routine. These routines will have some of the control and decision-making functions of the program. The module structure then becomes hierarchical.

The company president could assign duties to V.P.s in a variety of ways. One approach would be to select three people as follows:

- 1st V.P.—Manage all employees with names beginning with A–I
- 2nd V.P.—Manage all employees with names beginning with J–R
- 3rd V.P.—Manage all employees with names beginning with S–Z

More than likely, however, the president would assign duties based on the major functions the company has to perform, for example, marketing, production, and research and development. Similarly, in a program the second-level routines are the major functional subdivisions of the program. Then these modules would be further subdivided into lower level modules.

Returning to the example of the on-line banking inquiry, the hierarchy chart can

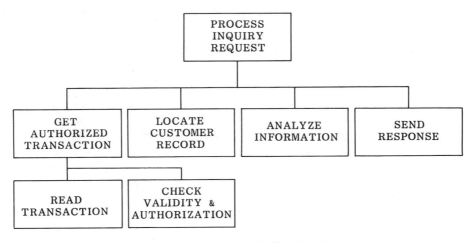

Figure 2-8. Example of a hierarchy chart.

be expanded, putting further processes under those that control them. At this point you may be adding to or refining the processes that you had in the data flow diagram. Thus the next version might be as shown in Figure 2-8.

Hierarchy charts do not show data flow, order of execution, or when and how often each module will be invoked. There is no order of execution implied by placing modules within a given level. People tend to think in a left-to-right manner, and there is no harm in arranging the boxes in that fashion. Certainly, in this example, there would be no point to placing them intentionally in a different order. However, when reading a hierarchy chart, don't *assume* that the modules will be executed always in a left-to-right order. The logic determining the control of the frequency and order of execution is inside the boxes and isn't shown on the chart.

For example, assume that in reading an inquiry from a terminal, an error is detected. Rather than entering ANALYZE INFORMATION, SEND RESPONSE may be entered next in order to notify the terminal user of the problem. In this case ANALYZE INFORMATION would never have been executed.

If the lines don't show order of execution, what do they show? They show *flow of control*. Each module is invoked by the one above it, and when completed, returns to its caller. This *called* routine is, therefore, subordinate to the module above it and superior to those below it. Continuing the analogy of the organization chart, it receives "orders" from its "boss" and reports back to the manager the outcome of its action. To complete that action, it may need to invoke one or more of its subordinate modules before it can report back.

Achieving Vertical Control

Flow of control proceeds only along the vertical lines that connect the modules in the hierarchy chart. This means that any module can invoke another module at a lower level and then have control returned to it when the lower level module is completed. To ensure that vertical movement or control, the following guidelines are given:

1. A module must return to its *caller*. The only exception to this rule might be in the case of detected errors that are unrecoverable and require immediate program termination.

2. A module may call another module below the level on which it appears; it may not call another module on the same or a higher level. (However, a module may call itself as in the case of *recursive* programming.) By allowing communication only with a module immediately above or below in the hierarchy chart, intermodule data flow is simplified. Sometimes, however, the need does arise when it is necessary to have a higher level module invoke a module several levels below its own level. This is permissible, but in that case show the module as appearing more than once in the chart at the appropriate levels. Recurring modules should be so indicated in the hierarchy chart. For example, extra vertical lines might be added to the box.

Of course, when the module is actually coded, it would appear only once in the collection of modules that makes up the program.

3. Major decision making should be placed at as high a level as possible. Typically, the top module (first level) contains the main decisions of a program. The top module is a synopsis of the entire program.

4. A lower level module should not make decisions that a higher level module must follow. To illustrate this point, return to the analogy of the organization chart. We would not expect employees to make decisions that their manager, their manager's manager, or other departments would have to follow. We would expect them to receive directions from their manager and report back as to whether or not they were able to carry them out successfully. A module, therefore, would not take actions which would force a change in program flow. It would not, for example, invoke a routine at its own (or a higher) level. It would not determine which routine is executed next by actually setting the address (that is, using an ALTER in COBOL or label variables in PL/I) in a routine which is above it or on the same level. Regardless of what occurs during a module's execution, it will always return to the module that invoked it (i.e., to the point where it was called within the module). The lower level module can send back to a higher module some indication of results achieved or conditions observed. Based on these results, the higher module can decide what action is to be taken. Thus, if a module detects an input error, indication is sent back to the higher module. The higher module, now, can decide which module(s) to call.

There are several advantages to keeping the flow of control *vertical*:

1. When someone is reading the program, the logic is easier to follow.

2. Reading the top module would reveal the general logic of the entire program.

3. It is easier to modify or add to the control flow at a later time.

4. Coding and testing higher level modules before lower modules reveals validity of the modular design and finds logic flaws sooner.

After all subfunctions of the higher level modules have been defined, lower level modules are specified. For example the ANALYZE INFORMATION module in Figure 2-8 is *decomposed* only after all modules which are subfunctions of PROCESS IN-

QUIRY REQUEST have been specified. This helps to minimize omissions or incomplete analyses of higher level functions.

Each level of boxes in a hierarchy chart represents modules as defined in this chapter. For example, even if ANALYZE INFORMATION is further qualified by the addition of four lower level modules, it is still a module that will ultimately represent program code.

At the very minimum, this module will contain statements to invoke its related modules on the third level.

Evaluating a Hierarchy Chart

When a hierarchy chart is finished, spend some time evaluating it to see if it can be improved. The first question to ask would be, "Is it indeed finished; have I refined it far enough"?

The designer of hierarchy charts may not know, in all cases, whether each box represents a manageable amount of code. Subfunctions may be specified that are either too large and need further subdivision or so small that they may not warrant being made into modules. Generally, it is better to go too far in modularizing rather than not far enough because it is easy to combine parts of a function. Adding missing subfunctions later on may be more difficult.

To determine if you have decomposed the chart far enough, look at each module to see if:

- the function can easily be understood

- the implementation can be readily grasped

- the module has potential to be used elsewhere

When you feel that these conditions have been met, you have probably finished the chart.

Now look at each module to check that it is performing one well-defined function, not *multiple* or *scattered* functions.

To illustrate multiple and scattered functions, consider the programming task of editing data within records. This editing might consist of such things as checking fields for all numeric or alphabetic characters, performing limit checks on numeric fields, verifying the presence of special characters, or inserting characters for output fields. An example of the multiple function would be a module which edits two completely different record types. An example of the scattered function would be designating two modules, each having part of the function of editing data fields within a single record type.

One way to evaluate a module is to look at its name. Modules, like processes, should be named in a verb-object format, with perhaps an adjective. Thus, SEND RESPONSE, and LOCATE CUSTOMER RECORD fit this format and probably represent single function modules. If, however, the word AND is needed, you probably have a module performing multiple functions. Thus, in our example, CHECK VALIDITY

AND AUTHORIZATION appears to be doing two things. Even though they are related, they should be separated into two modules, as in Figure 2-9.

If the object is a plural, or is a vague or general term, the module may be performing a group of functions. It may be the infamous "logical" module described earlier. Thus, examine carefully modules with names like EDIT DATA or PRINT RECORDS, if they are on the lowest level. If so, they probably are doing multiple functions. If PRINT RECORDS has modules below it that handle different kinds of records, it would be satisfactory.

Another way to evaluate a hierarchy chart is to mentally execute the program it represents and examine the data that is passed between modules. *Arguments* should be passed explicitly wherever possible, rather than shared in some commonly accessible storage. This makes it clear which items are being used by the module and helps to enforce the guideline of having few arguments.

The number of arguments (data) passed to a module may be a sign that a separation of functions is needed. For a large number of arguments being passed to a module, try to divide the module into smaller parts where each part's function is smaller in scope. The purpose of small modules here is to reduce the number of arguments passed or data shared between modules.

One of the advantages of a modular structure in which the number of data items shared is small, the data is explicitly passed, and control passes back to the caller or down to a lower module is that testing of the module is simpler. Results are more predictable and test time may be shorter.

Haney[6] makes the point that designers should do all they can to reduce the

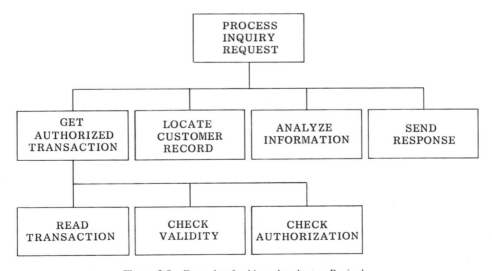

Figure 2-9. Example of a hierarchy chart.—Revised.

[6]F.M. Haney,"Module Connection Analysis," *Proceedings of the* 1972 *FJCC*, AFIPS Press, pp. 173-180.

interdependence of modules. When many shared data items exist between modules, maintainability becomes a problem. He describes how an operating system developed by his employer required 296 *initial* changes, which resulted in almost 3000 changes being made[7] Thus, when many dependencies exist, a few changes can have a rippling effect. Functional design should help this potential problem as well as keep the number of data items shared to a minimum. Also, passing data via an argument list and allowing communication only to those modules immediately above or below a module in a hierarchy chart will minimize the rippling effect.

A clean separation of functions is the key to good hierarchy charts, but this is not always possible. Then it will be necessary to compromise and select the design which most nearly achieves a clean separation of functions.

CASE STUDY

As a means of tying together the guidelines for top-down design and hierarchy charts, consider a sequential file update problem. The application is inventory control. Transactions have been batched together and are sorted into collating sequence based on inventory part number. There are three types of transactions indicated by a code in the transaction record:

1. Add a new inventory record (new item being added to the product line).

2. Change (receipts of additional quantity or issuing of existing stock).

3. Delete an existing inventory record (item is being dropped from the company's product line).

The master inventory file is a sequential file in which the inventory records are also in collating sequence. The transactions are processed against the old master file. A new master file is created by adding the new records, deleting some old records, and updating other old records as to quantity on hand. In addition, a log of all transactions processed is written out for audit purposes. The data flow diagram for the Inventory Update Problem is shown in Figure 2-10. It shows two inputs, transaction and old master, and two outputs, new master and change log.

To convert the data flow diagram to a hierarchy chart, start by looking for the last place where data can be considered as coming into the program. Next, look for the first place that output is generated. What is left is the processing portion. Thus, everything to the left of PROCESS TRANSACTION would be input and everything to the right, output. The first cut at a hierarchy chart would be as shown in Figure 2-11.

Now, examine the modules in the chart to see if all modules perform only a single function. Thinking about the PROCESS TRANSACTION module, it really performs the functions of adding a new master record, changing an existing one, and deleting an

---

[7]Richard G. Canning, "The Search for Software Reliability," *EDP Analyzer*, Vol. 12, No. 5, May 1974.

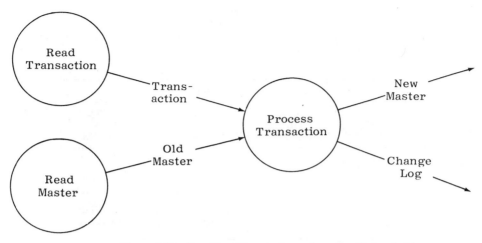

Figure 2-10. Data Flow Diagram for an Inventory Update Problem.

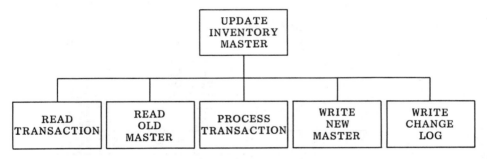

Figure 2-11. Inventory hierarchy chart—first try.

old one. Therefore it should be broken into three separate modules. Figure 2-12 shows the revised hierarchy chart.

Now examine the ADD, CHANGE, and DELETE modules to see if they perform more multiple functions. Since CHANGE handles both Receipts and Issues, it should be further subdivided. Figure 2-13 shows the second revision of the hierarchy chart.

You would now want to expand and refine the hierarchy chart. In thinking about the three modules, ADD, CHANGE and DELETE, each of them would need to see if a master record with the corresponding inventory part number exists. Therefore a new module, GET MATCHING MASTER would need to be added. Each of the three processing modules would need to test the relationship between the key in the transaction record and the one in the master record. Table 2-1 shows the various relationships and the specific operations to be performed.

Figure 2-14 shows the third revision of the hierarchy chart. Now a clean separation of functions is depicted and flow of control is clear and straightforward. The GET

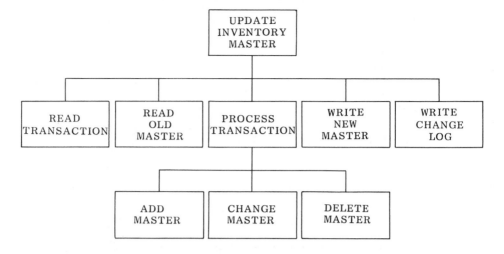

Figure 2-12. Inventory hierarchy chart—Revision 1.

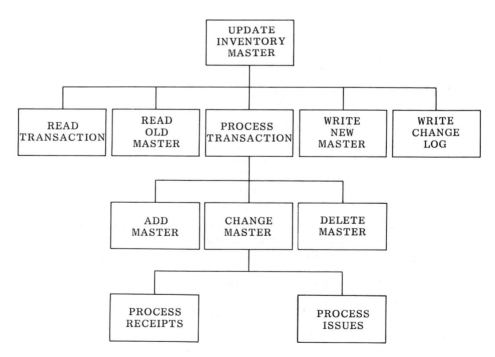

Figure 2-13. Inventory hierarchy chart—Revision 2.

Table 2-1. Design for Testing Transaction Key/Master Key Relationship

Condition	Action(s)
Transaction key = Master key	1. For ADD, print error message 2. For CHANGE (issues or receipts) or DELETE, update or delete the master record
Transaction key > Master key	1. Copy old master record into new master file
Transaction key < Master key	1. For ADD, write transaction into new master file 2. For CHANGE or DELETE, print error message

MATCHING MASTER is a reusable module where the module's results are used differently by the invoking modules. The ADD, CHANGE, and DELETE modules all call GET MATCHING MASTER, which will return to the respective invoking module

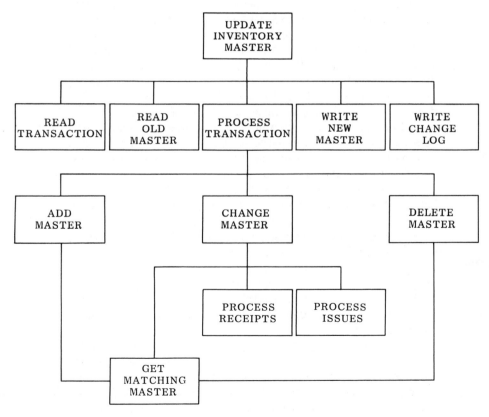

Figure 2-14. Inventory hierarchy chart—Revision 3

an *indicator* of whether or not there is a master that matches the transaction key. A *yes* or *no* indication, of course, has a different meaning to each of the three modules on level three. A *yes* indication to the ADD module is an error whereas a *yes* indication to the DELETE module is not.

As you think about this update problem, you will see that the actual updating of the inventory records is straightforward. The more challenging logic is to handle the two files and keep them synchronized. This is especially true when you consider that there are many records which will not be updated and merely need to be copied to the new master.

GET MATCHING MASTER, therefore, may be given a transaction whose key is much higher than the current master key. It would need to copy master records until the required one is found. Thus the READ MASTER and WRITE NEW MASTER modules need to be invoked from it.

Should these two modules be moved from their present position, or should they appear in both the current and new positions? Can all the copying of the master file be done from GET MATCHING MASTER? The one place where it can't be done is for the master records that have higher keys than the last transaction. When there are no more transactions, PROCESS TRANSACTIONS will no longer be invoked. Thus to copy the remainder of the file we need a new module. This module, COPY REST OF MASTER will call READ OLD MASTER and WRITE NEW MASTER. Figure 2-15 shows the new place of these modules and shows them as occurring more than once in the chart. In actuality, the code would appear only once for these two modules. Since one of the purposes of the hierarchy chart is to show flow of control, that flow is depicted by drawing the repeated modules as required.

Does anything else need to be added to the hierarchy chart? There will probably be some end-of-job processing to be done. Files will need to be closed, and perhaps a final message printed showing total number of transactions processed. You might want to add a small module to "wrap up" the program. Note that this module would actually perform two different functions—closing files and printing a message. However, since both of these are very short and very simple, it would be acceptable in this case.

Now you need to determine if the hierarchy chart has been refined to a sufficient degree. If each module represents a manageable amount of code, and the programming of it seems apparent, you are finished. That appears to be the case with these modules. Next, you should examine the data that needs to be passed between each pair of modules to see if any two modules are too closely coupled (try that with this example). If the number of data items passed is few, and they are not being used to control the actions of the other module, then the chart is completed. Figure 2-16 shows the final hierarchy chart.

After completing the hierarchy charts, it is advisable to review them for completeness and accuracy. If the program will be used by someone else, then review the charts with the user(s)—that is, conduct a structured walk-through. The data flow diagram is another good tool to clarify what the program is supposed to do. These documents, which are user-oriented, should also be reviewed with the user to obtain concurrence before embarking on further development. But don't show detailed charts or internal design. The procedure is illustrated as follows:

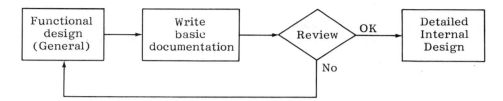

It has the obvious advantage of helping to ensure that the *requirements* and *specifications* have been understood by both parties and agreement reached regarding the desired results. At the end of the design phase, these conditions should exist: (1) the number of modules is known; (2) the relationship (function and flow of control) of various modules is depicted via hierarchy charts; and (3) all work to date has been verified by users for accuracy and completeness.

MANAGEMENT IMPLICATIONS

A key consideration for the organization as a whole is that independent modules can be assigned to various individuals for programming. If modules are ill defined, or require knowledge of the internal workings of other modules, the entire program may need to be written by one person. Functional modules provide for more flexibility in utilizing programmers and often permit more accurate estimates of the time to create them. They also allow for maintenance to be performed by someone other than the original developer. Thus well-defined modules lead to more efficient and complete utilization of the programming staff.

The successful use of top-down development depends on management's commitment to the use of this tool. If it doesn't have management's backing, it won't be fully accepted and implemented by all programmers in an installation. In addition to management commitment, there must be training programs for the DP organization and adherence to installation standards.

The transition period will not be easy for many DP professionals. People are conditioned to operate in the old familiar methods. The new ideas take rethinking and, in some cases, drastic changes in the way work is done. Even if they believe in these new ideas, they may still have to overcome the reluctance of others.

A related problem is that most people are more comfortable with well-defined tasks. Given a list of chores, most people tend to do those that are relatively simple, of short duration, and those they know how to do well. Thus, an employee may spend a lot of the day filling in forms, writing memos or reports, answering telephone calls, reading or cleaning up some technical item that needs work. Many would do any or all of these rather than tackle a larger, more complex problem whose solution is not obvious—even though the complex problem is more important.

Here again is the need to defer the well-defined task of coding and address the more ambiguous problem of defining module structure and identifying interfaces.

However, the benefits are so great for the organization that management needs to encourage the acceptance of top-down design. The lowered cost of developing, and especially maintaining, programs is an important consideration. Well-defined functional modules, placed in a common library, can dramatically simplify program development.

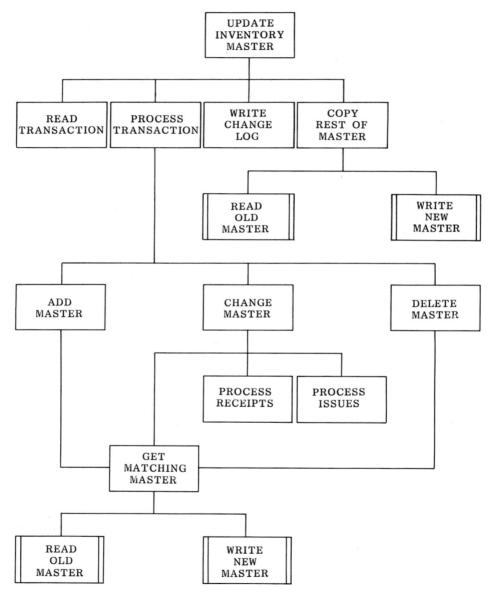

Figure 2-15. Inventory hierarchy chart—Revision 4.

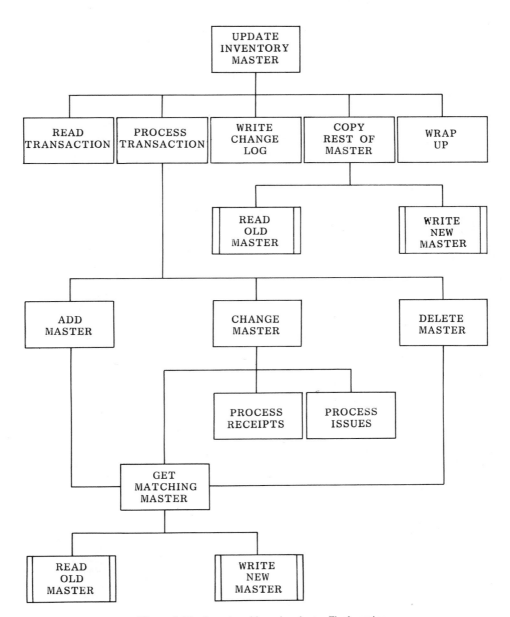

Figure 2-16. Inventory hierarchy chart—Final version.

SUMMARY

This chapter introduced two of the newer tools for program design—the data flow diagram and the hierarchy chart. Decomposing a program into its component modules requires that you work from the general to the specific. First, modules are identified based on their functions. The principle, *one module, one function*, must be applied. Then the modules are combined in a hierarchy chart based on levels of abstraction. Thus, the top module's function is a summary or synopsis of the entire program. Each subsequent level of defined modules is related to the programmer's understanding of the levels of abstraction of the problem. Knuth[8] relates programming talent and levels of abstraction in this way:

"I have felt for a long time that a talent for programming consists largely of the ability to switch readily from microscopic to macroscopic views of things, i.e., to change levels of abstraction fluently." Knuth mentioned this[9] to Dijkstra, and he replied with an excellent analysis of the situation:

I feel somewhat guilty when I have suggested that the distinction or introduction of 'different levels of abstraction' allows you to think about only one level at a time, ignoring completely the other levels. This is not true.

You are trying to organize your thoughts; that is, you are seeking to arrange matters in such a way that you can concentrate on some portion, say with 90 percent of your conscious thinking, while the rest is temporarily moved away somewhat towards the background of your mind. But that is something quite different from 'ignoring completely': you allow yourself temporarily to ignore details, but some overall appreciation of what is supposed to be or to come there continues to play a vital role. You remain alert for little red lamps that suddenly start flickering in the corners of your eye.[10]

In addition to function and levels of abstraction, hierarchy charts show flow of control—that is, "who is invoked by whom."

Of course, to design a program in top-down fashion, a clear understanding of the requirements of the program is imperative. Communicating with the people for whom the programmer is writing a program is essential. This communication should take place *before*, *during*, and *after* the program design phase. An essential step for improving the communication process after the program design phase is to write a user's manual for the program. This manual and related documents are then reviewed with the user before the next development phase is entered.

[8]Donald E. Knuth, "Structured Programming with go to Statements," *Computing Surveys,* Vol. 6, No. 4, December 1974, p. 292. Copyright 1974, Association for Computing Machinery, Inc., reprinted by permission.

[9]Donald E. Knuth, "A Review of 'Structured Programming'," Stanford Computer Science Department Report STAN-CS-73-371, Stanford University, Stanford, Calif., June 1973, 25 pp.

[10]Edsger W. Dijkstra, personal communication, January 13, 1973.

REVIEW QUESTIONS AND EXERCISES

1. Distinguish between a system, a program, and a module.

2. List as many characteristics of a module as you can recall.

3. Define *function*.

4. What are the advantages of modularizing based on *function?* Of keeping module flow of control *vertical?*

5. Why limit the complexity of a module?

6. What are the trade-offs (advantages/disadvantages) of various methods of limiting module complexity?

7. Comment on the accuracy of the following statements:

   a. When reading a hierarchy chart, it is all right to assume that the modules will be executed in a top-to-bottom and left-to-right order.

   b. Even if a second-level module needs to call a fourth-level module, it can't because a module may communicate only with modules immediately below and above its own level.

   c. If a lower-level module detects an error (during its execution), it has the authority to take corrective action by altering the normal sequence in which the other modules in the program are executed.

8. Establish a set of guidelines to follow in the design of specific modules.

9. List some ways in which you can tell if two modules are too closely coupled.

10. Draw a hierarchy chart for your life. That is, decide what your overall goal is. That will be the top box. Then decide what must be accomplished to meet that main goal. Continue by subdividing into lower functions.

11. Draw a hierarchy chart of the functional oganization of a car. Be sure to keep it functional rather than procedural. That is, concentrate on the jobs to be performed in order for a car to operate, rather than the order in which they are done.

12. A file of employees' records is to be processed in the following way: For each department the mean and standard deviation for salary and years of experience are to be computed. The mean and standard deviation for all employees in those two categories are also to be computed. Draw a data flow diagram and hierarchy chart for the program.

13. Sales data is stored by product. You want to determine which product has had the greatest sales this month. That information is to be included in an electronic message to be sent to all department heads. Draw both a data flow diagram and a hierarchy chart for this program.

14. Draw a data flow diagram and a hierarchy chart for a personal budgeting program. There will be a budget of estimated expenses for the year in various categories. You will be keeping a record of all checks written by category. Summarize expenses by category, compare with budget, and write a report.

3

Top-down Development:
Planning and Implementation

Top-down development can be thought of as a three-step process:

Each step is a phase in the system life cycle. The hierarchy chart is a key document developed during the design phase. It is also the working document in the next phase—planning. The importance of planning is gradually being recognized so that we may now think of it as a separate or specific activity in the development of a program.

Why plan? With a plan of action, things are better organized, people work more effectively, and the resulting work product is of a higher quality.

What do you plan? Estimates of personnel and computer requirements are made early in the system life cycle and then revised as the *planner* moves through the various phases of the project. This is usually a management task, but a manager will probably ask a programmer for an estimate of the time needed to do a certain project and what the estimated resources will be.

The management considerations for these two resources—people and computers—will be discussed in the Management Implications section of this chapter. In addition to resource planning, the order in which modules are to be coded and tested must also be planned.

PLANNING

Planning Module Development Order

Before coding any of the modules in a program, it is necessary to evaluate the alternative sequences in which modules may be coded and tested. Of course, they should be done in a top-down fashion, but there are variations within the top-down approach. For example, do you code *all* the modules on one level before moving down to the next level, or do you code all the modules on one leg (e.g., highest level to lowest level modules) of the hierarchy chart? The sequence selected is the one which provides for the most complete testing of the modules, enabling you to discover major problems as soon as possible. The best module-development sequence is a combination of two approaches: hierarchical and execution-order. We will explain each approach separately and then show how these two techniques may be combined to give an optimum sequence for coding and testing. Testing of modules must also be planned. We will introduce testing and its impact on the module-development order; however, this subject is covered in greater detail in Chapter 7.

Hierarchical Approach   In this approach a program's modules are coded and tested based on their position in the hierarchy chart. All modules at one level are coded and tested before modules at a lower level. Figure 3-1 illustrates this approach, using the bank inquiry example from Chapter 2. The numbers above the boxes indicate the sequence in which the modules are to be developed. In the level-by-level method the top module is first coded and tested, using stubs for the second-level modules. Each stub is a brief skeleton of what will later be expanded into a module. It contains whatever is needed to permit a complete test of the higher module.

After the top module is tested, then stubs on the second level are expanded into modules and tested with stubs for the third-level modules. The hierarchical approach, however, does not specify the order in which the modules on a particular level should be created. In Figure 3-1, for example, on level III it would have been possible to write CHECK VALIDITY *after* CHECK AUTHORIZATION rather than the left-to-right sequence shown. The order chosen would probably be that which permitted the most

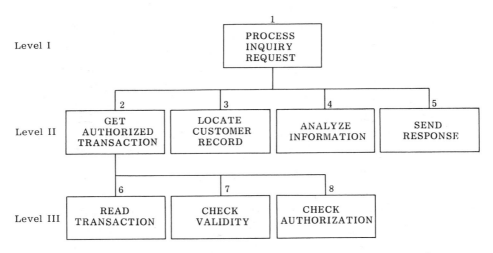

Figure 3-1. Development order of bank-inquiry program—hierarchical approach.

thorough testing. The above sequence might have been chosen if CHECK VALIDITY uses data items that are created or modified by CHECK AUTHORIZATION. The requirement that a module has for data produced or modified by another module is called *data dependency*.

Data dependency might also exist between modules at different levels. For example LOCATE CUSTOMER RECORD might depend on the data that is input by READ TRANSACTION. If the level-by-level method is used, LOCATE CUSTOMER RECORD cannot be tested completely because it will be written before READ TRANSACTION. One solution would be to redesign the hierarchy chart so that READ TRANSACTION is at the same level as LOCATE CUSTOMER RECORD and can therefore be written before it. This, however, may not be a logical organization, or it may tend to create a hierarchy chart with too many modules on the same level. Another solution is to write the stub for READ TRANSACTION to include the necessary input statements, and then code and test LOCATE CUSTOMER RECORD with this stub. If a stub, however, ends up being complex, it would probably be best to code the complete module rather than to spend time writing a complex stub. Thus, here is a case where a departure from the strict hierarchical approach might be desirable.

This departure from the hierarchical approach is *not* a departure from the topdown philosophy. Top-down philosophy means that higher level modules are written and integrated before the modules that are below *them*. In Figure 3-1 GET AUTHORIZED TRANSACTION is written before the modules that are subordinate to it. Choosing to develop one leg of a hierarchy chart before modules on higher levels (but different legs) can provide for better testing and perhaps reduce the programming effort required.

There are two points to remember when using the hierarchical approach:

1. Data dependencies, or flow of data between modules, may make it difficult to code and test in a level-by-level method.
2. Adherence to a strict hierarchical approach tends to leave the bulk of modules to be done toward the end of a project. This could create computer scheduling and personnel allocation problems.

Execution-Order Approach   In the execution-order approach the modules are developed in the order in which they are to be executed when the program is fully developed and becomes operational (Figure 3-2). The order of module development is determined by the *planner* mentally executing the program. However, the execution order will usually vary because input data items vary. Thus, as with the hierarchical approach, there are still decisions to be made as to the exact sequence for coding and testing.

One advantage of the execution-order approach is that the data dependency problem is minimized. Because modules are generally added in the order in which they will be executed, those that produce data needed by another will usually be written earlier. One disadvantage of this approach is that it implies a sequence of coding and testing where the programmers assigned to developing modules must do so "in their turn." Thus, the programmer coding SEND RESPONSE in Figure 3-2 must wait until the

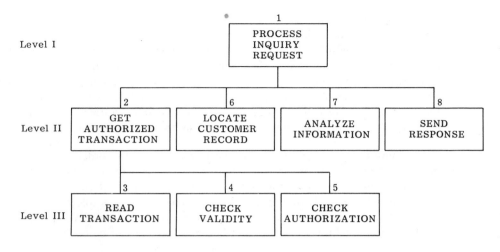

Figure 3-2. Development order of bank inquiry program—execution-order approach.

programmers handling all other modules have finished their work. This can present manpower scheduling problems and cause all modules to end up on the *critical path*.

A second area of difficulty is in the technical aspects of the execution-order approach. For example, in Figure 3-2 assume that SEND RESPONSE produces all output for this program. If the execution order is followed strictly, SEND RESPONSE will be the last module written.

Thus, during development of all other modules, output for the purpose of checking results would have to be provided by a stub. Once again, this might require a large stub of code not needed when the stub becomes a module. To avoid this problem, there are several solutions:

1. Redraw the hierarchy chart.
2. Use special debugging output routines which have previously been written and can be used without extensive program modifications.
3. Code easy-to-use output statements (such as PUT DATA in PL/I) in the stub.
4. Depart from the strict execution-order approach.

Item 1 may be too time-consuming and lead to inferior design. Items 2 and 3 are not always available; thus, item 4 is the most often selected solution. In this example it would mean coding SEND RESPONSE early, perhaps immediately after PROCESS INQUIRY REQUEST. An added bonus of doing this is that it provides the user with a sample of the program's results. (It is when the user sees the program output that s/he is most likely to say, "That's not what I wanted!" If that is the case, you would certainly like to know it as soon as possible.)

Wrap-up routines are another case in which the execution-order approach may be altered. These routines handle such things as the closing of files, printing final totals, and displaying an end-of-job message. Assume in the bank inquiry example that there is another module on the same level as SEND RESPONSE, but executing after it. Its function is to perform the closing of files. For smoother testing of the other modules using files, it could be written out of order as far as execution is concerned.

Combination Approach   The best approach to the order of module development is a combination of the hierarchical approach and the execution-order approach. Here the planner weighs the trade-offs of each approach in determining the sequence of module development. Different sequences, of course, are possible for the same hierarchy chart. But in all cases, in order to preserve the top-down development technique, the following conditions must be met before a module can be coded:

1. The control path to the module must have already been established. That is, the chain of modules through which control passes to a new module must already be a part of the running program.

2. All data values that a module needs must be available, either from modules that create or modify the data or from stubs for those modules.

In determining module-development order, four considerations have been discussed: (1) data dependencies, (2) availability of resources, (3) requirement for a module's output early in the testing sequence, and (4) need for a wrap-up module earlier in the sequence. A fifth consideration is *complexity*.

It is tempting to code the easy modules first to "get them out of the way." However, complex modules should usually be coded first. They don't get any easier with aging and may cause two problems by being developed later:

1. They may be more complex than anticipated and take longer to develop than estimated. (At the later stages extra time is at a premium.)

2. Hidden in that complexity may be some things that have been overlooked or inadequately defined. Coding the complex module early will point these out. Thus in Figure 3-2, ANALYZE INFORMATION is probably complex and should be written early.

A sixth consideration is *handling exceptions* related to invalid data. Modules that process valid data should be coded and tested before modules that are involved with invalid data. Thus, CHECK VALIDITY and CHECK AUTHORIZATION would be coded and tested later in the module sequence because they are designed to detect invalid input. A general principle is first to get the program to process valid data and produce correct output. Then code the portions that check for and handle invalid input or exceptional conditions.

There is no general rule for applying these considerations to a particular program. In fact, it often happens that these considerations are in conflict with each other. Each situation must be evaluated individually where the trade-offs are carefully weighed. This is why top-down planning takes time and capable people.

One method of establishing a workable order of development is to mentally execute the program in as much detail as possible. At least two people should be involved with this activity. One person verbally explains to the other(s) what occurs at each stage of the program and what each module is expected to do (i.e., the module's function). Generally, it is better to start with an execution-order approach rather than a hierarchical approach because the execution-order approach tends to assure that both the control-path and the data-availability criteria are met for each module.

The process of mentally executing the program may point up some deficiencies in the design of the modular structure or in the documentation for each module. (Each module should have an associated description of its data dependencies.) In the case of design errors, the hierarchy chart may have to be restructured; in the case of incomplete documentation or module specifications, the missing items must be defined before continuing with module development. (For further discussion of mental execution of a program, see Chapter 6, "Structured Walk-throughs.")

In order to test anything at all, it may be necessary to code and execute more than just the top module. These modules make up the *nucleus* of the program. The nucleus would then be tested with whatever stubs are required. The order of the remaining modules would be chosen so as to be able to test as completely as possible and minimize redundant work.

Figure 3-3 shows a possible development order using the combination approach. Several of the considerations for module order previously mentioned were used to

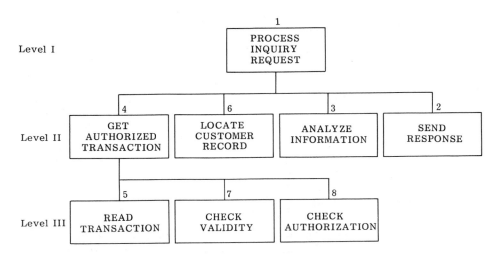

Figure 3-3. Development order of bank-inquiry program—combination approach.

determine this order. SEND RESPONSE would be done next after the top module. Thus it would be available to provide output for the remainder of the modules. ANALYZE INFORMATION is done next because it is the most complex. LOCATE CUSTOMER RECORD follows GET AUTHORIZED TRANSACTION as it uses data created by GET AUTHORIZED TRANSACTION. CHECK VALIDITY and CHECK AUTHORI-ZATION are last because they are simple and handle exception input.

Departures From the Top-down Sequence   There are several cases where the top-down sequence may not be feasible. These situations are depicted in Table 3-1 along with some alternative solutions. From this table we note that for problem area I the top-down solution is to redraw the hierarchy chart. This has two potential draw-backs: First, the chart may be more logical and understandable as it is. Second, when hierarchy charts are redrawn, there is a tendency to group too many modules on the second level. In these instances the solution *not* using top-down might be preferable. In problem area II an advantage of the top-down approach of coding a module before its specifications are firm is that it forces specification decisions to be made sooner, thus still leaving time to incorporate them. In problem area III the strict top-down approach is in conflict with the situation. The programmer must make sure the manager under-stands the situation and is aware that the program may cost more and be delayed by limitations in availability of people.

Table 3-1 Possible Departure from Top-down Sequence

Problem Area	Solution Not Using Top-Down Sequence	Solution Using Top-Down Sequence
I. Low-level module to be invoked by several higher level modules	Code and test early and put in subroutine library or source statement library	Redraw hierarchy chart, so that the module is invoked by a higher level module
II. *Module* specification still subject to change	Delay coding and testing	1. Code module anyway in anticipation that changes won't be that significant 2. Redraw hierarchy chart
III. More programmer labor available in early stages than later	1. Code in parallel even though the invoking modules are not finished 2. Negotiate with management for different programmer allocation	1. Don't use extra labor initially, although the project may require longer completion time 2. Negotiate with management for different man-power allocation

Planning for Test Data

Along with planning the order of module development, the entire program's test data should also be planned. At this point the type of tests should be decided. For example, one test might cause the program to run to completion without handling exceptional conditions. Here a sample of valid data might be used. For the first module test, a selected sample of three to five data records might suffice. Then a second sample of 100 to 250 records might be used. Of course, in the final testing, a complete set of actual data should be used.

Another test might involve data selected to exceed the typical range anticipated by the program. Yet another test might involve incorrect data, (e.g., negative when it should be positive or numeric when it should be alphabetic). When working with files whose records have *keys* associated with them, duplicate keys, nonexistent keys, invalid keys, and wrong-length keys should be included. For each test planned, the anticipated output should be defined. (For further information on test planning see Chapter 7.)

Why specify test data before coding?   There are several reasons for specifying data before coding:

1. It precludes the possibility of test data being designed to fit an already written program. It minimizes the possibility that the same omissions or errors made in coding will be made in test-data selection.
2. It promotes a better understanding of data requirements because many modules have interface dependencies that occur through the data.
3. It forces decisions and clarifications to be made earlier in the development cycle.
4. It focuses on the completed program from the beginning. By specifying test data first, the programmer concentrates on the final output that a program produces.
5. It provides continuity throughout the program phases: data established first, used during development, and then run against a completed program producing planned results.

Sometimes it is necessary to change the test data or add to it. This does not imply that early test-data definition should be postponed, anticipating that the data will be revised as the project proceeds. It simply means that, by defining a comprehensive test data set, if omissions and inconsistencies are found later, the test data can be changed accordingly.

It is not always possible to define a complete set of test data before coding begins. For example, in a large project it may take weeks to assemble all of the needed data for testing. Usually only a few people will be involved with this task. During this time what are other people on the project doing? For a better personnel utilization it might be convenient to code the top modules in parallel with test-data activities—providing that the data items are available before the module is first executed. Although this approach weakens the benefits of planning before coding, it may be necessary for the maximum use of resources.

Some installations use or write programs to generate test-data samples. These *data-generator programs* might use the data declarations (i.e., DATA DIVISION in

COBOL or DECLARE in PL/I) of the program to be tested. If this approach is used, the data definitions would be written first. Thus, some coding has been done before test data has been established. It would not be necessary, however, to create executable code at this time.

Who specifies test data?   Experienced and competent people—familiar with the application—should be responsible for test-data specifications. The users of the program should always be involved because they can often think of situations that programmers may be unfamiliar with. In addition, having users specify test data will help them to think through detailed requirements. Other people involved might be the systems analyst and the team leader. In other words, test data should be specified by a person other than the one writing the program to avoid one activity's influencing the other. This is not to say, however, that the programmer shouldn't also be thinking of test-data possibilities as he or she is developing the program.

IMPLEMENTATION

The *implementation phase* involves the actual preparation of test data, the creation and execution of the *job control language* (JCL), if any, and, finally, the coding and testing of the nucleus and the other modules or stubs.

Test-Data Preparation   The preparation of test data involves taking source documents on which data items have been specified and keying the data into the computer to prepare for testing.

Job Control Language (JCL)   If your system uses JCL, the next step is to define and code the complete JCL to be used by the finished program. This JCL will be used during the coding and testing to create the environment that will exist during the production run. (Here again, the emphasis is on the completed and running program.) To test the JCL statements, it may be necessary to run them with a null program which would be a stub for the main module. The advantage of coding and testing the complete JCL is that it forces details to be resolved sooner in the development cycle. These details might include specifications of file environments, amount of secondary storage needed, and number and size of internal data buffers. Specifying JCL before coding enhances the programming process by helping to avoid omissions or oversights in data definition, module interfaces, and module linkages.

Nucleus   A *nucleus* may consist of one or more top-level modules. The top module would be a part of the nucleus. The top module already written as a stub to test correctness of the JCL would be expanded first. If other modules are to be included in the nucleus, then the programmer must decide the order in which they will be added to the skeleton.

Stubs   In order to test programs from the top down, it is necessary to write stubs for the next level modules which have not yet been completed but are to be invoked by the current modules. This enables the invoking module to have a control path to the subordinate modules. The contents of the stubs can vary. Some kinds of stubs are:

1. Null

This would contain only the minimum necessary to return control to the routine that invoked it. The contents of a null stub vary based on the programming language being used as shown below.

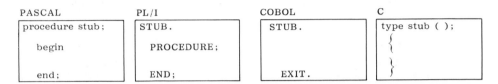

PASCAL

```
procedure stub;

  begin

  end;
```

PL/I

```
STUB.

  PROCEDURE;

  END;
```

COBOL

```
STUB.

  EXIT.
```

C

```
type stub ( );
  {
  {
  }
  }
```

You would use a null stub for a module when the rest of the program that is being tested doesn't need any data or processing that this module performs. For example, an output routine that provides an additional optional formatting of results could first be written as a null stub.

2. "Got Here"

A small extension to the null stub would be to have it print a message containing its name, thereby indicating that it had been invoked. This simple addition gives a trace of program flow. With the output messages it is possible to establish that modules have been invoked the proper number of times and in the proper order. Some language compilers contain a feature which automatically gives trace information. If this is the case, it might be more desirable to use that feature of the compiler rather than add the "got here" message to the otherwise null stubs.

3. Set Indicator

We have stated that lower level modules should not take actions that control the operation of higher level modules. Rather, modules may return to the calling module indications of what has occurred during their execution. Thus, the routines are linked by the passage of data items or indicators so that the function of acting on these items is separated. When a module is in the stub status, the communication of results must be taken into account. Some stubs must be written so that indicators are set appropriately if the invoking routine depends on them for its correct execution.

Consider the CHECK VALIDITY module in the previous bank inquiry example in Figure 3-3. It is invoked by GET AUTHORIZED TRANSACTION, and needs to send back to it an indication of whether or not the current transaction is valid. The invoking module then needs to check that indicator to determine whether to continue processing the transaction or cancel it. To test the statement in the GET AUTHORIZED TRANS-

ACTION module that makes that check, it is necessary to have the CHECK VALIDITY stub send back each of the two possible outcomes. Thus, the first time it is invoked it might send back an indication of a valid transaction, and the second time, an invalid one.

Note that the validation is not now being performed by the stub. All that the stub needs to do is send back to its invoker the various possibilities for the indicator.

Similarly, any error or unusual condition that a module could detect and return to its invoker should be included in the stub version of the module. The conditions would be simulated in that only the dummy indication of their occurrence would be returned. This type of stub allows for full testing of upper modules. (When functions are clearly separated, the number of indicators sent back to a calling module should be relatively few.)

4. Provide data

A stub might provide or modify data that is used by its invoker or other modules in the program. For example, the GET AUTHORIZED TRANSACTION module reads and validates transactions for the other modules to process. When written as a stub it still needs to make these transactions available. Instead of actually doing the reading and verifying, however, it could merely send back "dummy" data. That is, a list of valid transactions could be placed into the stub, and at each invocation it could return one of them.

Processing of the dummy record is done by the higher level module; thus, it could be determined that a valid record is properly handled. Later the stub is expanded to actually read a message (record) from the terminal and perform the verification required.

As another example, consider a module that takes a list of data items passed to it and sorts it into ascending sequence based on the first ten characters. It could be written as a stub to ignore the list sent to it and to send back a second list that contains the items presorted. Or consider a module that reads input records and updates an existing file. Each input record is to be sequence checked and validated for data being within prescribed ranges. When written as a stub, this module could read a small file in which all records were in sequence and had data within the prescribed limits. These are examples of stubs that perform a subset of their final data-handling function. This subset may require a few lines of code that may or may not remain when the module is expanded.

If the stub is to return a large amount of data, or send back many indicators, then it may be easier to write the complete module first. You do this if the stub is half or more as long and complex as the module—especially if a large part of the stub is throw-away code.

Whichever of these types of stubs you use, you employ the principle of only doing as much as is needed to completely test the rest of the program. Afterward, each stub is expanded into a full module and tested with *its* stubs. In this way you proceed adding modules and stubs in the top-down order you have previously determined.

Module Libraries   By following the principles presented you will be creating modules that

- perform a single function, and
- are independent of the other modules in the program

There is a high probability that some of these modules will be usable in other programs. You should build up a library of reusable modules to simplify and reduce later programming. If you are in a company where others are developing similar types of programs, then a common library is a must.

To make libraries of reusable modules work, it is necessary to adopt some guidelines to ensure consistency. Such things as how modules are named and described need to be standardized so that it is possible to search for an existing module easily. Some organizations have created extensive libraries that can be used as building blocks for various programs. This follows easily from the principles of structured programming and can be a great value. Not only does it reduce the amount of new coding needed, but since pretested modules are being used from the library, testing is also easier.

MANAGEMENT IMPLICATIONS

Top-down development tends to produce modules that are independent of each other. However, this is not always true, as in the case of data dependencies discussed in this chapter. As a manager you need to be aware of these dependencies and attempt to minimize them. Otherwise there can be a chain of modules each dependent on the previous one for its data. Then these modules need to be developed serially, which leads to all of them being on the *critical path*.

Resource Utilization

The top-down development of a program or system has major ramifications in terms of traditional project resource utilization. Typically, in traditional projects, people are assigned to a project for the life of the project. This may result in people being tied up when actually not required. Often a large amount of machine time near the end of the project is required as there is a recycling through other phases for a second or third time. With top-down design both personnel and computer usage patterns will differ from those of traditional projects.

Personnel Allocation   The project workload expands as the system grows. At the beginning of the implementation stage, only a few people are needed to write the higher level modules. As coding proceeds to lower levels and more modules, additional people need to be assigned to the project. An advantage of top-down development is that this increase in personnel can be predicted.

The independence of modules facilitates dividing the modules among several programmers so that they may work on various parts simultaneously. Dr. Harlan Mills has suggested that a "meaningful" piece of work for one programmer might be 2,000 lines of code. Thus, one programmer may be assigned several large modules (e.g., one leg) in a hierarchy chart or perhaps 20 small modules.

Top-down development suggests that a larger portion of project time be devoted to planning and less to implementation. The additional time in planning will involve only a few people even on a large project. One approach to top-down planning is to involve at least two people: one individual responsible for the completed plan, and one or more people responsible for selection of test data and test planning.

Computer Allocation   In bottom-up development there is often a large increase of machine usage at the end of the project. Figure 3-4 contrasts typical bottom-up machine usage with an example of top-down usage. The top-down usage depicted was part of the Skylab Mission, where computer usage was reported as being constant from the ninth to the 24th (and last) month of the project.[1]

The total machine usage is not usually any greater with top-down development; frequently, it is less. At first it might seem that additional time is needed because (1) the testing period is stretched out over a large part of the implementation stage, or (2) testing one module at the bottom of the hierarchy necessitates executing many other modules before it. However, this increase in early use of resources is offset by greater reductions in machine usage in later stages. Thus, there is not the usual peak at the end of a project.

Project Management

In top-down development, part of the program is running very early in the project, even if it is trivial. This part is constantly expanding during the project. This has several advantages:

1. Programmer morale is raised by seeing initial results early.
2. This boost in morale continues and grows as additional capabilities are continually being added. Confidence builds.
3. Progress is more easily scheduled and measured. Dates are established for specific functions to be available in the growing program and then used to determine completion of a milestone.
4. An incremental approach to completion can be used; that is, a date set for the availability of the final program, along with earlier dates for portions of it. Thus a subset of the types of transactions can be handled or one of the two types of output allowed.

---

[1] F. T. Baker and H. D. Mills, "Chief Programmer Teams," *Datamation*, December 1973. Reprinted with the permission of DATAMATION® Copyright 1973 by Technical Publishing Company, Greenwich, Connecticut 06830.

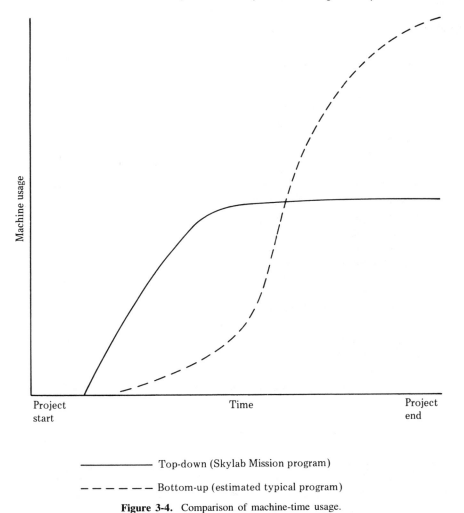

Top-down (Skylab Mission program)

– – – – – – Bottom-up (estimated typical program)

Figure 3-4. Comparison of machine-time usage.

Top-down development really lets you manage a programming project. It puts specifics into a phased development and gives you the means to measure progress.

Quality

The top-down approach to early testing verifies the correctness of the program, especially the high-level routines which contain the overall logic and control. Of course, the design, planning, and implementation phases take preparation, understanding, time, and experience to do well. However, the benefits of timely (or even early) completion—of having a program with a high level of reliability and one which is less expensive to maintain and modify—are worth several times the initial cost of using top-down development.

SUMMARY

In top-down development, there is an emphasis on planning carefully before implementing. Not only is it difficult to discipline oneself to defer coding but it's also difficult to actually do the planning. Lack of familiarity and experience in top-down planning will make it more difficult the first time. Subsequent attempts will be easier as techniques and expertise are refined, but planning will probably remain a time-consuming and exacting task.

Top-down development requires a more complete job of designing modules and establishing data dependencies between the modules. Planning the creation of stubs and the testing procedure requires great attention to detail to ensure that the test sequence is possible and that the tests will be sufficient. This is particularly true for more complex programs where the number of modules, interfaces, and data dependencies among them is large. It is here that planning is invaluable. Inadequate planning could cause redesigning, recoding, and retesting, all resulting in additional costs and delays.

Figure 3-5 summarizes the basic steps to be taken in the planning and implementation stages of a program-development effort. The planning stage establishes the order of module development and testing. This development order may not be strictly by levels as determined by the hierarchy chart, nor strictly in order of execution, but usually will be a combination of the hierarchical and execution-order approaches. A deep knowledge of the interrelationships between the modules is essential. The investment of time and effort to determine the coding and testing plan is usually repaid by the absence of large delays and costs caused by inadequate design or testing. The effective use of resources and specification of test data should also be planned before coding begins.

The implementation stage focuses on the completed program throughout the development process. Thus, test data and JCL should be prepared before the nucleus is coded.

A nucleus is created first and then modules are gradually added, expanding its capabilities. In testing the modules it will be necessary to write stubs for some of the unwritten lower modules. Stubs may range from a simple return statement to a skeleton of the module that provides some data to permit testing of the module above. Each module is added separately, and problems are identified and corrected before proceeding to lower levels. As each stub is expanded into a module, it generates the need for additional stubs at the next lower level and the process repeats. At all times an executable program is being tested. Each new section of code is tested against established code in an environment comparable to actual operational use.

Top-down-development schedules can be set by functional or module milestones. For example, we might state something to the effect: "As of April 15, we shall be able to run all file-update transactions. This will include modules A, D, and E." The type of statement to avoid is "As of April 15, the project will be 30 percent completed." The statement should indicate when specific functions (i.e., specific modules) will be finished and incorporated into the program. Thus, when a module can be demonstrated

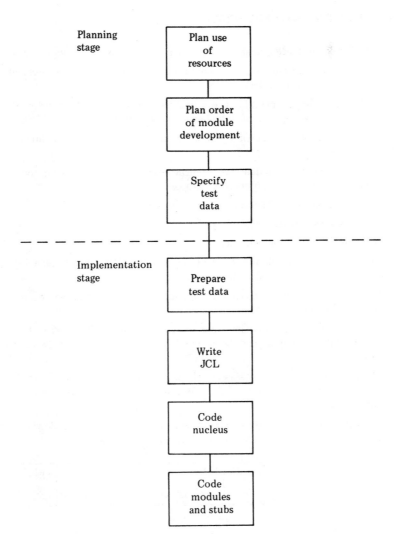

Figure 3-5. Steps in top-down development.

by running with planned test data, there is no doubt as to whether or not the milestone has been achieved.

Top-down development leads to projects whose progress is smooth and predictable, whose module interface and integration problems are minimized, and whose resources are more evenly distributed.

REVIEW QUESTIONS AND EXERCISES

1. Top-down development is a three-step process. What are these steps?

2. What are two problems that could arise when using a strict hierarchical approach in planning module-development order?

3. What types of modules (i.e., functions) justify departure from a strict execution-order approach in planning the module-development order?

4. To preserve a top-down-development approach, what two conditions must be met before a module can be coded?

5. In planning the module-development order, is a departure from top-down sequence a management problem or a programmer problem? Why?

6. Why specify data before coding a module?

7. Who specifies test data? Why?

8. What is a program nucleus?

9. In top-down development, where more emphasis is given to planning *before* implementing, how is manpower typically allocated?

10. Contrast computer resource requirements in a traditional approach with those where top-down development is used.

11. Refer to the development order shown in the hierarchy chart in Figure 3-3. List the stubs each module will require and the actions each stub must take (e.g. create data, set indicator, print output).

12. Refer to the hierarchy chart in Figure 2-16. List the modules in the order in which you would code and test them. Give the reason for each module's position in the sequence and list the stubs it will require.

13. Define as reasonably complete a set of test data for the following record (N = numeric digit, A = alphabetic character, X = alphameric character):

ITEM NO.	DESCRIPTION	QTY	PRICE
NNNNAA	XXXXXXXXXXXXXXXXXXXX	NNNN	NNN.NN

4

Structured Programming

"GOTO is a four-letter word"[1]

It has been proved that *sequence*, *choice*, and *repetition* structures are sufficient to solve any logic problem. The result is based on a theoretical foundation defined by Bohm and Jacopini.[2] The proof is something that you, as a programmer won't need to know unless you're so inclined. Mills[3] provided essentially the same proof. It is centered around converting each part of a program to one or more of the three basic structures—leaving the remaining parts of the program smaller than before. By sufficient repetitions the remaining unstructured portion of the program can be reduced until it is nonexistent or not needed. The proof demonstrates that the result of this process is an equivalent program that needs only the basic structures. This proof might lead to the thinking that the way to write structured code is to write unstructured code and then *convert* it. However, this is not the case.

The proof applies only to proper programs. A *proper program* has these characteristics:

1. It has one entry point.
2. It has one exit point.
3. It has no dead (unreachable) code.
4. It has no infinite loops.

Sequence, choice, and repetition are proper programs in the sense that they also have these characteristics. In this chapter we define the basic structures in detail as well

---

[1]Paraphrased from, "The use of four-letter words like GOTO can occasionally be justified even in the best of company." Donald E. Knuth, "Structured Programming with **go to** Statements," *Computing Surueys*, Vol. 6, No. 4, December 1974.

[2]Corrado Bohm and Guiseppe Jacopini, "Flow Diagrams, Turing Machines, and Languages with Only Two Formation Rules," *Communications of the ACM*, Vol. 9, May 1966, pp. 366-371.

[3]Harlan D. Mills, *Mathematical Foundations for Structured Programming*, IBM, Form No. FSC 72-6012, February 1972.

as several optional structures and then present the pseudo code for expressing these structures. (*Pseudo code* is a means of expressing a program's logic that can be used instead of flowcharts.) A person fairly new to programming will find the last section of this chapter of particular value, as it deals with programming techniques and style in structured programs.

PROGRAM STRUCTURES

Symbols

The symbols used in describing these logic constructs include process, decision, and collector symbols and connector lines.

Process Box   The symbol for a *process node*, which is also called a *functional node*, represents an operation that is to be performed. It consists of a rectangle with one control path leading into it and one leading out.

The process *a*, which appears in the box, may be a single executable instruction, a call to and return from a subroutine, another logic structure, or a number of logic structures forming a subprogram or subroutine.

Decision Symbol   The decision symbol, also called a *predicate node*, specifies a test operation. It consists of the standard decision box and is characterized by one control path leading in and two paths leading out. The specification *p* (for predicate) represents a test to be performed. One or the other output path (but not both) is taken as a result of the test.

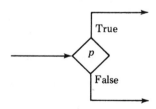

Collector Symbol   The collector symbol is a circle where control paths converge.

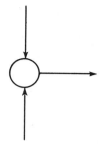

No operation is performed at the node. It is simply a junction which typically has two entries and one exit. Normally, no symbol is written in the collector node.

Connector Lines   Connector lines represent the passing of control from one of the above symbols to another in the direction of the arrow:

These four symbols are the only ones needed to draw any of the basic structures.

Sequence Structure

Sequencing indicates that control flows from one process box to the next in sequence.

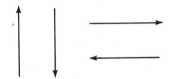

Because a single process block can be replaced by a sequence structure (two process blocks), a sequence structure can be expanded by repeating this procedure to provide for the sequential execution of any number of functions.

For a *complete* process to be performed, it may be necessary to execute code that is *out of line*. This point is illustrated as follows:

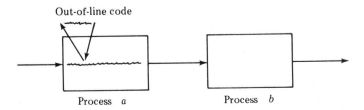

Out-of-line code

Process   *a*   Process   *b*

The out-of-line code represents a subroutine or subprogram. Control may pass out-of-line as long as control returns to the next sequential step. The integrity of the sequence structure is preserved by each subroutine or subprogram itself being a *proper program*.

The out-of-line code could be a group of programming statements (such as paragraphs in COBOL or internal procedures in PL/I) to which control is passed to be subsequently returned. Thus, a sequence structure is one in which a series of operations is performed in order, with perhaps some detours, but always returning to the main stream and proceeding in a forward direction.

Choice Structure

This structure, an IFTHENELSE, provides for a choice between two alternatives. In the following diagram the logical expression *p* is evaluated, where *p* could be a single variable representing a true/false, yes/no, on/off, or similar binary condition, or combination of variables in an expression.

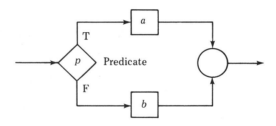

The expression specified must be capable of being resolved into the true/false condition. If the expression is true, then process *a* is executed. If it is false, process *b* is executed. Both processes *a* and *b* flow to a common point.

The two flow lines emerging from the process blocks meet at the collector node; logic continues along the same line. Thus, it is possible for the reader of the flowchart or the program to determine that control passes from one point to another with only the question of which alternative path is taken.

As with the sequence structure, the process block can be expanded to include as many statements as desired. The process block(s) may also be replaced by another structure. Also, it is possible to *nest* an IFTHENELSE structure within an IF-THENELSE structure (Figure 4-1). In fact, it is possible to nest them to any depth as long as readability is preserved. Readability decreases as nesting increases.

Repetition—DOWHILE

This structure provides for the repetitive execution or loop operation required by most computer programs. It is drawn as follows:

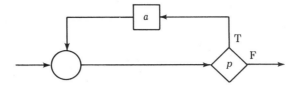

In this structure the flow passes through the collector node to the decision symbol where a test is made. Here the logical expression *p* is evaluated. If it is true (T), then process *a* is executed and *p* is evaluated again. If the expression tested is false (F), then *a* is not executed. Because the expression *p* is evaluated *before* any process statements are executed, it is possible that the coding contained with process *a* may never be executed. If *p* contains a variable which would be initialized prior to entry into the structure, this variable would then be modified as a part of process *a*. The modification of the control variable affecting the test is a necessity; otherwise, the program would be in an endless loop—thus violating one of the rules for a proper program. The process block of the DOWHILE could contain sequence structures, choice structures, or other repetition structures in any combination to represent any kind of logic.

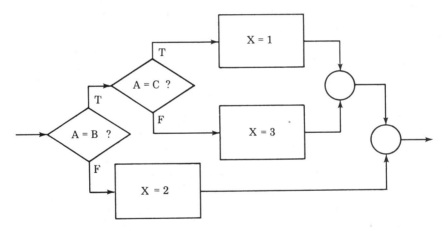

Figure 4-1. Nested IFTHENELSE structures.

Figure 4-2 shows a structured flowchart to find the largest value in a table of 100 numbers. The three basic structures have been used and are labeled in the flowchart. However, structured flowcharts do not include the name of the specific structure. Each of these structures is itself a *proper program* in that it has only one entry and one exit point and has a control path from the entry to the exit for all its process blocks.

Some people have added a variation to the DOWHILE structure. In the DOWHILE the condition is tested only once for each repetition, at the beginning of the loop. But suppose that under certain circumstances you want to terminate the loop somewhere in the middle. For example, an error might be detected that requires that

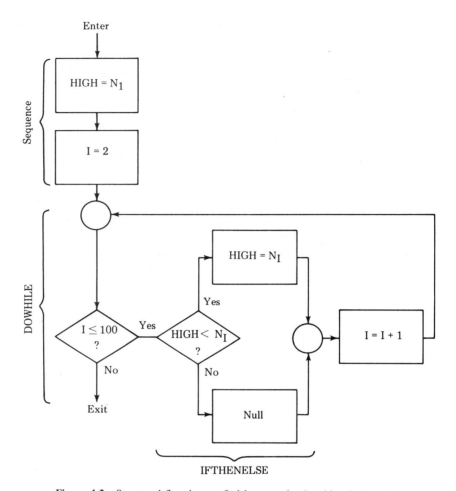

Figure 4-2. Structured flowchart to find largest value in table of 100 data items.

processing be discontinued. The variation to the DOWHILE permits a test to be made for this condition somewhere in the loop. If the condition were found to be true then the loop is exited early. Essentially, control passes to the end of the loop. Notice that this does not destroy the one-entry one-exit rule, because the loop always terminates at the same point.

Although these structures are sufficient to write any program, several additional structures have been proposed because they allow, in some cases, greater programing convenience without detracting from the goal of program readability. DOUNTIL and CASE are discussed here.

Repetition—DOUNTIL

DOUNTIL is another type of loop structure. It is drawn as follows:

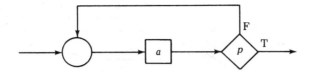

The DOUNTIL structure provides essentially the same loop capability as the DOWHILE, differing from it in two respects:

1. In a DOUNTIL structure the test is performed *after* the process *a* has been executed, whereas in a DOWHILE structure the test is performed *before* any execution of code within the range of the loop. Thus, a DOUNTIL loop will always be performed at least once, regardless of the value of *p*.

2. DOUNTIL terminates when *p* is true, whereas DOWHILE terminates when *p* is false. In other words, "do the loop operation *until* the condition tested is true."

The DOUNTIL structure is equivalent to the following sequence and DOWHILE structures:

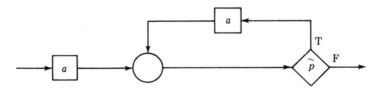

This concatenates a duplicate of box *a* with a DOWHILE structure. Because the DOWHILE exits on a false condition, the test for the predicate must be reversed (i.e., not *p*) to achieve the DOUNTIL logic. Thus, a DOUNTIL structure can be transformed into an equivalent structure containing simple sequencing and a DOWHILE.

Another approach that will accomplish the logic of the DOUNTIL is to specify a DOWHILE but set *p* true before entering the DOWHILE. This will cause the process block *a* to be performed at least once.

CASE Structure

The CASE structure is an extension of the choice structure. The need for it arises when the execution of one of many alternatives is to be selected based on a test. The structure may be drawn as follows:

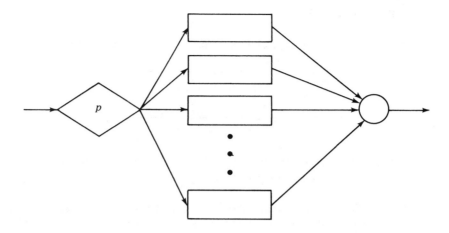

Here, as with the IFTHENELSE, the paths from the various process blocks merge at the same point and then continue in a forward direction. The flow will always be from the entry point to the exit point, with the exact path to be determined by the test.

The CASE structure is equivalent to the nested IFTHENELSE structure in Figure 4-3.

The justification for using the decision symbol to begin the CASE structure is that CASE is a variation of the IFTHENELSE structure. As an alternative, if it is desired to use a unique symbol to start the CASE structure, then these new symbols may be used:

Entry   Exit

The structure may be drawn as follows:

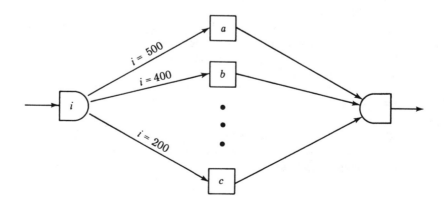

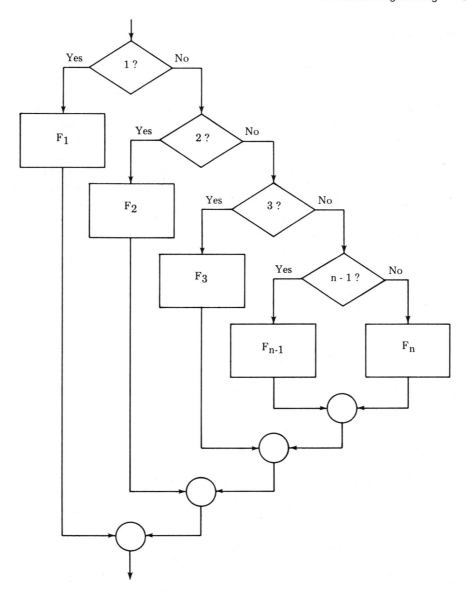

Figure 4-3. CASE structure equivalent.

Whether the decision symbol or these new symbols are used, they should be standard so all who need to can read each other's charts.

These structures may be varied somewhat, based on the programming language used (see Chapters 8–11). You may wish to add additional structures for convenience as long as they can be represented by a combination of the three basic structures.

PSEUDO CODE

Flow diagrams have been used to illustrate the various program structures described in this chapter. In Figure 4-2 it was suggested that these constructs are then combined to form a *structured program flowchart*. In structured programming detailed program flowcharts may be eliminated. (This is particularly good news to those programmers who draw program flowcharts—for documentation purposes—*after* a program is coded and debugged.)

It is still necessary, however, to describe a program's logic before the coding is started. An alternative method to detailed program flowcharting is to use a notation called *pseudo code*. It bridges the gap between native language and computer languages. It is an intermediate notation that allows expression of a program's logic in a somewhat formalized fashion without having to be concerned with syntax details of the programming language. Pseudo code resembles a programming language in that it can be used to express specific operations such as:

- Read next transaction
- Add daily sales to weekly sales
- Compute standard deviation

It differs from a programming language in two ways:

1. It can be used to express more complex or less specific operations. For example:

Find a matching record

2. It is not bound by any formal language syntactical rules. The only conventions are those related to the use of the structures themselves and the *indentation* that aids in reading the logic.

Pseudo code is used to design program logic *before* coding a problem. It is a vehicle for explaining how the program will operate. Thus, in installations where structured walk-throughs are used, another programmer would review the pseudo code program before it is coded in a programming language. One advantage to this approach is that it's easier to make changes to pseudo code than to a source program already prepared for machine processing.

When the final program is coded and tested, the pseudo code for simpler programs will probably be discarded if the source program is as readable as the pseudo code. For more complex programs the pseudo code must be maintained as part of the program documentation—in place of flowcharts or other specifications. (Of course, subsequent changes to a program must first be incorporated into the pseudo code.)

Expressing Program Structures in Pseudo Code

There is no single or formal definition of what form pseudo code should take. Pseudo code may contain whatever makes sense to the programmer. But here are some guidelines you may find helpful:

General Do not use any of the optional structures—for example, DOUNTIL— if they are not in the programming language you are using. Use capital letters for control structures.

Sequence Structure Write each statement on a separate line. For example:

```
Read next sales record
Multiply price by quantity giving sales amount
Compute roots of quadratic equation
```

Any line may later be expanded to show more detail.

IFTHENELSE Structure Because high-level programming languages contain an IF statement, using this keyword in your pseudo code is appropriate. For example:

```
IF amount passes edit checks
    Accumulate to total
ELSE
    Print error message
    Reject rest of record
ENDIF
```

The IF and ELSE are aligned vertically, and THEN may be written if desired. The purpose of the ENDIF is to explicitly mark the end of the structure. The ENDIF could be an aid to the reader of a program in that it emphasizes logic.

Write the words IF, ELSE, and ENDIF for a single structure in the same relative position. To indicate the true and false functions, use separate lines and indent. For a single IF, omit the ELSE if no action is to be taken (null ELSE). In nested IFs a null ELSE may be necessary to maintain proper logic. Nested IFs are indented to show structuring as illustrated here:

```
IF negative balance
    Call negative balance routine
ELSE
    IF zero balance
        Call normal balance routine
    ELSE
        Call positive balance routine
        Add balance to total
    ENDIF
ENDIF
```

DOWHILE Structure   Use a keyword that is appropriate to the programming language in which you are going to be coding. See Table 4-1.

Some COBOL installations use the DO because it is descriptive, shorter than PERFORM, and more standard. The terms LOOP and REPEAT may also be used. It is recommended that the end of a loop be explicitly defined by the terms ENDDO or ENDLOOP. They indicate which statments are to be included in the loop, and can be a reminder that they may translate into actual source statements. For example:

```
Read first record
DOWHILE more transactions
    Call validate record
    IF ok
        Call process record
        Call print
    ENDIF
    Read next record
ENDDO
```

Align the DOWHILE and ENDDO. For the statements contained within the range of the DO, use separate lines and indent.

DOUNTIL Structure   DOUNTIL is appropriate for this optional structure. As with DOWHILE, you may wish to replace DOUNTIL with a term relating to your programming language (e.g., PERFORM in COBOL). For example:

```
DOUNTIL number of months is greater than 9
    Call exponential smoothing
    Call output routine
ENDDO
```

If your standards and your programming language permit the early exit from a loop, you may wish to use an EXIT pseudo code statement. This terminates the loop, and control passes to the statement following the loop. For example:

```
DOUNTIL end of file
    Read a record
    IF read error
        EXIT LOOP
    ENDIF
    Process record
    Accumulate totals
ENDDO
```

CASE Structure   Because this structure is a variation of the IFTHENELSE, you may express the structure in a series of nested IF statements in which the ELSEs

Table 4-1 Examples of Pseudo code keywords

Language	DOWHILE Pseudo Code Example
COBOL	PERFORM UNTIL minutes > 60
C, PASCAL	WHILE minutes ≤ 60 DO
PL/I	DOWMILE minutes ≤ 60

are aligned under the first IF. Here only *one* ENDIF terminates the CASE structure. For example:

```
IF customer code = 100
      Call special account routine
ELSE IF customer code = 200
      Call thirty day account routine
ELSE IF customer code = 300
      Call revolving account routine
ELSE
      Call customer code error routine
ENDIF
```

A preferred approach is to use a pseudo code term such as CASESTART or CASEENTRY to indicate the beginning of the structure. This would be followed by the variable being tested to determine which of the various alternatives will be executed. Then each of the possible cases would be listed, indented from the CASESTART and including the value of the variable. The structure would end with ENDCASE. For example:

```
CASESTART customer code
      CASE 100
            Call special account routine
      CASE 200
            Call thirty day account routine
      CASE 300
            Call revolving account routine
      CASE none of above
            Call customer code error routine
ENDCASE
```

This chapter presented the basic and optional structures that you will be using. The next chapter shows how these structures are used to create a program. It shows a technique for taking a specification and, through a series of iterations, evolve the logic of the program. Later that logic can be written in the programming language you are using.

Structuring Unstructured Programs

You may sometimes be faced with the problem of taking an existing, nonstructured program and structuring it. There are several techniques for doing this which we will introduce shortly. However, you must seriously question whether it is worth doing for each individual case. Some of the considerations to take into account are:

1. All of the techniques available have limitations, and none work with programs that are highly unstructured. If you have a BS[4] program to convert they won't help you.
2. The techniques take a lot of time and effort. If you are experienced in structured programming, you may find it easier to rewrite the program from scratch.
3. In some cases the technique of structuring will actually make the converted program less readable. Wolberg[5] makes the point that you can even introduce errors during the structuring process.
4. The techniques result in a program that conforms to the rules of structured programming, but not necessarily the spirit. In other words, you will get the structures but not the other benefits, such as meaningful names, clear flow, and indentation, which make structured programs easy to read and maintain.

Despite the limitations just listed, you may still choose to structure some programs. For those that are close to being structured already and seem worth the effort, here are some techniques you can use:

Duplication of Coding   If the program jumps out of line to execute a few instructions and then returns, you could duplicate these instructions in line.

State Variable   In this technique, the program is subdivided into sections, each of which is branched to at least once. These portions of code are each assigned an arbitrary number. Then all of the program flow is controlled by setting a special variable, called a *state variable*. Instead of one routine branching directly to another, the first one merely sets this variable to be the number of that routine. Then it returns to a main controlling routine which examines the variable and branches to the respective portion of code.

Boolean Flag   For simple cases, such as a portion of code that has one entry but two exits, you can set a flag before entering it. Each of the two possible exits would then reset the flag appropriately and return control to the top of the section of code. There the flag is tested and the proper action taken.

[4]Bowl of Spaghetti.
[5]John R. Wolberg, *Conversion of Computer Software*, Englewood Cliffs, NJ: Prentice-Hall Inc, 1983.

For further discussion of these three techniques see the Yourdan, Ashcroft-Manna, and Gilbert references in the Bibliography.

CASE STUDY

In earlier chapters we stressed the importance of program readability. In this chapter, structures and the pseudo code for expressing those structures have been defined. As a means of tying together readability and structuring, a small sample problem is presented here.

Let us assume that a large office building monitors temperatures from the various floors over a given period of time. This is done to minimize energy requirements for the operation of the building. Of course, a *data-acquisition* or *sensor-based computer* is required to read temperatures and store them for processing later. Initially, the program is to count the number of temperatures (sampled once a minute for one hour) that are less than 64° or above 78°. Here is a pseudo code solution to be critiqued for readability and correctness.

```
LOOP 60 times
Read temp
IF temp < 64 increment counter 1
IF temp > 78 increment counter 2
ENDLOOP
Print counter 1 and counter 2
```

In the area of readability, things that are wrong with the code include (1) no indentation of the pseudo code, (2) nondescriptive data names, and (3) no ENDIFs marking the end of the IFTHENELSEs. With respect to program correctness, two faults should be noted: counter 1 and counter 2 were not initialized to zero, and the program will fail (i.e., abnormally end) if there are fewer than 60 values in the input file.

These problems suggest implementing a number of guidelines:

1. *Indent all code to show logic and highlight structures.*
2. *Use self-defining data names.* The terms *counter 1* and *counter 2* are too general. Had this section of code been part of a larger program, these names would not, in any way, be obvious as to their intent.
3. *Use long data names even if the programming language to be used does not permit them.* Thus, TEMP is less descriptive than TEMPERATURE—particularly since TEMP has been used in programs to mean a temporary variable or temporary storage. If necessary, the descriptive data name can be shortened when coding the problem.
4. *Use ENDIF to clarify IFTHENELSE structures.* This is particularly valuable when nested IFs are specified.

5. *Keep logic simple*. For example, simple IFs are easier to read for logic than nested IFs. In the previous example, two simple IF statements were specified. Each time through the loop, they both will be executed. Logically, however, it is not necessary to execute both IFs because if the first counter is incremented (i.e., temperature is less than 64°), it is not necessary to test the temperature for being greater than 78°. The second IF could be bypassed by using a nested IF. This would make the program run faster. If you are sure the logic is right and you are not sacrificing readability, coding first for clarity and then for efficiency is acceptable.

6. *Code the program to handle the end-of-file condition*. This sample program assumed there would always be 60 values to process. If there are fewer than 60 values, the program will fail because it is not designed to recognize the end-of-file condition.

With a structured approach to programming, some of the typical ways in which things "have always been done" must be reevaluated. One specific area is how to handle the end-of-file condition by using only the basic structures. Traditionally, GOTO statements were used to branch out of the normal processing routine. For example:

```
LOOP:  Read next record
       IF end-of-file GOTO EOJ
       Process record
       GOTO LOOP
EOJ:   Close files
End of job
```

This example is not structured, for there is a branch back to an earlier section of code as well as a branch to another section of code when an end-of-file is reached. A structured solution is to use the DOWHILE construct:

```
More records to process = yes
DOWHILE More records to process
         .
         .
         .
ENDDO
```

More records to process is an indicator which must be initialized (e.g., ON, YES, TRUE). When the end-of-file (EOF) is reached, the indicator should be turned OFF (or NO or FALSE) so that there will be an exit from the DOWHILE structure. How this is actually done depends on the programming language used. For pseudo code purposes we will specify *after* the READ statement how the end-of-file indicator is changed when EOF occurs. For example:

```
More records to process = yes
DOWHILE more records to process
    Read a record
        EOF sets more records to process = no
    .
    .
    .
ENDDO
```

Immediately following the READ statement it is necessary in the previous example to *test* the end-of-file indicator. This is because, following a READ, we typically process the record read. When end-of-file is detected, an alternate path (bypassing the record-processing code) must be taken. An IFTHENELSE structure could indicate whether *processing* or *wrap-up activities* such as printing final totals and closing files should be done following the READ operation. For example:

```
More records to process = yes
DOWHILE more records to process
    Read a record
        EOF sets more records to process = no
    IF more records to process = yes
        Process record
    ELSE
        Handle end-of-file activities
    ENDIF
ENDDO
```

Another way in which this could have been implemented is to handle the end-of-file activities outside the DOWHILE.

```
More records to process = yes
DOWHILE more records to process
    Read a record
        EOF sets more records to process = no
    IF more records to process = yes
        Process record
    ENDIF
ENDDO
Handle end-of-file activities
```

The structured method of reading and processing records may seem awkward to implement and, in some ways, more complex than the unstructured approach (one in which a GOTO is used). However, a number of common program bugs have in the past cropped up in these unstructured programs. Either the label indicating the beginning of the loop was placed on the wrong statement initially (or subsequently when program modifications were made), or the GOTO intending to return to the beginning of the loop operation was actually a GOTO to another label within the loop. Neither of these types of bugs can occur in the structured code.

Figure 4-4 shows the temperatures program again—this time with indented pseudo code, descriptive data names, ENDIFs, initialization of variables, and a structured approach to the handling of end-of-file.

```
Above  =  0
Below  =  0
More temperatures  =  yes
DOWHILE more temperatures
   Read a temperature
      EOF sets more temperatures  =  no
   IF more temperatures  =  yes
      IF temperature < 64
         Increment below
      ELSE
         IF temperature > 78
            Increment above
         ENDIF
      ENDIF
   ENDIF
ENDDO
Print results
```

Figure 4-4. Pseudo code to count temperature readings above or below given boundaries.

MANAGEMENT IMPLICATIONS

Programmer Acceptance

An interesting paradox is that highly competent programmers tend to accept structured programming more rapidly than the average programmer, but the latter appears to benefit more dramatically from the use of these technologies. One reason that competent programmers are attracted to and readily accept structured programming is that it extends and refines the general principles they have been following for years. In fact, some will state that there is nothing new about structured programming; it is the basic way they have been programming all along. One reason that the average programmer stands to benefit more is that structured programming offers a short cut method for learning techniques that usually come only after years of experience.

The reaction to structured programming by some, if not all, programmers may be depicted in stages of acceptance as follows:

Fear

↓

Neutrality

↓

Enthusiasm

If *fear* is the initial reaction, it may be because coding is delayed, thereby causing one to feel that structured programming will take longer. As the process becomes familiar, the programmer usually becomes *neutral*. After a couple of months of seeing the benefits of the new techniques, the overall reaction is usually one of *enthusiasm*.

The implication for management is not to force rapid acceptance of structured programming. Managers must allow time for the programmers to use the new techniques for a period of, say, three months. During this time the programmers use structured programming, but they know it is on a trial basis only. At the end of the three months their opinions are solicited and a decision is made as to whether or not to adopt it as an installation standard. When there is no force to change, there is more likelihood of willingness to accept the newer methods.

Efficiency

When a programmer first writes structured programs there may be some reduction in productivity. This reduction is only temporary. Productivity should return to its original point and then increase.

Comparisons made between structured and unstructured programs have not shown any consistent difference with respect to program efficiency. The programs are similar in terms of number of source statements required, size of object code, and speed of execution. The variations that result are sometimes in favor of structured programs and at other times in favor of unstructured programs. The difference appears to be more related to the ability of the programmer than to whether or not structured techniques are being used. A structured approach will probably keep very inefficient programs from being written. For those programs that do take more storage and execution time after having been structured, it is generally felt that the costs of program maintenance justify the reduced efficiency. This is especially true when the costs of program execution are compared with the costs of programming personnel to achieve execution-time savings.

Training

Learning the rules of structured programming is easy; applying them takes time. Therefore, the method of developing qualified structured programmers is to provide them with the opportunity to practice. In this way they encounter many situations, and in working out solutions their experience level increases steadily. One approach is to select a small group of highly experienced programmers and give them time to experiment, study, exchange ideas, and develop their expertise. Then they can advise the rest of the staff. Another approach is to use the *buddy system* in which two programmers learning structured programming can review each other's work. This idea can be expanded into a larger review session in which three or more people routinely review each other's work as suggested in structured walk-throughs (see Chapter 6).

Ideally, structured programming should be part of the entry-level training of all programmers. This avoids programmers picking up unstructured techniques and then having to unlearn them.

Standards

For structured programming to be effective, it is necessray to have a set of standards covering its use. The specific guidelines for structured programming may vary from one location to another, but within one group or project uniformity is needed. Standards should be based on criteria of readability and ease of modification.

Selection of standards will require some experimentation. Time will be needed to collect and synthesize programmers' reactions. If standards are to be accepted, the programmers must recognize their value, and they must be practical to implement.

One approach is to try structured programming first on a pilot project. A *pilot project* is not an experiment but is a project which is done in a carefully controlled and studied way. The people involved need to have an open mind in trying new techniques, evaluating the project, and recommending changes. The pilot project should be kept small and monitored closely to determine progress and evaluate the methods used. This approach should allow a workable set of standards to emerge. Other programming groups could see the suggested approaches, try them, and express their reactions. In this way standards will be more realistic and practical.

Several factors underlie a DP department's ability to achieve specified standards:

1. If people participate in the setting of standards, their willingness to follow standards is increased.

2. Because structured programs are more readable than unstructured programs, it is easier for someone to scan them to determine if standards are being met.

3. If the structured walk-through technique is used, the knowledge that a colleague is going to read a programmer's code subtly encourages a programmer to follow standards.

REVIEW QUESTIONS AND EXERCISES

1. The definition of a *proper program* includes four items. What are they?
2. Identify the following structures and label alternative paths where necessary.

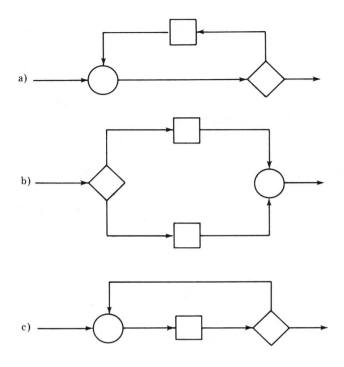

a)

b)

c)

3. Under what conditions may the CASE structure be needed?

4. What's wrong in terms of logic and structuring with the following summation problem that computes the *mean* of *n* input values?

```
Loop:    Read A
         IF A < 9999
            Increment counter
            Add A to sum
            Go to loop
         ELSE
            Compute average (Sum/counter)
            Print results
         ENDDO
```

5. Draw the basic program structures for each of the following steps. Indicate in each box what action is taking place. (Items a, b, and c should each be drawn as separate structures.)

a) Read three values A, B, and C and then call a subroutine named VERIFY-DATA.

b) IF A is greater than D, add A to B; ELSE

IF A is less than or equal to 0, add C to B.

c) Print A, B, and C.

6. Given the following program steps, draw the necessary structures to accomplish the task. Indicate in each box the program step. Connect each structure to the next one in sequence such that you have a program flowchart for the problem defined.

a) Read a record.

b) Call a subroutine named VERIFY-DATA.

c) IF input data verifies (i.e., it is ok), then compute EXTENSION (SALES-PRICE * QTY-ON-HAND) and print results.

ELSE, IF data is not ok, print error message.

d) Stop.

5

Stepwise Refinement

"Programming is a mirror of the mind."

Gerald Weinberg[1]

In the past, programming was rarely taught. The syntax of a programming language, yes; but, "how to create a program," hardly ever. Until recently little has been written on the process of designing or organizing program code. More experienced programmers would arrive, eventually, at their own procedure. But it was probably intuitive and not well defined or documented. Now some of these procedures are being refined and written down for others to use.

One such procedure is *stepwise refinement*. It is a step-by-step process that involves taking the function of a module and expanding it into subfunctions which are ultimately expanded into the necessary program steps. This process has a parallel in top-down program design in which the hierarchy chart is the tool for decomposing a program into its component modules. The hierarchy chart, of course, shows function and flow of control; it does not show the module's internal logic. Stepwise refinement, by contrast, is the tool for decomposing each module's function into the internal logic needed to carry out that function.

PSEUDO CODE

Stepwise refinement uses pseudo code in a specific and organized way. For example, consider a Library Information System as depicted in Figure 5-1. Three main programs are shown along with some possible modules for each program. The order that you use to code the modules depends on the principles discussed in Chapter 3. Assume you decided to start with the PROCESS BORROWER RECORDS module.

---

[1]Gerald Weinberg, "Primer on Programming," *THINK,* October/November 1974, p. 21. Reprinted by permission from THINK Magazine, published by IBM. Copyright 1974 by International Business Machines Corporation.

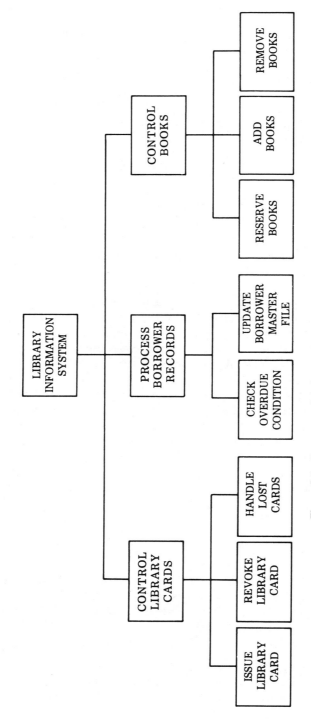

Figure 5-1. Programs and their modules in a library information system

There would be a file of records of the current borrowers. PROCESS BOR-ROWER RECORDS periodically reads that file to check for delinquent borrowers and to see if the records need to be updated. It contains the logic necessary to handle the file and determine what needs to be done. It invokes one or both of the two lower level modules, CHECK OVERDUE CONDITION and UPDATE BORROWER MASTER FILE. The pseudo code for the top module might be as follows:

```
Open file
More borrowers = yes
DOWHILE more borrowers
      Get next borrower's record
      IF Overdue
            Call Overdue Notice, with borrower's record
      ENDIF
      IF Any changes to record
            Call update, with borrower's record
      ENDIF
ENDDO
Close file
Print completion message
```

Then the module is coded in the programming language you are using and tested with the lower level modules written as stubs. Next you do one of the lower modules, say the CHECK OVERDUE CONDITION module. Let's continue with our example to demonstrate the use of stepwise refinement.

Begin by writing in pseudo code the basic actions that the module performs, in general terms. CHECK OVERDUE CONDITION will get a borrower's record from its invoking module and handle the overdue notices. Its initial logic might be:

```
Get next borrower's record
IF any books overdue
      Prepare overdue notice
```

Stepwise refinement is an *iterative* process in which more details are considered with each pass through the module. The first pass through the module produced the two previous pseudo code statements. The second pass involves taking one of the previous statements and expanding it. For example:

```
                          ┌ IF previous notice = 0
                          │       Print fines
Prepare overdue notice   ┤ ELSE IF previous notice = 1
                          │       Print invoice for lost books
                          │ ELSE
                          └       Restrict library card use
```

At this point you probably see how the term *stepwise refinement* was coined. The first step involved a very general statement. The decomposition of that first general step into a second or lower level sequence of steps causes a module's logic to be more precisely defined—that is, it results in *a refinement of a previous problem statement*. Thus, you can see how a module expands as these details are added and refined. It is like designing a building by first planning the beams of the entire structure, then the floors, dividing the floors into wings, then rooms, and finally deciding on the wallpaper, furniture, and details of the individual rooms. It would, of course, be possible to design one room completely before starting the next and plan the beams for the second floor only when the first was complete, but this would probably be more prone to error and fraught with missing specifications. Similarly, a module should be designed by first roughing out the overall logic and then returning to specify more and more detail with each iteration.

Continuing with the stepwise refinement of the overdue-notices module, the sub-function *Print fines* could be further decomposed into the following:

Print fines $\begin{cases} \text{Calculate fines due} \\ \text{Set previous notice } = 1 \\ \text{Print borrower's name and address} \\ \text{Print overdue book titles and fines} \end{cases}$

Then, at the next level of refinement, this step may be further decomposed:

Calculate fines due $\begin{cases} \text{Compute number of days overdue} \\ \text{Multiply days by rate} \end{cases}$

A convenient way to organize expansions is to draw a brace at the line to be refined and place the more detailed lines within the brace. As further expansions are made, additional braces would be placed to the right of the pertinent line. Thus, the refinements might appear in this general format:

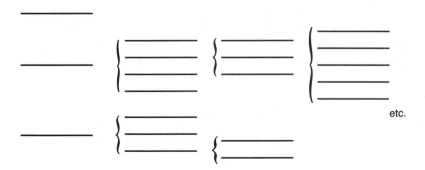

These charts are often called Warnier-Orr charts, after Jean-Dominique Warnier and Ken Orr.

If the program is large or complex, there will be many levels of refinement. You could use either a wide piece of paper or perhaps a chalkboard and expand your code horizontally as we have just shown. Another approach is to use a new sheet of paper for each line of pseudo code that requires further expansion.

In using pseudo code for stepwise refinement, each iteration describes the logic in greater detail. The initial version would be very general and close to the specifications, while the later versions would be closer to actual code. As a matter of fact, you have gone far enough in the stepwise refinement process when each pseudo code statement is directly translatable into one or two programming language statements. Thus, pseudo code statements at the first level of refinement are very general. For example:

> Process inquiry transaction
> Calculate weekly payroll
> Compute invoice amount due

At an intermediate level, the statements represent a portion of the module but not in enough detail to be coded:

> Update master record
> Find all factors of integer
> Edit input record

Lowest level statements will be directly translatable into programming language statements:

> Increment number of records counter
> Print error message
> Add gross pay to YTD gross pay
> Compute standard deviation

FLOWCHARTS

It is also possible to use flowcharts as the medium for stepwise refinement. The same iterative procedure is followed, but instead of pseudo code, flowchart symbols are used. What medium—pseudo code or flowcharts—will you use to express the refinements? Whichever you prefer. Both will be demonstrated here. At first, you may find flowcharts more familiar and therefore easier to use. However, because of the physical problems of drawing flowcharts (that is, limited page size), pseudo code is often the preferred method.

When using flowcharts in place of pseudo code, the same principle of expanding and nesting logic is followed. However, as a new refinement is made, the boxes representing it will replace the previous box. Therefore, it will be necessary to establish some procedure to effect this replacement. The brute force approach is simply to redraw the complete flowchart for each iteration or expansion. Another approach is to draw a general program flowchart—limiting the expression of logic to as many flowchart symbols as can fit on one page. Then you expand a portion of the general chart on a subsequent page, and so on.

Let us look at the library example shown earlier and see how the expansion could be performed by using flowcharts. Figure 5-2 shows the first pass in expressing the module's logic. This would be written on the first sheet of paper you are working with.

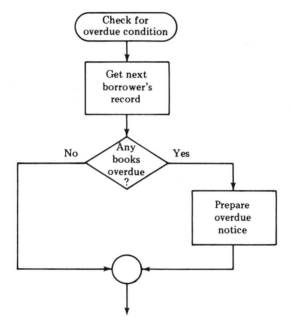

Figure 5-2. Stepwise refinement—first pass in library-overdue-notice module

The Prepare Overdue Notice box in this figure is further expanded on a separate sheet of paper. It is shown in Figure 5-3. And, again, the next refinement—that of Print Fines—is developed on a third sheet of paper; it is shown in Figure 5-4. Additional expansions would be performed as necessary. The iterative procedure would continue until each box in the flowcharts could be correspondingly written in programming language statements. These flowchart worksheets may or may not become part of the final documentation.

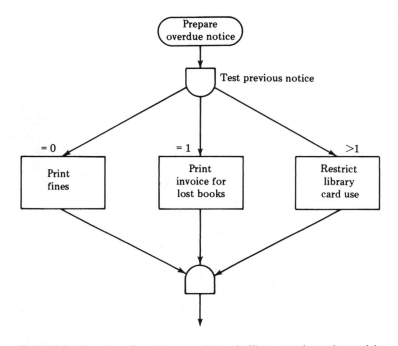

Figure 5-3. Stepwise refinement—second pass in library-overdue-notice module

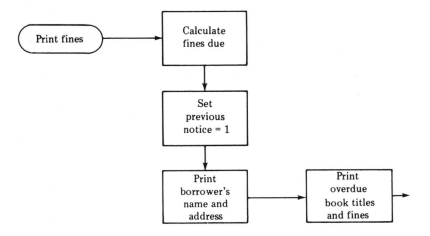

Figure 5-4. Stepwise refinement—third pass in library-overdue-notice module

GUIDELINES

Whether you use pseudo code or flowcharts, as you go through the iterative process of expanding and refining the function specified, there are several principles to keep in mind:

1. *Postpone details.* Do only a small amount of expansion each time. Do not get into the details too soon but concentrate on the major elements first.

2. *Consciously make decisions.* Each decision in the expansion process has consequences, some obvious, but others rather subtle. Proceed slowly; ask yourself a lot of questions. Try to understand the consequences of what you are doing: What are the implications of doing it this way? Am I starting down a path that I will later regret? Is there another way to do it? What are the trade-offs? Have I considered all reasonable alternatives?

3. *Consider data implications.* As you refine, the need for data items will emerge. Some of your decisions will have an effect on the amount of storage required, data types, and usage. Keep a list of data items needed and expand their definitions. These considerations may be part of the decision involving trade-offs.

4. *Be prepared to revoke earlier decisions.* There are times when unforeseen problems will arise. If they can be traced to an earlier decision, try an alternative approach on one or more levels of refinement.

CASE STUDY—STEPWISE REFINEMENT

A general approach to stepwise refinement has been illustrated. To apply the principles discussed, let us examine a program involving a fair degree of complexity. It is by design that we selected this problem, for it illustrates well the value of stepwise refinement as a programming tool. The example involves the reduction of air pollution data.

Assume you are working on program called AIR QUALITY. You have divided it into three modules as shown in the hierarchy chart that follows:

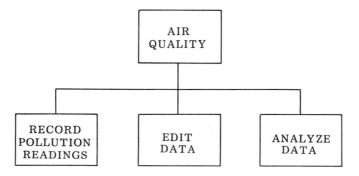

The RECORD POLLUTION READINGS module takes air pollution measurements once a minute for a 24-hour period near the smokestack of a large manufacturing plant. The pollutant-measurement value is expressed in parts per million (PPM). Normally, a measurement value is in the range of 10,000 to 90,000 PPM.

The EDIT DATA module will check the output of the RECORD module for completeness and validity. You are now working on the ANALYZE DATA module. It should do the following:

1. Compute the average pollution value for each hour of the 24-hour period.
2. Maintain a count of violations per hour. A violation occurs when the pollution value is above 100,000 PPM for five consecutive minutes. (Thus, ten consecutive minutes above 100,000 PPM count as *two* violations; the maximum violation count in one hour would be 12.) A violation can span hour changes; assign such violations to the hour in which they are completed.
3. Write a report that contains the hour, the hourly mean PPM value, and the hourly violation count for each of the 24 hours. Output is in the following format:

HOUR	MEAN (PPM)	VIOLATION COUNT
01	50,000	1
02	60,000	2
03	75,000	1
04	100,500	12
05	98,000	4
06	76,000	3
07	70,000	1
.	.	.
.	.	.
.	.	.
24	45,000	0

As the mechanics of stepwise refinement are being illustrated, both the flowchart and the pseudo code solutions will be shown. In actual practice, you would use one or the other. The refinement begins with a single statement:

Process pollution data for 24 hours

Next, two more general statements could be added that are very typical in most programs. These are

Initialize
Wrap-up

The first stage of refinement is shown in Figure 5-5, where the three basic steps have been established. A logical place to begin refinement is with the

Process data 24 hours

statement (as opposed to *initialize*) because as *process* is developed, items that need to be initialized become apparent.

Because the processing of data frequently involves a repetitive or loop operation, a general question that might be asked is, "What is the largest or 'outer' loop in the

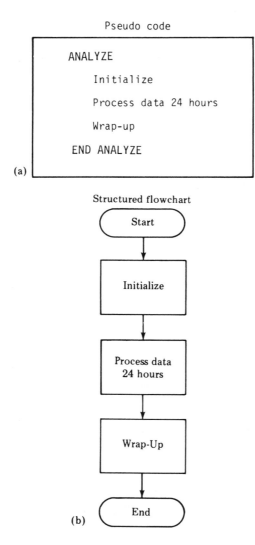

Figure 5-5. First stage of refinement

program?" In this example the processing of data is to be done for each hour in a 24-hour period. Thus, it seems the program should loop 24 times. With each pass through the loop, to process one hour's worth of data, three steps can be identified: (1) Read data for this hour, (2) Process data for this hour, and (3) Print results for this hour. Here we are following the rule about postponing details. The amount of refinement is small. Even so, at this point we should be evaluating what has been done. At each stage of refinement, study the intended expansion to see what decisions about design have actually been made and what the consequences of those decisions are.

In this example what decisions have we made? One is that all data for each hour will be input before processing any of the data. What are the implications of this decision? Storage for 60 data items will be needed. The coding will involve subscripting or indexing to address the individual data elements. What are the alternatives? One would be to read in one measurement at a time and process it before reading in the next one. In that case, a READ statement would be executed 60 times to read each hour's worth of data. What are the implications of that approach? Subsequent or previous data items are not available to the program. Is this acceptable, or is it possible that these items may be needed later? Another alternative is to read all 24 hours' data at one time. There are other decisions to be evaluated (e.g., print results at the end of each hour as compared to printing all 24 hours' worth at the end). What we are trying to demonstrate is the type of thinking that must be done in weighing the consequences of the various alternatives. The point is that there is no one correct solution.

At this time a list of data items will be started. These are the counters, indicators, and temporary storage items needed by this module. First, 60 storage locations are needed for the readings each hour; we will call the storage area PPMVALUE. Two results are to be printed, MEAN and VIOLATIONS. Because we have decided to print results each hour, we will need only one location for each. A counter to keep track of the number of iterations through the loop, called HOUR, is also needed. In addition to identifying the needed data items, the characteristics of the data items must be considered. In particular, the range of values that the data can have should be specified at this stage of development. It is necessary to know the maximum size of a data item so that enough storage is assigned to that item. A *data list* for this problem at this stage of refinement is shown in Table 5-1. As new data items are required, they will be added to

Table 5-1 Data List after Second Stage of Refinement

Data Name	Description	Range	Initialization
PPMVALUE	Pollution measurements per minute in parts per million, 60 elements	0–1,000,000	
MEAN	Average reading of PPMVALUE for each hour	0–1,000,000	
VIOLATIONS	Number of violations per hour	0–12	Not needed
HOUR	Counter for hour's loop	0–24	Not needed

this list. As attributes (range, initial value) become apparent, they will also be added to the chart.

So far we have not determined any data item initialization requirements, but there are some other initialization considerations. For example, do files need to be opened? In some programming languages they do not; in others they do. If files must be opened, this would be an initialization step. Because results are printed in the loop, the printing of a heading must be done outside the loop—making it an initialization step.

Another initialization step might be to set the hour counter to 1. However, a **for** in PASCAL or C, a DO in PL/I or a PERFORM in COBOL automatically handles the initializing, testing, and incrementing of the index variable in a loop operation. Thus, in the languages mentioned, this initialization step is not necessary. The closing of files, if required, would be shown in the *wrap-up* step. Figure 5-6 shows the refinement to this point.

Let us now examine the three steps in the loop:

Read data for this hour
Process data for this hour
Print results for this hour

The first step does not require further expansion because the operation can be easily coded as a programming language statement.

The details (e.g., syntax, file name) can be deferred because they do not have any influence on the logic being developed. In other words, the steps to consider are those whose expansion is necessary to the further refinement of the problem. Thus,

Process data this hour

is a logical choice for expansion.

There are 60 input values (one sample per minute) associated with the processing of data for a given hour. Another repetition structure is needed to control the execution of statements for a total of 60 times. For any loop operation, we specify an *initialization* step before it and a *wrap-up* step following it. As refinement proceeds, you may discover that you do not need these steps—in which case they can be discarded when translating from pseudo code or a structured flowchart to a programming language code. Figures 5-7 and 5-8 show the third stage of refinement for the pollution problem. We have identified one more data item, a counter, for MINUTES. We add it to our data list but don't need to initialize it for the same reason we didn't initialize the HOUR counter. The current data list is shown in Table 5-2.

The next step to be expanded is the

Process data this minute

statement. It will be further expanded into two parts specifying the operations to be done for each measurement: (1) Accumulate the sum preparatory to computing the

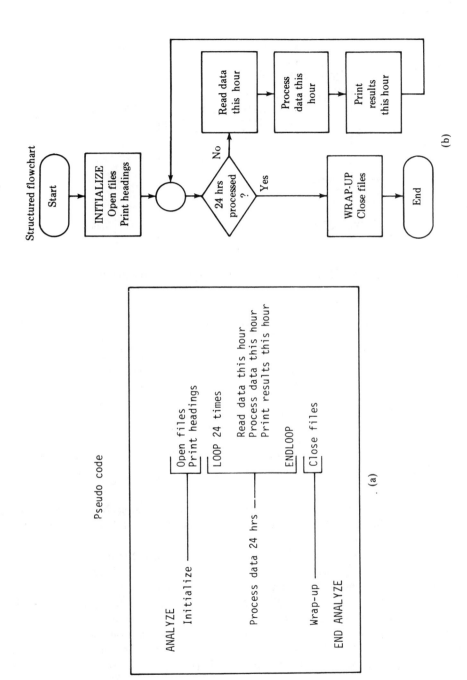

Pseudo code

```
ANALYZE
    Initialize ── Open files
                  Print headings

Process data 24 hrs ── LOOP 24 times
                              Read data this hour
                              Process data this hour
                              Print results this hour
                       ENDLOOP

    Wrap-up ── Close files
END ANALYZE
```

(a)

Structured flowchart

Start

INITIALIZE
Open files
Print headings

24 hrs processed ?

No → Read data this hour → Process data this hour → Print results this hour

Yes → WRAP-UP Close files → End

(b)

Figure 5-6. Second stage of refinement

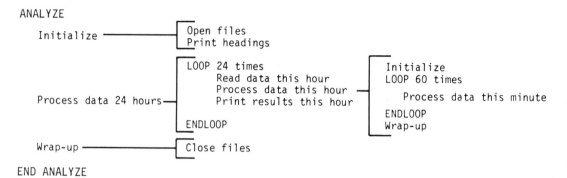

Figure 5-7. Third stage of refinement—pseudo code solution

hourly average, and (2) Check for readings exceeding the maximum (possible violation).

Table 5-2 Data List after Third Stage of Refinement

Data Name	Description	Range	Initialization
PPMVALUE	Pollution measurements per minute in parts per million, 60 elements	0–1,000,000	
MEAN	Average reading of PPMVALUE for each hour	0–1,000,000	
VIOLATIONS	Number of violations per hour	0–12	
HOUR	Counter for hour's loop	0–24	Not needed
MINUTES	Counter for minute's loop	0–60	Not needed

The *accumulation* step does not require further expansion, but it does point to the need for an additional data item. This item is an accumulator called SUM into which all readings for an hour are totaled.

Now, we must ask ourselves, at what point(s) should SUM be initialized to zero, modified, and subsequently reset? The initialization must be done before the start of each minute loop, and the modification will occur within the loop. (*Reset* occurs when the initialization step is executed a subsequent time.) At the end of the loop, SUM must be divided by 60 to obtain the average—a step to be added to *wrap-up* for the inner loop. The *check* for violation step will require further expansion, but that will be done in a later iteration. Figures 5-9 and 5-10 show the fourth stage of refinement. SUM is added to the data list which is shown in Table 5-3. We will now expand the step

Check for violation

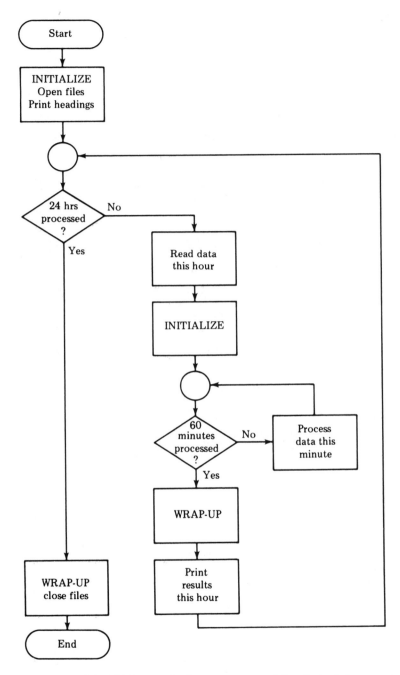

Figure 5-8. Third stage of refinement—structured flowchart solution

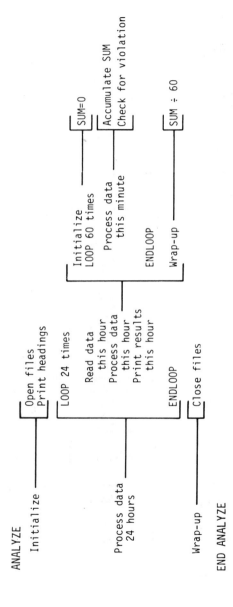

Figure 5-9. Fourth stage of refinement—pseudo code solution

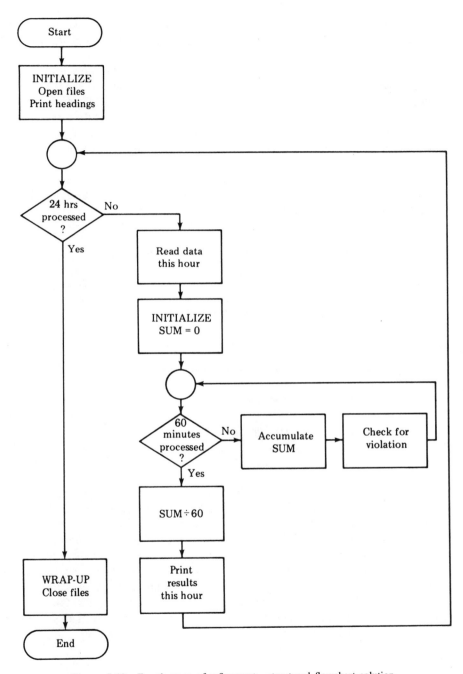

Figure 5-10. Fourth stage of refinement—structured flowchart solution

We have stated that a violation occurs when the pollution value is above 100,000 for five *consecutive* minutes. Also, if a violation spans the hour change, it is assigned to the hour in which it is completed.

As part of this expansion a test must be made to determine if the current reading is greater than 100,000. If so, we will have to check further to see if five in a row have occurred. To do that, we will need to have a second counter. The first, called VIOLA-TIONS, counts the number of times this hour that five consecutive excess readings have been observed. The second one will count the consecutive high readings. We will refer to this as the INFRACTIONS counter. When it reaches five, it will indicate that a violation has occurred.

Because we have now established a new data item, we should ask ourselves more about it. Does this counter need to be initialized? When an infraction is detected, we will want to increment the current setting.

Table 5-3 Data List after Fourth Stage of Refinement

Data Name	Description	Range	Initialization
PPMVALUE	Pollution measurements per minute in parts per million, 60 elements	0–1,000,000	
MEAN	Average reading of PPMVALUE for each hour	0–1,000,000	
VIOLATIONS	Number of violations per hour	0–12	
HOUR	Counter for hour's loop	0–24	Not needed
MINUTES	Counter for minute's loop	0–60	Not needed
SUM	Total of PPMVALUE readings per hour	0–60,000,000	Set to zero at start of each hour

For the first infraction we need to be assured that it has a zero value. Where should this initialization take place? Clearly, it needs to be done before the first hour's data is processed, but should it be reset to zero for each hour? No, because a string of consecutive infractions can cross hour boundaries. Thus, it should be initialized only at the beginning of the module. It will be reset to zero after five infractions have been counted, but that is a detail that can be postponed to a later stage of refinement. For now we can simply say, for the true branch of the test, "process infraction."

What is to be done if the current reading is not over 100,000? This breaks the (possible) string of consecutive infractions; therefore, INFRACTIONS should be set to zero. Figures 5-11 and 5-12 show the fifth stage of refinement.

The final refinement is to expand the statement

Process infraction

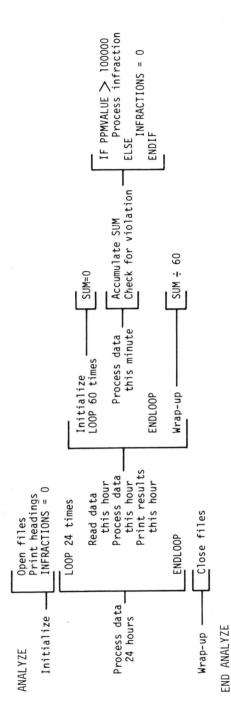

Figure 5-11. Fifth stage of refinement—pseudo code solution

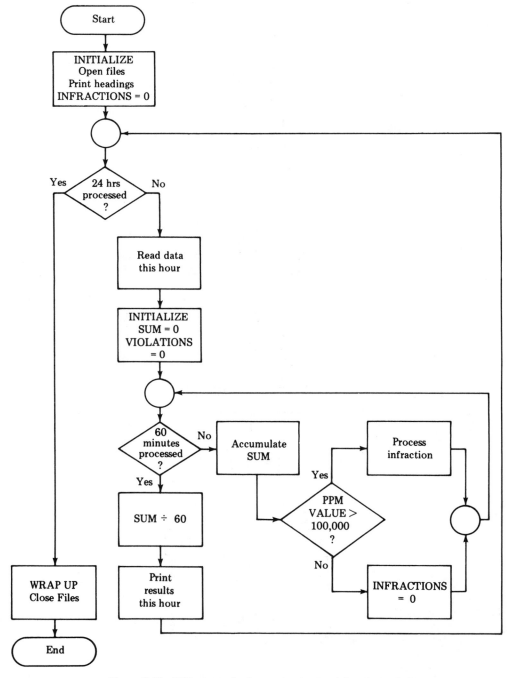

Figure 5-12. Fifth stage of refinement—structured flowchart solution

First, we need to increase the current value of INFRACTIONS by one. If this counter has now reached five, we need to increment the VIOLATIONS counter by one and reset the INFRACTIONS counter to zero. If the INFRACTIONS counter has not yet reached five, there is no further action to be taken. We have now completed the refinement of the logic of the program.

At this point we review the list of data items for completeness. We also check that initialization, resetting, and testing have been done in the proper places. The completed data list is shown in Table 5-4. The 60 PPMVALUE measurements are read in each hour and will not need to be initialized. MEAN is computed at the end of each hour and needs no further attention. HOUR, MINUTES, SUM, and INFRACTIONS have already been initialized; but VIOLATIONS has not. Should it be initialized at the beginning of the program as was INFRACTIONS? No, because, unlike INFRACTIONS, it needs to be reset to zero at the beginning of each hour because we are counting violations per hour, and all violations ending during each hour are charged to it. Thus, VIOLATIONS is set to zero at the initialization step within the loop for the hours and does not need to be included in the initialization step for the entire program.

Table 5-4 Final Data List

Data Name	Description	Range	Initialization
PPMVALUE	Pollution measurements per minute in parts per million, 60 elements	0–1,000,000	Not needed
MEAN	Average reading of PPMVALUE for each hour	0–1,000,000	Not needed
VIOLATIONS	Number of violations per hour	0–12	Set to zero at start of each hour
HOUR	Counter for hour's loop	0–24	Not needed
MINUTES	Counter for minute's loop	0–60	Not needed
SUM	Total of PPMVALUE readings per hour	0–60,000,000	Set to zero at start of each hour
INFRACTIONS	Count of consecutive PPMVALUE readings 100,000	0–5	Set to zero at start of program

This completes the refinement, with the final program structure shown in Figures 5-13 and 5-14. Before transforming the pseudo code into the programming language you are using, you may wish to *telescope* some or all of the code. That is, replace a line that was expanded with its expansion. The pseudo code would then be in line and more directly translatable into programming steps. For large programs you may want to keep some of the expansions on separate pages. See the sections on segmenting in Chapters 8–11. If you are writing in a COBOL compiler that doesn't allow in-line PERFORMS,

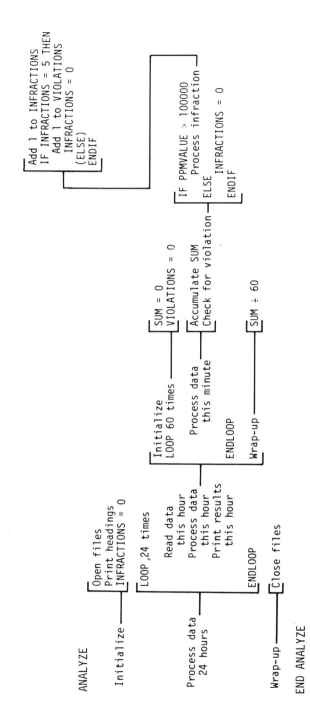

Figure 5-13. Sixth stage of refinement—pseudo code solution

```
ANALYZE

   Initialize ─┬─[ Open files
               │   Print headings
               └─  INFRACTIONS = 0

   Process data ─┬─ LOOP,24 times
   24 hours      │
                 │    Read data
                 │     this hour
                 │    Process data
                 │     this hour
                 │    Print results
                 │     this hour
                 └─ ENDLOOP

   Wrap-up ──[ Close files

END ANALYZE
```

```
   Initialize ─┬─[ SUM = 0
               └─  VIOLATIONS = 0

   LOOP 60 times

   Process data ─┬─[ Accumulate SUM
   this minute   └─  Check for violation

   ENDLOOP

   Wrap-up ──[ SUM ÷ 60
```

```
   Add 1 to INFRACTIONS
   IF INFRACTIONS = 5 THEN
      Add 1 to VIOLATIONS
      INFRACTIONS = 0
   (ELSE)
   ENDIF
```

```
   IF PPMVALUE > 100000
      Process infraction
   ELSE
      INFRACTIONS = 0
   ENDIF
```

106

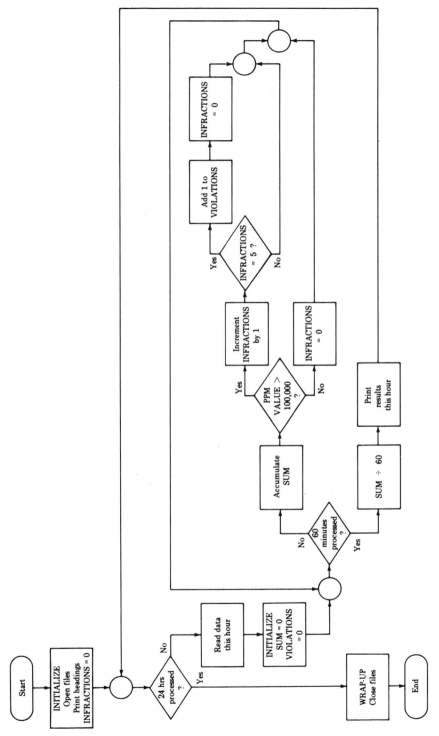

Figure 5-14. Sixth stage of refinement—structured flowchart solution

107

then all repetitions will need to be written as separate paragraphs. For those situations you would not want to telescope.

Figure 5-15 shows the entire program written in line. For COBOL without in-line PERFORMs, Figure 5-16 shows the final pseudo code with partial telescoping.

```
ANALYZE
   PRINT HEADINGS
   INFRACTIONS = 0
   LOOP 24 TIMES
      READ DATA THIS HOUR
      SUM = 0
      VIOLATIONS = 0
      LOOP 60 TIMES
         ADD VALUE TO SUM
         IF VALUE > 100000 THEN
            ADD 1 TO INFRACTIONS
            IF INFRACTIONS = 5 THEN
               ADD 1 TO VIOLATIONS
               INFRACTIONS = 0
            (ELSE)
            ENDIF
         ELSE
            INFRACTIONS = 0
         ENDIF
      ENDLOOP
      MEAN = SUM ÷ 60
      PRINT RESULTS THIS HOUR
   ENDLOOP
ANALYZE
```

Figure 5-15. Pseudo code in composite form

```
ANALYZE
   OPEN FILES
   PRINT HEADINGS
   INFRACTIONS = 0
   PERFORM HOUR LOOP 24 TIMES
   CLOSE FILES
END ANALYZE

HOUR LOOP
   READ DATA THIS HOUR
   SUM = 0
   VIOLATIONS = 0
   PERFORM MINUTE LOOP 60 TIMES
   MEAN = SUM ÷ 60
   PRINT RESULTS THIS HOUR
END HOUR LOOP

MINUTE LOOP
   ADD VALUE TO SUM
   IF VALUE > 100000
      ADD 1 TO INFRACTIONS
      IF INFRACTIONS = 5
         ADD 1 TO VIOLATIONS
         INFRACTIONS = 0
      ELSE
         NULL
      ENDIF
   ELSE
      INFRACTIONS = 0
   ENDIF
END MINUTE LOOP
```

Figure 5-16. Pseudo code in composite form—COBOL without in-line PERFORMs

SEGMENTING

Modules which are large (100 to 200 executable statements) could be subdivided into *segments*. A segment is both a logical and a physical subdivision of a module. Logically, it is a subfunction of the module's function. Physically, it is limited to the number of source-code lines that will fit on one printer page of source output (50 to 60 lines).

Segmenting is a method for presenting a *picture on a source-listing page.* It is a technique where the control logic is coded in higher level segments and the details are pushed down to lower level segments. This approach should simplify the coding and testing of a module, make a module easier to read and understand, and simplify the changes that are made to a module at a later time.

During stepwise refmement it is easy to identify segments. As you expand the module into more detail, it will be apparent whether or not the total code will fit on a single page. If not, and you wish to segment the module, select a portion of the pseudo code (or the flowchart) to be a segment. Which part should you take?—a *subfunction that requires further expansion*. For example, if a module's function is to print a report, a segment might handle the page overflow subfunction of printing the heading at the top of the first page as well as on all overflow pages. Code that is executed from more than one point in the module is another good choice for a segment.

It is also possible that a segment, when expanded, might itself be more than a page in length. If so, a lower level segment can be defined. In this way the module is organized into single pages in such a way that you are gradually led into greater details. Looking at the top segment you should see the overall flow and main processing loop. Subsequent pages would expand on this outline.

Each segment should be a *proper program* and return control to its higher segment. This facilitates the reading and understanding of any segment without having to examine the lower segments.

There are two ways in which control can be passed to segments:

1. Use appropriate invoking statements (e.g., PERFORM, CALL to an internal procedure, or function reference).
2. Use a *source statement library* (e.g., COPY in COBOL, # **include** in C, INCLUDE in PL/I) to develop the segments. When the module is compiled, the segments will be logically placed in line, and control will flow in and out of them sequentially. If possible, the source statement listing should show the segments on separate pages so that the single-page orientation will be preserved.

There are occasions when a segment may be longer than one printer page. For example, a routine with a large number of statements that are always executed in sequence might be better expressed in one continuous stream rather than arbitrarily segmented. Thus, an output module that is placing a long list of items in the output area and then issuing the write statements would still be readable if left as one continuous sequence.

It is also desirable to have a flexible limit established for the maximum segment size to allow for subsequent additions to the segments. If a segment fills its page and then later requires an additional few lines of code, it would probably be better to leave the main structuring as it is and allow the segment to spill over into the first few lines of the next page. This is preferable to artificially creating additional segments to avoid exceeding the one-page limit.

CASE STUDY—SEGMENTING

Segmenting is top-down design at the program-coding level and is best done at the stepwise refinement stage. To illustrate the process of segmenting, let us consider a sales analysis program with these four modules:

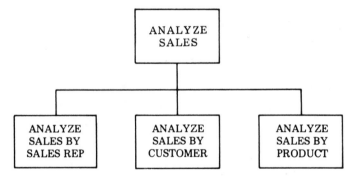

The left-most module on the second level could be further subdivided into these modules:

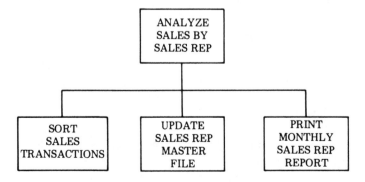

The module we will develop into segments is the UPDATE SALESREP MASTER FILE. The master file contains records in the following format:

SALESREP record

Sales rep number	Sales rep name	Gross sales this month	Returns this month	YTD gross sales	YTD returns

This file will be updated from transactions which have been sorted into ascending sequence by sales rep number. The transaction sales records are in this format:

SALES Transaction Record

Code	Customer number	Sales rep number	Invoice number	Invoice date	Item number	Qty Sold	Price	Description

The monthly gross sales are to be computed for each sales rep from the individual records. The *total sales* is to be computed from these input records for each sales rep and stored in the GROSS SALES THIS MONTH field (shaded area in the SALESREP record). Assume, for now, that *returns* are handled by another module.

There may be more than one transaction sales record for a sales rep. Sorting these transactions by sales rep causes each sales rep's records to be grouped together. The logic for this module must take into account *control breaks*. Because each sales rep's records are grouped together, whenever there is a change in the sales rep number read (i.e., a *break* in the sequence of numbers), it means that it is time to write the previous sales rep's *total sales* and start computing a new total for the next sales rep.

In handling the control break, two program *variables* must be specified:

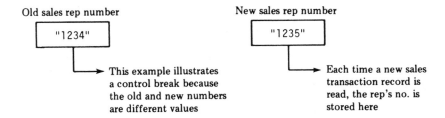

These two variables will have to be compared to determine the break in the sequence of sales rep numbers. After each comparison the *new sales rep number* will be moved (copied) into the *old sales rep number*.

The first time through the program—that is, when the first sales record is read—it will be necessary to simply copy the new sales rep number into the old sales rep number *without* comparing these two variables. This situation creates the need for a *first-time* program switch. This background information allows us to study the solution in Figure 5-17.

The solution begins with initialization steps followed by the basic loop control for reading sales transactions and either processing those transactions or handling the end-of-file condition.

```
Total sales = 0
More transactions = yes
Record found = yes
First time through module = yes
Open files


DOWHILE more transactions
  Read a sales transaction
    EOF sets more transactions = no
  IF more transactions
    Process transaction
  ELSE
    Wrap-up
  ENDIF
ENDDO
Exit program


Process transaction.
  IF first time through module = yes
    Move new sales rep no. to old sales rep no.
    First time through module = no
  ENDIF
  IF new sales rep no. = old sales rep no.
    Compute extension
    Add extension to total sales
  ENDIF
  IF new sales rep no. > old sales rep no.
    Read sales rep master
      Key error sets record found = no
    IF record found = yes
      Move total sales to sales rep master
      Rewrite sales rep master
    ELSE
      Print error message
    ENDIF
    Move new sales rep no. to old sales rep no.
    Compute new extension and move to total sales
  ENDIF
IF new sales rep no. < old sales rep no.
  Write transaction sequence error message
ENDIF


Wrap-up.
  Update last sales rep's record with new total sales
  Print end-of-job message
  Close files
End-of-job.
```

Figure 5-17. Pseudo code for update of sales rep's monthly sales

The section dealing with the processing of a transaction provides three consecutive IF statements testing the relationship between the *old sales rep number* and the *new sales rep number*. These tests indicate whether or not a control break has occurred or if there is a sequence error in the transaction file.

When the *new sales rep number* is greater than the *old sales rep number*, it is time to update the previously read rep's record with the accumulated total sales. Assuming that the master file to be updated is stored on a direct-access device and its records are accessed by means of a key, this code is required:

```
Read sales rep master
    Key error sets record found = no
IF record found = yes
    Move total sales to master sales rep record
    Rewrite total sales to master sales rep record
    Rewrite sales rep master
ELSE
    Print error message
ENDIF
```

The last section of pseudo code in the module in Figure 5-17 is entered when the end-of-file is detected. Assume, for the present, that the following code had been specified (as it actually was when we developed this solution). Is there a potential problem?

```
Wrap-up.
    Update last sales rep's record with new total sales
    Print end-of-job message
    Close files
End-of-job.
```

Yes, there is a problem. When the end-of-file is reached, it is necessary to update the last sales rep's accumulated sales total into the master record. The one time this program would fail—with, typically, "strange" error messages—is if there were no records in the transaction file at all. This is an obvious mistake—but one which we have seen from time to time. Of course, if there were no records in the sales transactions file, there is no total sales to write into the last sales rep's record. Here we can use the *first time through the program* indicator to condition whether or not the total sales would be written into the last sales rep's record. Here is that code again:

```
Wrap-up.
    IF first time through program = no
        Update last sales rep's record with new total sales
        Print normal end-of-job message
    ELSE
        Print no sales transactions error message
    ENDIF
    Close files
End-of-job.
```

The updating of the sales master record would be expanded as previously shown.

Now that we have developed the general solution, what should be segmented? The *initialization* and *main loop* could form the top segment. Logically, *process transaction* would be a segment and so would *wrap-up*. If program efficiency is a consideration, the updating of a sales rep's record could also be a small segment because the identical program steps are required from two places within the module: once in the *process transaction* segment and once in the *wrap-up* segment.

Figure 5-18 shows a four-segment hierarchy chart for this module. Unlike top-down program design where the hierarchy chart is drawn *before* coding begins, the segment chart is drawn *after* the pseudo code has been developed. The segment hierarchy chart does show a module's subfunctions and the flow of control between segments (i.e., "who is invoked by whom").

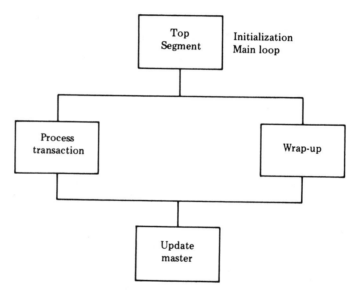

Figure 5-18. Segmented module for update of sales reps monthly sales

Figure 5-19 shows the revised pseudo code solution. Each segment has a segment name and the segments have been arranged in general execution sequence to enhance readability. Within the PROCESS TRANSACTION segment, nested IFs replace the three consecutive IFs that compare *new sales rep number* with the *old sales rep number*.

```
Top segment.
  Total sales = 0
  More transactions = yes
  Record found = yes
  First time through module = yes
  Open files

  DOWHILE more transactions
    Read a sales transaction
      EOF sets more transactions = no
    IF more transactions
      Process transaction
    ELSE
      Wrap-up
    ENDIF
  ENDDO
  Exit program

Process transaction.
  IF first time through module = yes
    Move new sales rep no. to old sales rep no.
    First time through module = no
  ENDIF
  IF new sales rep no. = old sales rep no.
    Compute extension
    Add extension to total sales
  ELSE
    IF new sales rep no. > old sales rep no.
      Update sales master
      Move new sales rep no. to old sales rep no.
      Compute new extension and move to total sales
    ELSE
      Write transaction sequence error message
    ENDIF
  ENDIF

Update sales master.
  Read sales rep master
    Key error sets record found = no
  IF record found = yes
    Move total sales to sales rep master
    Rewrite sales rep master
  ELSE
    Print error message
  ENDIF

Wrap-up.
  IF first time through program = no
    Update sales master
    Print normal end-of-job message
  ELSE
    Print no sales transactions error message
  ENDIF
  Close files
```

Figure 5-19. Segmented pseudo code for update of sales rep's monthly sales

SUMMARY

You will probably want to use stepwise refinement for every module you write. In a few isolated cases you may write the final code without going through the stepwise refinement process. For example, a module that simply formats data for printed output may consist of many lines of code to convert the data, space it on the output form, and print it. But these program steps are relatively simple and do not require any complicated logic. Most modules that you write will have more substance to them, in which case stepwise refinement will help to ensure a valid and structured program.

Stepwise refinement is a technique in which major elements are considered first. Then subordinate items are nested within the overall logic. As the program expands, the newer parts are inserted into the basic structure. Each process step is studied carefully, and only a small amount of expansion takes place. If too many expansions are included at each iteration, it may dilute your attention, so postpone details for as long as possible.

At each iteration there are choices as to which part to refine next and what these refinements will be. Because some decisions will have a profound effect on the final design of the program, decisions should be made after careful thought and weighing of alternatives. Frequently, there will be several solutions, all of which are correct but which differ in efficiency, expandability, or ease of understanding. In difficult or critical programs, do the refinement process twice. The second solution will usually be an improvement over the first.

As each expansion is made, examine what consequences might result from that decision. The implications of each step should be compared with the implications of alternate choices. In some cases a simple-appearing refinement may have far-reaching consequences on the design of the rest of the module. While every attempt should be made to foresee this situation, it will occasionally happen that the undesirable effects are not discovered until later in the refinement process. In this case it will be necessary to revoke the earlier decision that caused the problem, thereby deleting several levels of refinement. However, this is a simple and inexpensive change. What is more costly are changes *after* the module has been coded.

At each iteration, decisions about data are also being made. The term *data* is used here not in the sense of major input and output but to mean the data definitions within a module (counters, switches, temporary storage areas, etc.). Record formats will have been defined before the refinement process begins. As refinement progresses, requirements for additional data items will become apparent. For each data item consider the definition of the item, when it is initialized, when it is used (tested, accumulated, moved), and when it is reset. Thus, the data and logic for a module will be developed in parallel.

Whether or not modules should be segmented is an installation decision. Some installations specify that a module should be no more than 50 to 60 lines of source code and therefore do not even consider segmenting. Basically, segmenting is top-down program design at the lowest level of module development. The top segment may consist of the main processing loop for the program as well as the module's initialization steps. Lower level segments are logical subdivisions of the module's general function. After you have developed the module's logic by using the stepwise refinement technique, it is apparent which groups of code can logically be segments.

REVIEW QUESTIONS AND EXERCISES

1. Explain stepwise refinement.

2. How do you know when you have gone far enough in the stepwise refinement process?

3. As you proceed through the process of expanding and refining, what principles should guide you?

4. What are the trade-offs of pseudo code versus flowchart solutions in the stepwise refinement process?
   a. Advantages of flowcharts:
   b. Advantages of pseudo code:

5. Is the stepwise refinement process to be used in all programs that you might develop? Why or why not?

6. In making a *data list* what kinds of infomation should be included?

7. In the air pollution example the assumption was made that all data for the 24 hours was present. No test was made for end-of-file. Redo the stepwise refinement for this problem without that assumption. That is, include a test for end-of-file before the end of the 24 hours of data. In the event that it occurs, *no* further output is to be produced other than an error message.

8. In Figure 5-17 would the logic shown comparing new with old sales rep number in the PROCESS TRANSACTION segment have been as clear had nested IFs replaced the successive IFs? What are the advantages of nesting IFs? Advantages of successive IFs?

9. Modify the pseudo code solution in Figure 5-19 to include a test for CODE = SR to verify that a sales record is, in fact, just that. If the CODE field is in error, bypass the input transaction and print an appropriate error message.

10. Add the required pseudo code segment(s) to Figure 5-18 to handle *returns this month*. Assume the returns, if any, for each sales rep will be grouped together by sales rep, and follow the sales record(s) for a given sales rep. In the illustration SR = Sales Record and RR = Returns Record:

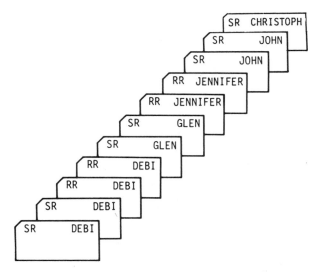

Note that there may be *sales records* only or *returns records* only for a given sales rep as well as both types for one sales rep.

11. Write the pseudo code module to generate a report from the information contained in the SALESREP RECORD file. The file contains these fields:

Sales rep number	Sales rep name	Gross sales this month	Returns this month	YTD gross sales	YTD returns

Output should include:

```
NAME          NUMBER   GROSS SALES    NET SALES     YTD GROSS     YTD NET SALES

XXXXXXXXXX    XXXX     XXXXX.XX       XXXXX.XX      XXXXXX.XX     XXXXXX.XX
XXXXXXXXXX    XXXX     XXXXX.XX       XXXXX.XX      XXXXXX.XX     XXXXXX.XX
XXXXXXXXXX    XXXX     XXXXX.XX       XXXXX.XX      XXXXXX.XX     XXXXXX.XX

     TOTALS            XXXXXX.XX      XXXXXX.XX     XXXXXXX.XX    XXXXXXX.XX
```

Net sales is computed as *gross sales this month* minus *returns this month*. Year-to-date (YTD) net sales is computed as *YTD gross sales* minus *YTD returns*.

In the SALESREP RECORD file, accumulate the monthly fields (sales and returns) into the corresponding year-to-date fields and reset to zero the monthly *gross sales* and *returns* fields.

12. Write the pseudo code to calculate the number of quarters, dimes, nickels, and pennies to be given as change from a dollar for any given amount.

6

Structured Walk-Throughs and Inspections

"If I have seen further it is by standing upon the shoulders of giants."

Sir Isaac Newton

"Scientists stand on each other's shoulders. Programmers stand on each other's toes."

Anonymous

A classical management tool for tracking the progress of a data processing project has been the *project review*. Checkpoints are made throughout the project for the purpose of spotting problem areas before they reach emergency proportions and while there is still time to take corrective action. From a management point of view, the concern is whether or not the project is ahead of or behind schedule, whether more resources are needed, or how the project stands in terms of the planned budget. Of course, management is also interested in having the completed project meet the design objectives of the system.

A tool that ultimately benefits management but is a *technical tool* for the technical people on a project is a *structured walk-through*. The term *structured* is used because the reviews are a regular, planned part of development cycles and are carried out in a well-defined and predetermined manner. The term *walk-through* is used because the material being reviewed is mentally executed in a step-by-step fashion. A structured walk-through is designed to detect errors in a problem-solving and non-fault-finding atmosphere in which everyone, especially the *developer*, is eager to find the errors as early as possible.

A variation of the structured walk-through, called an *inspection* will also be discussed in this chapter. The inspection is more formal than the structured walk-through and is more rigorous. It involves different people and includes additional activities. It is similar in that it is a structured review to detect errors early on.

Figure 6-1 shows a *phased-development cycle*. The area under the curve represents a growing commitment of resources (e.g., people, budget) to the DP project. Walk-throughs are held throughout the life of this project—starting as early as possible and continuing through the implementation phase. Frequent sessions, in which a small amount of material is reviewed, are preferable to longer but infrequent meetings.

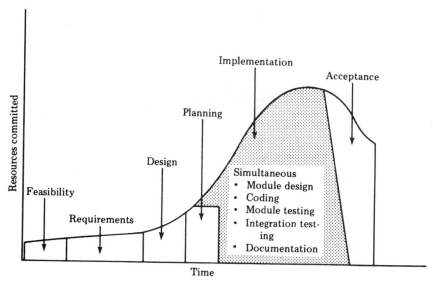

Figure 6-1. Phased-development cycle (See glossary for definition of phases.)

Advantages of frequent walk-throughs are that a manageable amount of material is reviewed and major flaws are detected sooner, thereby reducing the possibility that work already completed will have to be done over.

Table 6-1 shows items which might be reviewed by using structured walk-throughs, or inspections at various times during a phased-development effort. One of the first walk-throughs, to be conducted during the *requirements phase*, is a review of the system specifications. Here the specs must be reviewed for completeness and must be understood by those technical people who will work to satisfy them. Then a sample data flow must be walked through during the *design phase* to verify that the specs are being met. During the *planning phase*, walk-throughs concentrate on the plan for module-development order and the test plan. Specific test case selection criteria and test data would be reviewed to determine whether adequate tests are being planned. During the *implementation phase*, reviews would cover the detailed program design, module interfaces, and documentation being produced. Finally, during the *acceptance phase*, the deliverable product is again reviewed.

STRUCTURED WALK-THROUGHS

Who Attends?

The developer of a product to be reviewed selects the reviewers and the time and date of each review. The manager[1] is not usually invited, because one of the essential ingredients of an effective walk-through session is an open and nondefensive atmosphere. The

---

[1]*Manager* here implies control over salary, promotion, and firing,

Table 6-1 Items to Be Reviewed by Using Structured Walk-Throughs and Inspections

Project phase	Items to be reviewed	Most likely problem
During requirements phase	• Project plans	• Omissions
	• Schedules	• Unrealistic
	• Scope of project	• Unavailability of key users
Beginning of design phase	• System specifications	• Missing tasks
	• Problem definition	• Ambiguous
During design phase	• Program functional specifications	• Incomplete
	• Program design (hierarchy charts)	• Flow of control not vertical, or functions not well defined.
	• Exception handling	• Incomplete detail
	• Controls	• Incomplete coverage of requirements
During planning phase	• Module-development-order plan	• Data dependencies not fully identified
	• Module-test-order plan	• Incomplete coverage of requirements
	• Test data	• Not complete set
During implementation phase	• Detailed program design	• Departure from overall logic design
	• Module interfaces	• Unstated assumptions
	• Documentation (users' guides)	• Ambiguous or wrong level of detail
	• Pseudo and source code	• Logic errors
Acceptance phase	• Final documentation	• Criteria for good documentation not established
	• Finished product (results versus specs)	• Change in specs

walk-through is not an evaluation tool, but the presence of a manager might make it so. Occasionally, there are manager/employee relationships in which employees feel at ease in having errors made visible to the manager. Even though a mutual respect might exist, it is usually impossible for the manager to avoid evaluating the employee or for the employees to feel comfortable revealing mistakes or omissions to their manager.

By contrast, a project or team leader would be an ideal candidate for the review, because the leader is accountable for the technical success of the project. In fact, it is desirable that the team leader attend most, if not all, walk-through sessions. The team leader is one of the most qualified reviewers to spot problems. The leader will undoubtedly meet with the manager and relate project progress and problem areas, including that of an individual whose work needs improving. Thus, a manager can be informed of progress without having to attend the walk-through sessions—which are basically technical in nature.

The attendee most motivated to find problems and errors is a reviewer who has a vested interest in the success of the project. For team projects, then, reviewers would be the team members. If a test group exists, then members of that group are also motivated to trouble-shoot, because their job is to validate the program product. It is essential that test group personnel be included in walk-throughs, beginning at the earliest stages.

In addition, every installation seems to have a small group of individuals who are known and respected for their high degree of technical competence and facility for trouble-shooting. These individuals seem to enjoy this reputation and are usually willing to advise anyone who comes to them for help. The developer should identify these people and invite one or more of them to the scheduled walk-throughs.

During the early phases of a project, overall system objectives are specified. In these sessions it is valuable to have the user of the finished product attend the walk-throughs. The walk-through is not in lieu of other meetings and communications with the user; it is an additional vehicle for improved communication between the systems analysis/program development group and the user-department group. With this approach better design specifications should emerge. There should be a higher degree of commitment to the design on the part of users because they participated in the specification of the system rather than had the DP department "tell them what they needed." With this kind of early involvement, users should be less inclined to complain about the system or request major changes when it is completed.

Also, at the early stages of a project, the developer should invite a representative of the *operations group* to the design walk-through. The mechanics of operations are best understood by operations personnel; thus, they are best qualified to review the design from an operational standpoint.

Walk-through sessions usually involve three to six reviewers. In small installations it may not be possible to have that many people attend. (It has been suggested that a one-man shop can have a walk-through in front of a mirror.) In small installations walk-throughs may involve only two technical people because there are only two in the department. In fact, in the small installation the president or vice-president of the firm could be directly involved in the data processing effort. In this case either of them would participate in walk-throughs.

The team leader, team members, test group and operations personnel, user-department representatives, and good trouble shooters are all candidates for those who might attend structured walk-throughs. Of these, the developer should select the attendees who will give diverse viewpoints and opinions, to insure the most useful and thorough reviewing.

Walk-through Atmosphere

Assume you are a developer in a walk-through session. If you are open rather than defensive, you make it easy for your reviewers to help you create a better product. If your reviewers see themselves as problem solvers, not problem creators, then the walk-through is a helpful and cooperative session. What can be done to foster this atmosphere? We see at least five positive steps that can be taken:

1. *You and everyone senior or junior to you have your work reviewed.* With this approach there is no stigma attached to the fact that a developer is having a review. (If walk-throughs are selectively scheduled, a developer might feel his work is being singled out for lower quality—an approach that might cause some people to waste time proving their work is good rather than trying to find problems and solve them.) If you are a team leader, try to have your work reviewed first. An open attitude on your part could set a standard for other reviews.

2. *You are not evaluated on the number or severity of errors found DURING your walk-throughs.* Suppose you were asked to take a test that would be graded by someone else. The test giver, however, is trying to validate the test and is interested only in what questions a group of test takers misses. After taking the test, you are to turn the test in *without* your name on it. Then you are given the correct answers to the test so that you may learn from your mistakes. No one else knows how *you* specifically did on the test. How do you feel about taking this type of test? Relaxed? Comfortable? Did you see it as an opportunity for personal growth? To learn something new? In approaching a walk-through, it is this type of feeling that needs to be perpetuated. It should be as though your name has been removed from the work product being reviewed—all that you are trying to accomplish is the validation of that product.

3. *You are evaluated on the number or severity of errors found AFTER all walk-throughs have been completed.* Some installations keep track of errors found subsequent to the walk-throughs. If there are a large number of problems found later, you may be held responsible for them. If there is not a satisfactory explanation (complexity of problem, newness of application), then the noted errors could affect your evaluation. Knowing that this evaluation approach is used should increase your desire to view the walk-through as a vehicle for improving your evaluation with your manager.

4. *Your reviewers focus on detection, not correction, of errors.* When an error is detected, it is assumed that you will correct it later. The reviewers do not make specific changes to your work. It is important not to discuss which of several alternatives is the better solution. The point is for the reviewers to help you find the errors, and for you to decide on the best way to implement the corrections.

5. *You concentrate on major problems, not trivial errors.* Early detection of major problems saves time and effort to correct later. Trivial errors, such as syntax errors, are found soon enough and are easily corrected.

How It Works

When you think you are ready for a walk-through select the time and invite your reviewers. This is not to say, however, that walk-throughs "just happen." Initially, an overall plan should be developed by you and your manager, specifying target dates for specific walk-throughs. Try to be as realistic as possible in the setting of dates.

After the reviewers have been invited and have indicated that they can attend, give them a copy of the work to be reviewed several days in advance of the session. This work may be a specifications narrative, system flowcharts, forms design, record layouts and file descriptions, data-base structure, hierarchy charts, pseudo code, or even program coding sheets. As you can see, much of the material to be reviewed in the walk-throughs later becomes documentation for the project. As reviewers are studying this material in advance of the session, they can note small or typographical errors on these documents, which are returned to you after the walk-through session. In this way, not only is the work itself reviewed, but also the documentation is updated for completeness, accuracy, and readability. Thus, the walk-through provides the opportunity for documentation to be produced during various phases of development when it can be of use to you as well.

At the session, one of your reviewers acts as a *recorder* and notes all issues that have been raised. A *list of exposures* (errors) is generated and given to you as well as to all reviewers. A copy is *not* sent to your manager but would be sent to the team leader should this person be unable to attend the walk-through.

Another reviewer acts as a *moderator*, whose job is to establish a positive atmosphere. A moderator must be sensitive to a variety of intangibles—pace, timing, and tone of the presentation, to name a few. A skillful moderator knows when to end discussion and how to move along without offending anyone. This individual does not allow the session to degenerate into *arguing* over issues or suggesting better solutions.

The session should begin with a statement of its *objectives* which should be expressed in terms of a *measurable action* or behavior; for example, "The purpose of this session is to *trace* the flow of data through the program's modules and *find* interface and/or logic errors." Compare this with the statement, "The purpose of this session is to understand how a program's modules interface with each other." (How do we know the reviewer *understands*?)

The reviewers come to the session with their comments. If there are any questions or problems about the documents they received prior to the walk-through, they are discussed at the start of the session. Following the comments on the distributed material, you give a brief tutorial on your work, if necessary. (If the reviewers are not familiar with the total project, the overall system may have to be discussed. This tutorial should be at the concepts level and should provide only the essential information needed to conduct a profitable review.)

The main part of the session now follows. This is the time in which the work is studied in detail. You explain what every portion of your design or code is doing, why it is there, and how it will work. This is a step-by-step process. Perhaps you have had the common experience of being unable to find an error in your program and going to someone for help. In order to explain what your program is doing and what the problem is, you start at the beginning and go through the program, describing each part. Then you suddenly find the error yourself, thank your listener, and return to your desk. The error was found by your explaining the program without your *helper* having said a word. The same situation often occurs at a walk-through session. The mechanics of the review point out errors which frequently you see first. If not, one of the reviewers usually does.

One of the most effective ways to find errors is to follow data through a program. The sample data could be selected from the test data that will be used to test the program when it is operational. The program is executed mentally by you with the reviewers questioning as you proceed. Encourage questions, especially those of the "What if . . ." variety. The atmosphere is one of a group studying the solution to a problem rather than being told that the solution is correct. When issues are raised that need attention, they are noted by the recorder before the moderator moves the group on to another area. Your reviewers should look for errors of omission as well as commission, and for deviations from the specifications. They should be looking for problems with interfaces and problems with handling exception conditions.

Should a reviewer point out *gross* program inefficiencies to you? There are two schools of thought on this: one is to establish that the program will work correctly; solve the problem at hand. Spending time looking for better ways of doing the same thing (especially if that will also need to be verified for accuracy) may be wasteful. The other viewpoint is that this is a good way for everyone attending to learn better techniques. Comments of this type can be helpful if handled properly. Perhaps a compromise is best, as was implied by the use of the word *gross* earlier. If a major savings can be obtained, then a discussion of program style and other properties can be instructive. However, the moderator should limit discussions which appear to refer to minor savings of space or time or are controversial.

If minor errors or marginal improvements in style are noted by the reviewers, then the moderator could suggest they *write* their comments to you. This approach does not take time from the session, avoids embarassment, and can be enlightening to you. If the list of errors noted by the recorder exceeds preestablished limits, either in number or severity of items, then a second walk-through can be scheduled. Otherwise, you simply correct the problems after the session. Normally, there is no formal follow-up to ensure that the corrections are made, but you may wish to send a memo to your reviewers when the corrections have been completed so that they know the current state of the project. This is necessary if they are interfacing with your work.

In some locations a list of errors is accumulated for all developers. This cumulative error list serves two purposes:

1. It indicates areas of *common* problems. Tutorials could be scheduled for developers to improve their skills in the particular areas.
2. It is a guide for future walk-through reviewers. Knowing what errors are likely to occur may direct reviewers' attention to those areas.

The entire walk-through session should take approximately one and a half to two hours. Shorter sessions would not allow sufficient depth of study; more than two hours may make the walk-through a hardship for those reviewers who have heavy demands on their time.

Figure 6-2 summarizes the operation of a walk-through.

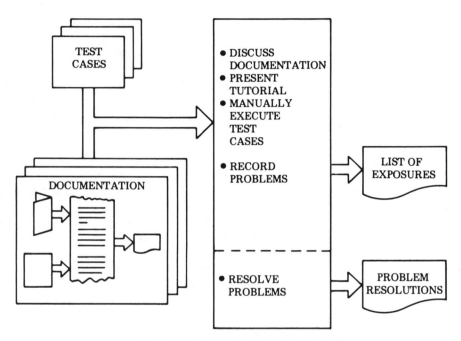

Figure 6-2. Operation of a walk-through

INSPECTIONS

Inspections are a more formal and rigorous version of the structured walk-through. They are similar in that they

- find errors early
- are a group review
- look at the work in great detail

Inspections differ from structured walk-throughs in the following ways:

1. There are specified criteria for a successful completion of an inspection. Work does not proceed on the next phase until this formal approval is obtained.
2. The session is run by a specially-trained moderator, *not* part of the develop-

ment team. In a walk-through you select the review team. In an inspection the moderator is selected *for* you, and it is the moderator who selects the rest of the review team.

3. Walk-throughs are scheduled by the developer. Inspections are scheduled by the moderator or management.

4. In a walk-through you present your own work. In an inspection, someone appointed by the moderator does the "reading" of your work.

5. In walk-throughs we recommended keeping track of common errors. In inspections this idea is extended and formalized. The compilation of error lists is mandatory, and the errors are accumulated into a data base. They are then sorted and analyzed in various ways. For example, statistics on the most common errors by phase are accumulated. These are then used by later inspection teams as a guide of what to look for. For sample lists of common errors, see Myers.[2]

6. In an inspection the errors found are recorded in a data base. The moderator follows up to ensure that the author has reworked the material satisfactorily.

7. Managers do not attend walk-throughs or inspections. However, in walk-throughs they are not informed of the results; in inspections, they are. In this way they are apprised of both the error rates and of the amount of time taken for rework and testing.

While inspections sound more threatening than structured walk-throughs, experience has shown that they become accepted as standard practice. The results have been outstanding in finding errors and learning more about common errors so that they can be minimized.

MANAGEMENT IMPLICATIONS

Structured walk-throughs and inspections have proven to be very effective tools in detecting errors early, when it is inexpensive to correct them. Often errors are found that are difficult to locate in any other way. In addition, the cause of the error, not merely the symptoms of it, is usually seen.

These techniques are quite valuable for an organization. The main question for you to answer is how formal and rigorous you want the reviews to be. You would probably want them to be in keeping with the general attitude in the organization. You may even wish to compromise, and define a review procedure that is somewhere between the walk-through and the inspection as here defined. For example, you may wish to have trained moderators, and have them appointed for a review, but allow the other reviewers to be selected by the developer. Thus, your structured walk-through may have more of the characteristics of an inspection.

[2]Glenford J. Myers, *The Art of Software Testing* (John Wiley and Sons, 1979).

The structured walk-through can make a major contribution to the success of a project. To ensure this success, here are some pitfalls to avoid:

1. *Using results of walk-throughs as an employee evaluation tool*. If reviewers and developers think that management is using the walk-through as an evaluation tool, then they may subconsciously agree for mutual protection not to find problems in each other's work.

2. *Scheduling insufficient time for walk-throughs*. Walk-throughs do take time, especially at the beginning of the development cycle. Walk-through time should be incorporated into the overall manpower schedule as well as into each individual's schedule. In estimating time needed by each individual, realize that two to four hours of time may be needed by the developer to prepare for a review that takes two hours. Also, the reviewer not only spends time in the walk-through session but also needs time to review the material before the session. In some projects, then, review sessions may require many man-weeks of time. A poor use of time? Not at all! In projects using structured walk-throughs (and other structured programming technologies), programmers not only completed the job as scheduled but also eliminated the redesigning at the end of the cycle that was typical in their traditional development efforts. Participating in walk-throughs should be a scheduled part of everyone's job. It is important that developers *not* regard reviewing as time away from their work. If a walk-through is shortened in an effort to save time (thereby becoming a quick run-through), then only simple or glaring errors are found.

3. *Becoming concerned that the walk-through is carrying a poor developer who would otherwise have been identified sooner*. If the reviewers are finding errors for the developer, is the developer doing an adequate job, or is the group doing his work for him? A walk-through does not *carry* a poor developer for very long because it is still up to the developer to make the necessary changes.

Structured walk-throughs locate design and logic errors early in the development cycle. These reviews become meaningful milestones which contribute heavily to productivity.

The role of the reviewers is one of preparation, probing, and problem definition. If the reviewers are teammates, it is common for them to discover hidden relationships between what they are developing and what is being reviewed. Ambiguities will come to light, necessitating further clarification and definition. If for no other reason, management should value the walk-through as an effective communication tool for the developers.

Walk-throughs can motivate both the developer and the reviewer to pursue a higher level of excellence. It is natural to try to do the best work possible before a review in hopes that only a few errors exist. Thus, walk-throughs contribute to program quality, even when few or no errors are found during the session. The reviewers usually feel satisfied at having helped improve a product. The developer feels a sense of achievement at having met a milestone of the project.

For you as a manager walk-throughs are a good measure of project progress. Knowing that specific walk-throughs have been conducted is better than merely asking a developer for an estimate of the status of the work.

Structured walk-throughs should be combined with other techniques mentioned earlier. Thus, in top-down design, walk-throughs should be held for the design of higher level modules to ensure validity before lower level modules are developed. With structured programming the simplicity and clarity of the program make it easier to conduct the walk-through. Conversely, the walk-through can be used to ensure that proper structured programming conventions are being followed.

You will need to communicate to your staff the importance you place on walk-throughs and schedule time for these sessions. Essential ingredients for a successful walk-through include a positive attitude on the part of all participants—one that is open and nondefensive—and a belief that you are not evaluating them based on what occurs *during* a walk-through. A few walk-throughs may be required before people come to believe in and accept the real purpose of the walk-through. For this reason the first few walk-throughs may not be as successful as later ones.

SUMMARY

Experience with structured walk-throughs and inspections is most encouraging. Undoubtedly there are a number of ways they could be modified to fit other types of projects. By using the walk-through, some or all of these results may occur:

1. There is a vehicle for catching errors in the system at the earliest possible time, when the cost of correcting them is lowest.
2. The overall quality of the product is improved.
3. Employees are frequently motivated to pursue a higher degree of work excellence.
4. Developers feel more confident about the quality of their work.
5. Developers derive a greater satisfaction from their work.
6. Team spirit is enhanced.
7. Junior people have the opportunity to learn new techniques.
8. Experienced people often improve their skills.
9. New personnel on a project can be more quickly and adequately trained via walk-throughs than by other methods.
10. Management can track project progress and completeness.

REVIEW QUESTIONS

1. Name at least two ways in which a structured walk-through differs from a project review.

2. Name at least two ways in which a structured walk-through differs from the technique of asking a friend for help when you have a problem.

3. Name at least two ways in which a structured walk-through differs from an inspection.

4. Assume you are a developer who is going to have a walk-through. List the types of people you would invite, and give a reason for asking each one.

5. Assume you are a developer who is going to have your first walk-through. List as many things as possible that you, your manager, and your colleagues can do to help you become open and nondefensive.

6. As a developer would you prefer to have your work reviewed at a walk-through or an inspection? Why?

7. As a manager list some of the criteria you would use to decide whether to use walk-throughs or inspections.

8. What would you recommend as a follow-up procedure to make sure that the exposures identified do get corrected?

9. Plan a walk-through session. Decide on the items to be distributed ahead of time, the visual aids to be provided, and how the two hours will be allocated.

10. List at least two arguments for and two arguments against having the developer's manager attend the walk-through.

11. Name at least three uses for the list of exposures generated during a walk-through.

7

Testing

"The bitterness of poor quality lingers long after the sweetness of meeting schedules."

C. Weagle[1]

Testing is a process in which a program is validated. It is a *positive* activity that seeks to demonstrate that the program is correct and does, in fact, meet its design specifications. *Debugging* is a process in which program errors are removed. It is a *negative* activity in that it is centered around the elimination of known errors or bugs. Testing is complete when all desired verifications against specifications have been performed. Debugging is finished when there are no known errors. However, debugging is a process that ends only temporarily, because subsequent execution of a program may uncover other errors—thereby restarting the debugging process. (Reminds us of Mark Twain's comment about giving up smoking: "It's easy to do; I've done it many times.")

Because debugging is a reactive procedure which stems from testing, it cannot be planned ahead of time. The best that can be done is to establish guidelines of how to debug and develop a list of "what to look for." Testing, however, can and should be planned. It is a definable task in which the how and what to test can be specified. Testing can be scheduled to take place at a specific time in the development cycle.

Debugging cannot begin until the end of a development cycle, because it requires an executable program. Testing, on the other hand, can begin in the early stages of the development effort. Of course, the tests themselves must be run near the end of a project, but the decisions of what to test, how to test, with what kind of data, can and should be completed before the coding is started.

Whenever possible, the person planning the tests should not be the same person who designed and coded the program. This helps to ensure that the tests will discover errors in the program rather than repeat them blindly.

---

[1]C. Weagle, "Visit to a Programming Center," *THINK*, October/November 1974, p. 31. Reprinted by permission from THINK. Copyright 1974 by International Business Machines Corporation.

WHAT IS TESTED AND HOW?

Items to be tested include specifications, individual modules, and intermodule connections. These will be discussed in this section.

Testing the Specifications

Well-defined specifications provide the framework from which to plan and execute program testing. The specifications must be clearly stated so that the program can be tested against them. Thus, the first step is to test the *specifications* for completeness and clarity. One approach to analyzing specifications is to use *cause-and-effect* logic. A *cause* as used here means a *condition* or combination of conditions that could occur. An *effect* is an observable result or action to be taken (e.g., change a record, print a message). Hopefully, the specifications are written that way, but if they are not, then a meeting must be held with the user (and the designer if the user did not actually write the specs). As a result of this meeting (which may or may not be in the form of a walk-through), a list of cause-and-effect relationships describing the application's requirements should be developed. An example is shown in Table 7-1.

Table 7-1 Program Specifications in Terms of Cause-and-Effect Relationships

Condition (Cause)	Observable Action (Effect)
1. Transactions out of sequence	Print error message and terminate job
2. Invalid transaction code	Print error message and bypass transaction
3. A master record already exists for an ADDITION transaction	Print duplicate record error message and bypass transaction
4. ADDITION transaction is followed by an UPDATE transaction to that ADDITION *where* the ADDITION record was bypassed because of condition 3 above	Print error message and bypass *all* UPDATE records related to the rejected ADDITION transaction
5. Etc.	

Writing the specifications in this way helps to point up any omissions in them. If there is a cause that does not have an indicated effect, an omission has been identified. Similarly any effect without a condition specified will also be apparent. If, on the other hand, a narrative form is used for specifications, omissions are harder to spot. For example, consider the following portion of specifications for a program to update an inventory file:

Transactions are in part number sequence and may contain additions, changes, or deletions of master records. Each transaction is to be edited according to the attached criteria, and the specified error message produced. Additions which match an existing record, or updates and deletes for which there is no master record, should produce the indicated message.

What is the desired effect if a transaction is *not* in sequence? Should the program check for this? If found, is the job terminated? Is the current transaction discarded? What about the previous transaction? These need to be clarified before development continues.

Next, look for combinations of causes that are linked by AND or OR. For example, what is the effect if an addition transaction has edit errors AND also matches an existing record? Are both errors to be indicated? If only one, which one? The impact of the answer on the design and implementation of the program can be significant. Where possible, all combinations of causes should be considered. However, in some programs there are so many possible combinations of conditions that it is not practical to test them all. Identify the more important combinations and those most likely to occur in the event there is not time to test all combinations. Some combinations, of course, are not logically possible. For example, an *end-of-file condition* and a *transaction out of sequence* can't occur at the same time, so this combination would not be tested.

Black-Box Testing of Modules

One of the advantages of modular design is that it facilitates testing. As each additional module is to be tested, it is added in a top-down manner as discussed in Chapter 3. The methods of limiting module complexity discussed in Chapter 2 will not only aid program modification but also simplify module testing. In planning for the testing of functional modules, you may wish to develop a *list of functional variations*. A functional variation is one type of output from a module given a specific combination of input data items.

This type of testing is often called *black-box*, or specification-based, testing.[2] You are creating tests which derive directly from the definition of the module's function; that is, the description states that given certain input the module will produce certain output. Your tests, of course, provide the necessary input to determine whether the desired output is obtained.

Note that these tests do not take into account the internal design of the module. (For that, see "White-box Testing" later in this chapter.) The term *black-box*, then, indicates that you are just looking at the module from the outside. You will be testing with various kinds of input, both valid and invalid, to determine that the module meets its specifications. The first tests should always be those with valid data input and no exceptional conditions. Then the handling of various possible error and exceptional conditions can be tested.

Table 7-2 provides a sample list of functional variations for the sequential file update case study in the COBOL and PL/I chapters. This list, then, becomes the

[2]Philip Gilbert, *Software Design and Development* (Chicago, IL, Science Research Associates, 1983).

Table 7-2 Sample List of Functional Variations

	CONDITIONS			ACTION
Variation	Transaction Type	Edit OK?	Matching Master?	Effect
1	Add	Yes	No	Record added
2	Add	No	No	Error message #5
3	Add	Yes	Yes	Error message #3
4	Add	No	Yes	Error message #5 & #3
5	Delete	Yes	Yes	Record deleted
6	Delete	No	Yes	Error message #7
	•			
	•			
	•			

starting point for defining the desired test data. This definition of test data should probably begin in the design phase so that the sample data can be used in walk-throughs to test the design of an application. Of course, as discussed in Chapter 3, the actual test data is prepared *before* module coding begins. Each item in the list of functional variations becomes one test case. These variations should be repeated in a variety of sequences. For example, test data should include at least *two repetitions* of the same error *consecutively*. If practical, each type of error should be followed by an occurrence of each other type of error. This list of test cases is augmented by giving considerations to these situations:

1. *The first record in the file*. At least one test case is needed for each of the possibilities for the first record. This would include both valid and invalid records. You should also include an empty file—one with no records. What happens if *end-of-file* occurs on the *first* read?

2. *Last record*. For each input file there should be at least one test case where that file ends *first*. In addition, each input file should be tested with valid and error records as the last record in the file.

3. *Invalid data*. For each data item there should be an allowable range of values. These were developed during stepwise refinement (see Chapter 5). Tests of valid data are needed, including values at the upper and lower limits of the acceptable range. Also invalid data beyond these limits needs to be input as a test, as well as an incorrect number of data items. Be sure you include data that has invalid characters, zero, and negative values.

Each set of test data should combine as many tests as possible. However, in order to test different conditions, such as each file ending first, multiple sets of test data are needed. Table 7-3 shows an example of some test data sets for the file update program.

Table 7-3 Test Data Sets

Set	Errors	First Record	Last Record	EOF First
A	Transaction Code	Valid	Valid	Trans
B	Above, plus Add of duplicate record	Invalid	Invalid	Both
C	Above, plus Update and No Match	Invalid	Valid	Trans
D	Above, plus Edit Errors	Valid	Invalid	Trans
E	All types	Valid	Invalid	Master

Other situations requiring special consideration include:

1. *Large-volume tests.* It is important to simulate the eventual running environment as closely as possible. For large-volume tests, use actual data from the activity for which the program application is being developed.

2. *Multiple-volume tests.* Often large files are stored across several volumes (e.g., one tape file spans several tape reels, or one direct-access file is spread across several diskettes). Be sure to test data in every volume of a multivolume file, including the *first* and *last* records stored in each volume of the file.

Each developed set of test data requires planning and time for running and evaluating results. Thus, the sets of test data have to be kept to a manageable number. You may want to use walk-throughs as an occasion to plan testing. That is, early in the development cycle, a review session can incorporate a discussion of the test cases planned.

After the test data sets have been defined, a *master list of test data* should be created. A sample list is shown in Table 7-4. The master list includes all test cases, with the possible exception of actual or historical data used. For each item in the test data set, a unique identifying number (or name) and the functional variations are specified, along with the type of transaction (if applicable) and additional comments. This can be a time-consuming task, but the master list of test data is a useful tool for producing the *test plan*, for executing the test, and for verifying the results.

In addition to planned test data, actual data from the application should be used. If the present application is a *manual* system, then it may be desirable to create the needed data from actual source documents. If the existing application is being reprogrammed, then data from the existing application may be directly usable to test the new program. Try to establish the actual running atmosphere in the testing of programs.

To generate the planned test data, a *data-generator program* can be used. This is a general-purpose program in which specification sheets direct the type of data records to be generated.

Table 7-4 Example of Master Test Data List

Test Data Set					Type of Transaction	Part Number	Functional Variations	Comments
A	B	C	D	E				
√			√	√	Add	015237	1	Before first master
	√		√	√	Add	016440	3	Duplicate
√	√		√	√	Add	016441	1	
		√	√	√	Delete	016441	6	Delete new addition
√	√	√	√	√	Delete	016924	5	
		√	√	√	Add	016925	2	
	√	√	√	√	Add	033101	3	Duplicate
√	√	√	√	√	Change	040485	8	
					•	•		
					•	•		
					•	•		

Testing Intermodule Connections

So far we have been concerned with data that test the functions of the program as seen from outside the program. These are observable causes and effects initially described in the list of functional variations. The connections between modules must also be tested, because most modules pass data to and receive data back from other modules. Generally, we can say that the data passed to and from modules is of two types:

- External data (transactions, master records)
- Internal data (indicators or counters whose status is generated by alternate paths through a module's logic)

In planning for the testing of intermodule connections, a useful tool is the creation of an *input/output list* for each module in a program. Input/output as used here does not necessarily imply a READ or WRITE operation in the module. *Input* may be a data item *passed to* a module. It may be the complete record, part of a record, indicators, or counters. *Output* consists of items *produced by* the module. These are not necessarily final output items, as they may become input items to other modules. The same variable can be both an input and an output data item if the module alters its value. A sample *I/O list* is shown in Table 7-5. This list includes both external and internal data as previously defined.

An advantage of developing this I/O list is that it leads to a better definition of what each module is to do. (A module's function is the transformation of input to output.) If there are many items for some of the modules on the list, it can point to weaknesses in the design.

Because the I/O list identifies the interfaces (data passed) between modules, this list becomes a useful guide in the development of stubs. In the top-down testing of modules, stubs must be coded so as to be able to receive the input data *arguments* and return the required output data. (In some languages, such as Pascal, arguments are referred to as actual parameters.)

Table 7-5 Sample I/O List for a Program's Modules

Module Name	Input	Output
ADD	• ADD transaction • MASTER MATCH indicator	• New master record • NEW RECORD ADDED indicator
UPDATE	• ISSUES transaction • RECEIPTS transaction • MASTER MATCH indicator	• New master record
DELETE	• DELETE transaction • MASTER MATCH indicator	None
WRAP-UP Etc.	None • • •	• End-of-job message • • •

A tool that will assist in the organization of test data arguments is the *argument matrix* shown in Table 7-6. In this matrix all module names appear across the top. Include all data items that you think belong there. Unused data items can be easily deleted later. Each data item that is passed to or from a module should be identified with either an I, an M, or a U, where

I indicates that this data item is *initially* provided by this module (Data is either provided by an input operation or is established internally through initialization.)

M indicates that the data item could be or is *modified* by this module

U indicates that the data item is *used* by this module

Some modules in Table 7-6 have multiple symbols—such as QTY ON ORDER, which is both *modified* and *used* by the PROCESS RECEIPTS module. By examining these entries in the matrix, you may discover omissions or inconsistencies. For example, if the initialization of a data item has been overlooked, this omission should be detected here. If a data item is passed to a module but never used in that module, the inconsistency should be noticed. Having simple interfaces (i.e., few data items passed) will make this analysis practical.

The main use for the argument matrix is to serve as a basis for developing a top-down test plan. Since it shows data initialization and dependencies, it is very helpful in planning module testing and stub requirements. This will be explained in the next section.

Table 7-6 Argument Matrix Example
(I = Initializes data; U = Uses data; M = Modifies data)

		MAIN	READ TRANS	GET MATCHING MASTER	READ MASTER	ADD	DELETE	PROCESS RECEIPTS	··
Indicators	NEW RECORD	I		U-M		M	U-M		
	MASTER EOF	I		U	M				
	TRANS EOF	I-U	M						
	MASTER MATCH	I-U		M		U	U		
Master Record	ITEM KEY			U	I	U			
	DESCRIPTION				I				
	QTY ON HAND				I			U	
	TOTAL ISSUES				I				
	TOTAL RECEIPTS				I			U	
	QTY ON ORDER				I			U-M	
	ORDER POINT				I				
	REORDER QTY				I				
	TOTAL COST				I			U-M	
	AVERAGE COST				I			M	
	DATE LAST ISSUE				I				
Transaction	TRANSACTION TYPE	U	I						
	· ·								
	· ·								
	· ·								

Intermodule testing is another form of black-box testing. Here again the logic of the module is unknown, hence the term *black-box*. It is the results produced that are being tested.

White-Box Testing

Tests which verify the internal logic of a module must also be included. For these, look at the various paths that are possible based on the control structures (selection, repetition, case). Here you are looking at the details of the program rather than its input-output. Hence the module is a white box.

Be sure that sufficient tests are included so that every statement gets executed at least once. That means that for every IF, both the THEN and the ELSE part must be executed. For a DOUNTIL there should be a test in which the loop is not executed at all, and one or more where it is. Similarly all CASE possibilities should be executed.

Note that it will not usually be practical to test all of the combinations of logic paths. If your module has, say, ten IFs, you may wish to test all possible variations. That would mean 2^{10} or over 1,000 test cases. Similarly a DOWHILE can't be tested with all possible number of repetitions, for that would be infinite. You need to be selective. Test combinations of IF statements that are related to each other. Certainly those in a nest need to be tested with all combinations in order to get each part to execute. And loops need to be tested with a few of the possible number of repetitions.

DEVELOPING THE TEST PLAN

For each module indicate which tests must be run. For some modules, especially those at the top of the hierarchy chart, several sets of test data may be required. For some of the lower modules, *one test set* will suffice. Whenever possible, add one module at a time and test one module at a time.

There are several exceptions to this guideline. For example, two lower level modules that do not communicate with each other and are in different *legs* of the hierarchy chart might have their test data combined so that one test is performed on the two modules. Another exception is found in the case of adding a module that requires a specific stub. The problem is, however, that the stub is complex and would require almost as much effort to code as a stub as it would to code the entire module. In this case the stub is coded and the two modules are tested together. The other exception may be in the case of the top module(s), which may require several lower-level modules in order to execute anything at all.

Once you have decided which test will be run with each module, the next step is to identify the stubs that each module needs. The argument matrix (Table 7-6) will help you identify the data requirements for each module. For each data item that has an M or a U designated in a specific module, the module requires a stub to supply the data item. For example, the PROCESS RECEIPTS module in Table 7-6 has a U and an M designated for the data item, QTY ON ORDER. This item is initially provided in the READ MASTER module. Thus, in order to execute the PROCESS RECEIPTS module, READ MASTER must be provided either as a stub or as a module.

Any lower-level modules that are to be coded first as stubs and that contain I or M data items must, of course, provide that data. The I data could be read from an external file or simply compiled into the stub as program constants.

If data items are to be modified (M data items) by the stub, the stub could still return to the invoking module some predetermined results that were compiled into the stub as program constants. For example, ADD has a U for MASTER MATCH, and GET MATCHING MASTER has an M. Thus, to test ADD, a stub for GET MATCHING MASTER must send back both possible settings for the indicator.

The passing of indicators between modules and stubs is fairly easy to implement. If more than one indicator is being passed, try to test all combinations. Since indicators are binary, the number of test cases is 2^n where n is the number of indicators. Note that this is another reason to keep down the number of data items passed between modules.

The next step in planning module tests is to calculate, in advance of executing the module, the expected results. This is preferable to taking your computer output and calculating that the answers are correct. Expected test output should be defined in detail and might include:

- A listing of the sequence in which modules are to be executed, both for valid and for error transactions
- A record count (of all input and output records)
- A listing of modified records (*before* and *after* the update)
- The number and type of exception messages
- Adding machine results of calculations carried out by the program (as a check against program-generated round-off errors)

In addition to these tests, controls or audit trails would, of course, be incorporated into a program. These controls, although a permanent part of the program, can also aid in the testing process.

Another step in test planning is the specification of what constitutes a successful test for a module. Even in the case of some moderate-sized programs, completely testing every possible situation becomes impractical. Some of the conditions may be trivial, and some may be so unlikely as to warrant being ignored. The person specifying the tests must decide what constitutes a successful test. Are there some trivial errors that will be accepted? If so, they should be documented. For example, assume 300 sets of test data have been run against the latest module of a language compiler. Two of the test runs failed. Perhaps the tests depicted a rather obscure way in which the language *might* be used. Can this test be considered successful so that lower level modules can be coded and tested? The decision here, of course, is whether or not to make a program operational while debugging continues. Whatever the criteria for successful testing of modules, try to write the standards before the actual program tests are run.

Another item to specify is the procedure for correcting errors and retesting. Who will be retesting? How? Will one error be fixed and tested, or will the corrections be batched? If an error is discovered after a module has passed its tests, will you run *regression* tests? If so, how many? Which ones? For each expected problem, you are establishing a plan and a procedure to handle it. This should help to make the testing process less hectic and more orderly.

The last part of the test plan is the *acceptance test*. Here the user and the developer jointly agree that the program is a viable product that meets its design objectives. Before the implementation phase the user, the developer, and the tester should establish the criteria for acceptance. What does the user require? Ideally, the user is as involved in the evaluation of test results as the developer and tester.

EXECUTING THE TESTS

During the implementation phase you will be coding and testing the modules in a top-down order as specified in your test plan. However, because the test plan was written before the modules were coded, it will now need to be augmented to see that all branches in the code are tested. This should be done for both paths of each selection structure, although it may not be practical to test all possible combinations.

As part of your planning, you would have also estimated the time required to code and test each module. The running of the test and its successful completion becomes a milestone of progress on the project. Each test's output is compared with the anticipated results as set forth in the test plan. Where discrepancies are discovered, the *bugs* are found and removed. The results of each test should be documented for future reference. After the first few modules are tested, you may choose to run only a few of those tests as the lower level modules are being tested.

As tests turn up errors, corrections will be made, and the tests rerun to verify the corrections. But what if the correction actually introduces an error? In particular what if the new error affects a previously-run test?

To guard against this you must periodically rerun old tests to ensure that they still work. Ideally you rerun all tests, but that may not always be practical. In that case you will probably set up a representative sample to retest periodically. This collection would be augmented with new tests as more functions are available to be tested, a process called *regression testing*.

Perry[3] makes the point that in addition to test data you also need to make sure that your documentation and module descriptions remain valid as changes are made.

MANAGEMENT IMPLICATIONS

Testing, as described in this chapter, has some implications for management:

1. *Expenditure pattern will be different.* Because testing is started early in the development cycle, a greater commitment of resources is required sooner than in traditional projects. However, the total cost of testing should not increase. In some cases total cost has even decreased. The traditional and suggested expenditure patterns are shown in Figure 7-1.

2. *Testing costs are more easily identified.* In traditional projects the only specific cost associated with testing is that for System Test. Any costs associated with reworking a project due to poor design or inadequate testing usually come under the costs associated with development. Because testing costs are now more visible, management may have to spend more time justifying the expenditure. However, once justified, it is possible to closely estimate what the costs will be.

[3]William E. Perry, *A Structured Approach to Systems Testing* (Englewood Cliffs, NJ: Prentice-Hall, Inc., 1983).

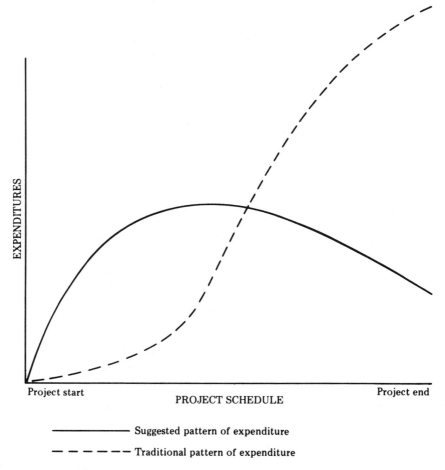

EXPENDITURES

Project start

PROJECT SCHEDULE

Project end

———————— Suggested pattern of expenditure

— — — — — — Traditional pattern of expenditure

Figure 7-1. Changed pattern of expenditure for testing activity

3. *The benefits of testing show up at the end of the development cycle.* In traditional projects the running of tests is often a chaotic 11th-hour rush that requires more time for the fixing of errors than anticipated. In projects using the new improved programming technologies, the usual problems and delays don't materialize. Greater benefits often accrue during production running, when maintenance problems and costs are reduced.

4. *Testing in parallel with the development effort requires personnel.* To implement testing as presented in this chapter, people will have to be assigned to the part- or full-time task of test planning and test running. Initiating this

kind of operation may require establishing new job categories and planning additional training. People doing development work may not be interested in an assignment as a *test planner* for they may view the job as a step down. This attitude might change once the test planner's job is firmly established as essential to the success of all projects.

5. *A new approach to testing may have some start-up costs associated with it.* As with any new idea or method, there are initial problems to be worked out. However, in the case of testing that starts early in the development cycle, the problems appear to be short-lived.

SUMMARY

Testing can and should be planned before coding begins. It is necessary to analyze and understand the program specifications in detail. Then you can define what is to be tested. Using cause-and-effect analysis can help to clarify specifications.

In addition to testing observable effects, you will want to test the connections from one module to another. For each module you should create a list of input and output data items. These could be arranged in an argument matrix to help organize your thinking.

Those tests that are designed to demonstrate that a module functions as it was defined to do are called black-box tests. Their objective is to examine what the module should produce given specified input. Other tests, called white-box tests, must be included to test the module's internal logic and control structures. They are designed to see that all paths through the module are exercised at least once.

A test plan should be drawn, showing tests to be performed on each module, stub requirements, and output expected. This is all done before program coding begins. When the modules are coded, then the tests can be run and the results compared with expected output.

Following these steps to testing will result in less *total time* spent in testing and debugging, fewer errors, easier detection and correction of errors, and better satisfaction on the part of both programmers and users.

The number of errors detected during module testing should be small. This is based on the principles stressed in this book. Functional design provides simple modules. Walk-throughs find errors before they get to the machine-testing stage. The discipline of using only the program structures results in more carefully thought-out programs and therefore fewer errors, The absence of the uncontrolled GOTO lowers the number of possible paths through modules—a factor in reducing complexity and making testing easier and more complete. When errors are found, they are more easily diagnosed and located because of the clarity of the program. Top-down testing distributes the detection of possible errors over a longer period of time, thereby allowing more time to correct each error.

REVIEW QUESTIONS AND EXERCISES

1. List at least three ways in which testing differs from debugging.

2. Why is it necessary to spend time and effort analyzing specifications?

3. Consider a program to determine the type of triangle formed by three sides. It reads in sets of three side lengths *a*, *b*, and *c* and determines the type of triangle as follows:
   - If the sum of two sides is not greater than the third, no triangle.
   - If two sides are equal, isosceles
   - If three sides are equal, equilateral
   - If one side squared equals the sum of the squares of the other sides, right triangle

Write specifications for this program, using cause-and-effect analysis.

4. Create a list of functional variations for the program in question 3.

5. What are the reasons you might need more than one set of test data for a program?

6. Create a list of test data for the program in question 3. Divide the test into sets which contain various types of valid and invalid data.

7. Assume the following hierarchy chart for the problem in question 3.

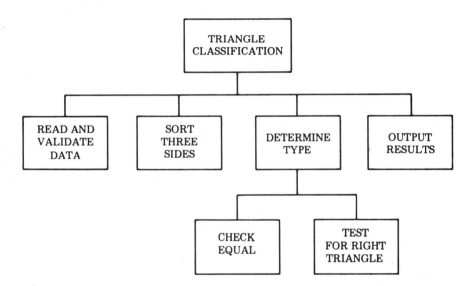

Create an input/output list (refer to Table 7-5) for each of these modules.

8. Draw an argument matrix for the program in question 7.

9. How does black-box testing differ from white-box testing?

10. Figure 7-1 shows a suggested expenditure pattern for testing. What are some of the activities that account for the higher expenses in the earlier stages of the project?

8

Structured Programming Using PL/I

"Now, said Rabbit, "This is a Search and I've organized it—"
"Done what to it?" said Pooh.
"Organized it. Which means—well, it's what you do to a Search when you don't
all look in the same place at once."[1]

A. A. Milne

PL/I (*note the Roman numeral* I) is a programming language that meets the needs of
both scientific and commercial programmers, affords a flexibility heretofore available
only to assembler language programmers, and takes advantage of new computer architecture developments. Its richness has encouraged use in a wide variety of applications.
Its syntax allows for easy coding of the basic structures—sequence, choice (IF-
THENELSE), and repetition (DOWHILE). The optional structures—DOUNTIL and
CASE—can be written in a way that is still easy to code and easy to read.

This chapter assumes familiarity with PL/I and discusses three structured programming considerations: modularity, structuring, and improving readability.

MODULARITY

Module Organization

Figure 8-1 shows a hierarchy chart of a number of modules in a customer billing
application. Each box in this chart represents a module in the application. Each of these
modules is an *external* procedure that may contain any number of *internal* procedures.
The modules pass control by use of the CALL statement or by a function reference. In
either case, data is communicated by use of a list of arguments. Thus the data that is
shared is explicitly known to someone reading the program. External modules are
separately compiled to ensure that data from one module is not being used by the other.
In this way you can follow the principles of *information hiding* introduced in Chapter 2.

[1]From *The House at Pooh Corner* by A.A. Milne. Copyright 1928 by E.P. Dutton & Co.; renewal, (c)
1956 by A.A. Milne. Reprinted by permission of the publishers, E.P. Dutton & Co., Inc. and Methuen
Children's Books Ltd.

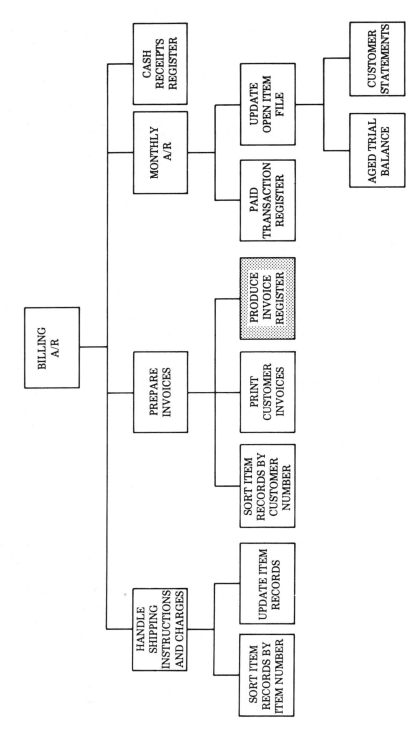

Figure 8-1. Modules in a billing/accounts receivable application

The modules in this figure are developed from the top down, where *one leg* of the chart probably would be fully developed before the next leg is designed in detail, coded, and tested. Assume that the left-most leg in the hierarchy chart has been completed and we are now down to the coding stages of the module (shaded box in Figure 8-1) that generates an Invoice Register. The invoice register layout is shown in Figure 8-2.

This module, like all modules, should be limited to a manageable number of executable source statements. A number of PL/I installations using structured programming techniques have found it desirable to limit the number of *executable* source statements to the 50 to 60 lines of code that can be contained on one printer page of output. Other installations have decided to allow larger modules and subdivide them into segments of 25 to 60 lines of code.

How to Segment a Module

Assume that the logic for the PRODUCE INVOICE REGISTER module has already been written in pseudo code. By examining this code, it is determined that the module will require more than 60 lines of source code. Thus, the module needs to be segmented. The *item records* to be processed by this module include, among other things, these fields:

Customer number	Salesman number	Invoice number	Item number	Quantity purchased	Price	Description

Segmenting is best handled at the stepwise refinement stage. After several iterations it will be apparent whether or not the module will require more than a page of code. In the invoice register example the logic produced through stepwise refinement is as follows:

```
On Endfile
    More item records = no
More item records = yes
DOWHILE more item records
    Read an item record
    IF more item records
        Validate data
        IF data ok
            Call process item record
        ELSE
            Call data error
        ENDIF
    ELSE
        Call final totals
    ENDIF
ENDDO
```

INVOICE REGISTER

INVOICE NUMBER	CUST NO	CUSTOMER NAME	MERCHANDISE AMOUNT	TAX	TOTAL AMOUNT
16799	14753	HOBBYRAMA	52.50	2.61	54.81
16800	14758	HOFF ELEC CO	86.12	4.30	90.42
16801	14764	HOLBRO PAINT CO	92.20	4.61	96.81
16802	14770	HOLLAND CO	80.15	4.01	84.16
16803	14775	HOVER CO	912.12	45.61	957.73
16804	14780	HOWELL CO	200.10	10.00	210.10
16805	14787	HOWKEN UTILITIES	315.00	15.75	330.75
16806	14790	HUGEL MOTORS	930.30	46.65	
16807	14792	IRVING TIRE CO.	1,950.00		
16808	14795	IVY BARN INC.			
16809	15800	JACKSON SALES	00	2.02	672.42
			1,050.10	40.00	840.10
			280.50	92.51	1,142.61
			555.10	14.03	294.53
16843	15970	ZACHARY BROS.	106.66	27.76	582.86
16844	15972	ZEPHYR ELEC CO	1,133.00	5.33	111.99
				56.65	1,189.65
		TOTALS	61,564.67	3,078.23	64,642.90

Figure 8-2. Invoice register layout

The pseudo code solution for handling the end-of-file is slightly different from the generic way in which pseudo code was presented earlier in this book. There is no formal definition of the form that pseudo code should take; simply write it in a way that closely approximates the language in which you will be programming. Hence, the ENDFILE on-unit, unique to PL/I, is included in the pseudo code. This pseudo code could now be translated into PL/I source code and form the *top segment* in this module.

The top segment is a synopsis of the entire module. A module, then, is segmented in the same hierarchical fashion in which a system or program is developed.

Figure 8-3 shows the hierarchy for the segmented module that will generate the invoice register. The lower-level segments may be internal procedures that are invoked via a CALL. However, assume that the *Validate Data* segment has already been coded and resides in the source-statement library. In this case the segment will be included via the %INCLUDE, and control will be passed to that segment by simply *flowing* into the segment.

At the point of beginning to code this module, both test data and the job control language should have been prepared. The top segment is coded first. Of course, any segments needed to test the higher level segments would either be coded as stubs first or completely coded if they are easy to code or relatively short. In the invoice register example, all of the segments (other than the top segment) could be initially coded as stubs. The top segment would then be tested, followed by the coding and testing of the other segments.

A combination of the hierarchical and execution-order approaches is the best method of *planning* the sequence in which the lower-level segments are coded and tested. Thus, the sequence of coding and testing might be (1) Top segment, (2) Process item record, (3) Final totals, (4) Validate data, and (5) Data error.

In formatting the source listing, it is desirable to have one segment per source listing page. (Occasionally, two or three small segments might appear on one printer page with spacing between the segments.) Most PL/I compilers provide the facility for spacing a source listing via (1) the preprocessor formatting option—%PAGE and %SKIP (*n*) where *n* is the number of lines to be skipped, or (2) column 1 of the source program (source statements would use columns 2 to 72) to indicate a carriage control character. For example, specify a "1" for skip to a new page, a blank for skip one line, and so on. Usually you must specify—through job control language or the PROCESS statement—that you wish to use either of these formatting features.

If the segmented invoice register module were formatted, one segment per source listing page, the source listing would probably appear as shown in Figure 8-4. (Some PL/I compilers provide *two* source listings—one with source statement library code appearing at the end of the source listing and the other with the source statement code inserted in-line where it would be executed.) In this example the DECLARE statements were grouped together at the end of the source program.

Each segment should be a *proper program* with these characteristics:

1. There is one entry at the top of the page.

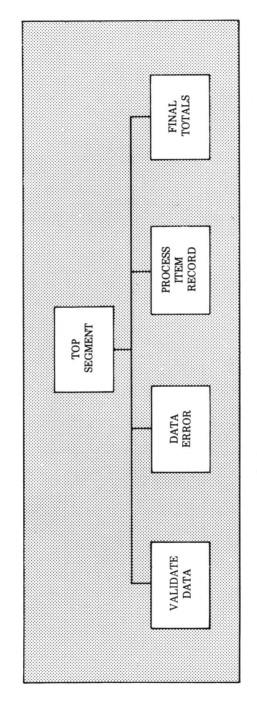

Figure 8-3. Segments in the invoice-register module

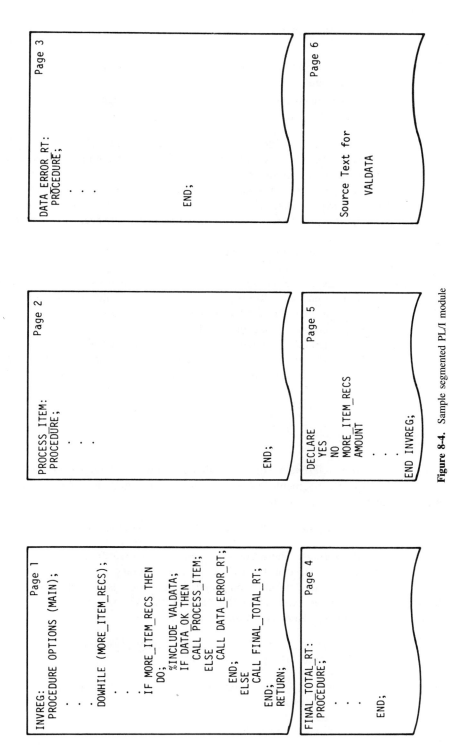

Page 1
```
INVREG:
    PROCEDURE OPTIONS (MAIN);
    .
    .
    .
    DOWHILE (MORE_ITEM_RECS);
        IF MORE_ITEM_RECS THEN
            DO;
                %INCLUDE VALDATA;
                IF DATA OK THEN
                    CALL PROCESS_ITEM;
                ELSE
                    CALL DATA_ERROR_RT;
            END;
        ELSE
            CALL FINAL_TOTAL_RT;
    END;
    RETURN;
```

Page 2
```
PROCESS_ITEM:
    PROCEDURE;
    .
    .
    .
    END;
```

Page 3
```
DATA_ERROR_RT:
    PROCEDURE;
    .
    .
    .
    END;
```

Page 4
```
FINAL_TOTAL_RT:
    PROCEDURE;
    .
    .
    .
    END;
```

Page 5
```
DECLARE
    YES
    NO
    MORE_ITEM_RECS
    AMOUNT
    .
    .
END INVREG;
```

Page 6
```
Source Text for

    VALDATA
```

Figure 8-4. Sample segmented PL/I module

2. There is one exit. It should be the last statement on a page and the return is to the invoking segment.
3. The logic flow is from the top to the bottom of the page.
4. Logically related code is grouped together.

Figure 8-5 shows a possible sequence or logical grouping of source code in a module. The source listing begins with one or two pages of comments describing the module and its method of solving the given problem. (You may wish to precede the source program with a general pseudo code solution as a vehicle for explaining the program.) When descriptive data names are used in structured programs, the need for comments throughout a program is minimized. Comments, however, might precede the more complex segments.

The DECLARE statements could be grouped together either at the beginning of a program—that is, *before* executable code—or at the end of a program. It is difficult to give concrete rules about the grouping of DECLARE statements because, in some cases, the programmer may wish to use the dynamic storage allocation feature of PL/I. Doing so would mean that DECLARE statements could also appear throughout a module in its various internal procedures or begin blocks.

There are four methods by which control may be passed to a segment:

Use a CALL statement: This is the most commonly used method. In the case of segments, the CALLs are always to *internal* procedures.

```
IF MORE__TRANSACTIONS THEN
    CALL PROCESS__TRANSACTION;
ELSE
    CALL WRAP__UP;
```

Use a function reference: This is another method by which subprograms in PL/I are invoked. Typically, segments invoked in this manner have a specific arithmetic or computational function. For example:

```
TAX__AMT = COMPUTE__TAX(MERCHANDISE__AMT);
```

Use the preprocessor: There are some restrictions regarding the types of source statements that may be placed in the source statement library. Check with the compiler you are using. In structured programming one common use is to include lines of code intended for execution in-line (as in the case of the Validate Data Segment in the invoice register module). Here is another example:

```
IF NEW__ITEM__NUMBER = SAVED__ITEM__NUMBER THEN
    %INCLUDE COMPUTE;
ELSE
    IF NEW__ITEM__NUMBER > SAVED__ITEM__NUMBER THEN
        %INCLUDE OUTREC;
    ELSE
        %INCLUDE SEQERR;
```

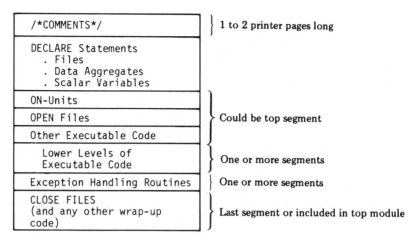

Figure 8-5. Sequence of code in a PL/I module

One advantage of the preprocessor is that the included source code will be executed in-line and does not require a CALL or function reference. Thus, there is less program overhead associated with these segments because the subroutine linkage statements are eliminated.

Use the GOTO Statement: As long as the general rule of *returning to the caller* (at the point of invocation) is incorporated into a segment's logic, a program is still considered structured, although it may contain GOTO statements. (What is unacceptable is the uncontrolled use of the GOTO.)

In summary, the basic approach is to organize a module's logic by page. It is the executable statements in a PL/I module that are to be segmented. Nonexecutable statements, such as DECLARE, are grouped together and may or may not be subdivided by page.

Modules and/or segments can contain source code copied from a source statement library via the preprocessor option %INCLUDE if this option is available. CALL statements to internal procedures are considered CALLs to segments, whereas CALLs to external procedures (separately compiled subroutines) are CALLs to lower level modules. Of course, all executable code is a combination of the basic structures plus any of the additional structures that are allowed in a given installation.

STRUCTURING PL/I PROGRAMS

Structuring involves taking the three basic structures as well as any additional structures and combining them to accomplish a given function or subfunction. These are briefly reviewed here with PL/I examples.

Sequence Structure

The sequence structure consists of two process blocks in which control flows from one box to the next in sequence. A box could represent a single statement such as READ, or it could represent a group of statements such as a DO group, an internal procedure, or a begin block. To review, the structure is represented as follows:

Choice Structure

The IFTHENELSE figure should be familiar to PL/I programmers. It specifies a test between alternatives to determine which of two process or function blocks will be performed.

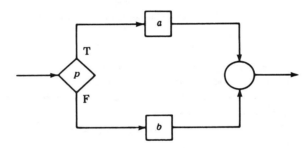

Using a structured IF statement, you may specify single statements (except the GOTO) following the THEN and ELSE clauses. For example:

```
IF BALANCE - PAYMENT - CREDITS = 0 THEN
    CALL ZERO_BALANCE_RT;
ELSE
    CALL NON_ZERO_BALANCE_RT;
```

Or, a DO group could be specified:

```
IF SUCCESSFUL THEN
    DO;
        A = B;
        C = D;
    END;
ELSE
    DO;
        A = X;
        C = Y;
    END;
```

Alternatively, the ELSE clause may be omitted:

```
IF QTY_ON_HAND < RE_ORDER_QTY THEN
    CALL WRITE_PURCHASE_ORDER_RT;
```

When using nested IF statements, use meaningful data names and keep the conditions tested as simple as possible. A nesting of more than three levels becomes difficult to follow. Nested IFs should be indented to show structuring.

```
IF DEGREE = BACHELORS THEN
    IF GRADE_PT_AVER >= 3.5 THEN
        PUT LIST ('HIRE' || NAME);
    ELSE
        PUT LIST('CONSIDER' || NAME);
ELSE
    IF COMPARABLE_WORK_EXP THEN
        PUT LIST ('HIRE' || NAME);
    ELSE
        PUT LIST ('DO NOT HIRE'ONAME);
```

The ELSE keyword is always paired (in the same column) with its matching IF. Nested IFs should always be contained within a single page on the source listing.

Repetition Structures

DOWHILE Structure   The DOWHILE figure provides basic loop capability by specifying that a function is repeated while a specified condition is true. The condition is always tested before the execution of the statements following the DO; hence the statements may never be executed. The structure is drawn as follows:

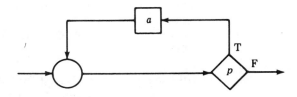

Here is a PL/I example:

```
I = 1:
DO WHILE (I <= NO_DAYS);
    TOTAL = TOTAL + TEMPERATURES(I);
    I = I + 1;
END;
```

When using the DOWHILE, a program must always provide for modification of the expression following the WHILE, so that eventually the expression tested is no longer true. Had the statement

$$I = I + 1;$$

not been included in the example cited, the program would have resulted in an interminable loop.

A variation of the previous solution could be to use this form of the DOWHILE:

DO I = 1 BY 1 WHILE(I <= NO_DAYS);

In this case the index variable I is automatically incremented each time through the loop. If there is no coding to terminate the DO, as in this variation of the iterative DO,

DO I = 1 BY 1;

the control variable will eventually be increased to the point where an overflow (FIXEDOVERFLOW or OVERFLOW) condition is raised.

Another form of the DOWHILE which will probably appear quite often in structured programs follows:

```
DO WHILE (MORE_TRANSACTIONS);
/*      •        └─→ AS LONG AS MORE_TRANSACTIONS
        •              IS TRUE, THE DO GROUP WILL
        •              BE REPETITIVELY EXECUTED.    */
END;
```

Other forms of the iterative DO are also defined as DOWHILE structures. Thus, the statements

```
DO I = 1 TO 100 BY 1;
DO J = -10 TO +10;
DO K = 10 TO 20, 30 TO 40, 50 TO 60;
DO L = 1,8,9,11,6,13;
```

still resemble the DOWHILE figure because the test for termination is performed prior to execution of the statements within the range of the DO. Of course, indexing and the WHILE clause may both be specified:

```
DO I = 1 TO 10 WHILE(P);
DO J = 1 TO 10 WHILE(A=B);
```

DOUNTIL Structure   As discussed earlier, the DOUNTIL structure provides essentially the same loop capability as the DOWHILE. It differs from the DOWHILE in two respects:

1. The test for loop control is done *after* the execution of statements within the range of the DO. Thus, the contained statements will always be executed at least once.

2. The DOUNTIL is terminated when the condition tested is true (DOWHILE terminates when the condition tested is false).

Here is .the structure:

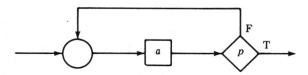

This form of the DO

DOWHILE (¬ expression);

indicates that statements within the range of the DO must be executed *while* the expression in parentheses is *not true*. This, then, is a convenient form to use for the DOUNTIL structure. For example:

```
        DECLARE DONE BIT(1);
        DONE = NO;
        DO WHILE ( ¬ DONE);
   /*       •
            •
            •                              */
        IF RESULT < 0 THEN
              DONE = YES;
     END;
```

CASE Structure

The CASE structure may be used when there is a test and subsequent execution of one of many alternatives. It may be drawn as follows:

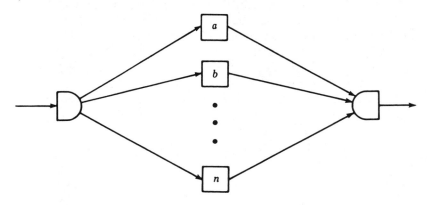

The paths from the various process blocks all merge at the same point and then continue in a forward direction. In some PL/I compilers the SELECT statement is provided as a means of implementing the CASE structure. For example, assume that the identifier CODE contains a value indicating how goods are to be shipped to a customer. The select-group could be coded as follows:

```
SELECT;
          WHEN (CODE = 110) CALL SHIP_PREPAID;
          WHEN (CODE = 120) CALL SHIP_FOB;
          WHEN (CODE = 130) CALL SHIP_COD;
          OTHERWISE CALL SPECIAL_HANDLING;
END;
```

Another method of expressing the CASE structure is to use a series of nested IF statements. For example:

```
IF CASE = 110 THEN
      CALL SHIP_PREPAID;
ELSE IF CASE = 120 THEN
      CALL SHIP_FOB;
ELSE IF CASE = 130 THEN
      CALL SHIP_COD;
ELSE CALL SPECIAL_HANDLING;
```

For a small number of alternatives, the IFTHENELSE method of expressing the CASE structure is acceptable. Occasionally, it may be necessary to have a CASE structure in which one of 50 or 75 or even 100 functions is to be selected. In this situation a *GOTO label variable* approach could be used as the method for managing the alternatives. For purposes of simplicity here, however, assume that one of four functions is to be selected, based on the numeric value of a variable called CODE. If CODE = 1, then a group of code labeled CASE 1 will be executed; if CODE = 2, then code beginning at label CASE2 will be executed; and so on. If CODE is greater than 4 or less than 1, an error routine is to be executed.

Figure 8-6 shows the initialization steps necessary to implement the CASE structure. An array whose bounds are from 0 to 4 is defined and initialized with the labels of the corresponding routines for CODE = 0, CODE = 1, and so forth.

Figure 8-7 shows a general way in which the CASE structure could be coded. The GOTO statement represents the beginning of the CASE structure, and the label END_CASE shows the exit point of the structure. Between the GOTO statement and the label marking the end of the CASE structure are the sections of code for the various

```
DECLARE
      CASE(0:4)   LABEL INITIAL(ERROR,CASE1,CASE2,CASE3,CASE4),
      CODE        FIXED BINARY(15);
```

Figure 8-6. Initializing for the CASE structure

```
GET FILE (SYSIN) LIST(CODE);
IF CODE<0 | CODE>4 THEN
    CODE = 0;
GO TO CASE(CODE);
ERROR:
    /* CODE FOR ERROR ROUTINE*/
    GO TO END_CASE;
CASE1:
    /* PROGRAMMING FOR CODE '1' */
    GO TO END_CASE;
CASE2:
    /* PROGRAMMING FOR CODE '2' */
    GO TO END_CASE;
CASE3:
    /* PROGRAMMING FOR CODE '3' */
    GO TO END_CASE;
CASE4:
    /* PROGRAMMING FOR CODE '4' */
    GO TO END_CASE;
END CASE:;
```

Figure 8-7. CASE structure simulated in PL/I

alternatives. The variable, CODE, is defined as FIXED BINARY for program efficiency and is initialized through a GET LIST operation. The IF statement tests for array boundary limits and, if boundaries are exceeded, sets CODE = 0, thereby forcing a *branch* to the error-handling routine.

The CASE method just described carefully avoided the use of GOTOs except where necessary. Currently there is a controversy between those structured programming practitioners who believe the GOTO should be avoided at all costs and those, such as Knuth, who reason that GOTOs are justified in specific and limited cases.[2] Knuth describes an *event-driven construct* in which a jump to an error exit is justified. Although he does not specifically relate event-driven constructs to on-units, on-units could be classified as such. If you belong to the camp that is more relaxed about the use of GOTOs, then these two alternative solutions for the testing statement in the CASE implementation might appeal to you:

```
IF CODE<0 | CODE>4 THEN
    GO TO ERROR;
ELSE
    GO TO CASE(CODE);


ON SUBSCRIPTRANGE
    GO TO ERROR;
(SUBRG); GO TO CASE(CODE);
```

[2]Donald E. Knuth, "Structured Programming with **go to** Statements," *Computing Surveys,* Vol. 6, No. 4, December 1974.

Another way in which the CASE structure might be implemented is to DECLARE an array to have the ENTRY attribute and initialize each element with the names of internal or external procedures. Then the appropriate procedure could be called with

```
CALL TABLE (ICODE);
```

for example.

SEARCH Structure

Because table look-up or table searching is a common occurrence in programming, a SEARCH structure has been defined. In table searching a *search argument* is compared with a *table argument*. (Usually an equal compare is being sought but not exclusively. You might be looking for the first entry *greater than* the search argument.) The *table function* is the actual processing of a record or other data once a *match* is found. An error condition occurs if there is no matching table argument for the search argument being used. Thus, there are two process blocks in a search operation: a *normal process* when a matching element is found and an *error process* when no matching item is found.

A SEARCH structure, which will handle serial or binary search operations, is shown in Figure 8-8. In this structure the flow begins at the top. Then the table entry to be compared with the search argument is determined. This would involve incrementing an index value for a serial search or averaging the high and low bounds for a binary search. Next, a test is made to determine if there are more table elements to be compared. If not, the table argument was not found—hence an error exit is required.

The second test compares the table argument with the search argument. If the condition tested (e.g., table argument = search argument) *is met*, the process block handles the operations needed (i.e., PROCESS TABLE FUNCTION). If the condition tested *is not met*, the loop operation continues. The structure has one entry and one exit. The flow continues to a common point in a forward direction. The comparison loop may be executed many times, but only one of the two process blocks will be executed.

In implementing the SEARCH structure for a serial search, the following solution, which uses a GOTO within the structure, could be specified in PL/I (LIMIT contains the number of items in the table):

```
            I = 0;
SEARCH_AGAIN:
            I = I + 1;
            IF I > LIMIT THEN
                CALL ARG_NOT_FOUND;
            ELSE
                IF SEARCH_ARG = TABLE(I) THEN
                    CALL PROCESS_TABLE_FUNCTION;
                ELSE
                    GO TO SEARCH_AGAIN;
```

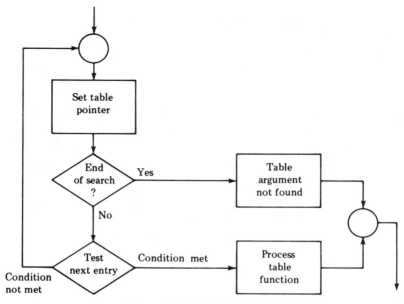

Figure 8-8. SEARCH structure

Of course, a number of algorithms for table searching have been developed. For example, the following algorithm is correct:

```
DO I = 1 TO LIMIT WHILE(SEARCH__ARG ¬= TABLE(I));
END;
IF I <= LIMIT THEN
    CALL PROCESS__TABLE__FUNCTION;
ELSE
    CALL ARG__NOT__FOUND;
```

However, the reader of that solution has to spend time understanding the null iteration (i.e., there are no explicit statements within the range of the DO). This is tricky code and, according to Knuth, "is almost never a good way to search an array."[3]

An algorithm for a serial search (not using the SEARCH structure) could take this structured form:

```
ARG__FOUND = NO;
DO I = 1 TO LIMIT WHILE(¬ARG__FOUND);
    IF SEARCH__ARG = TABLE(I) THEN
        DO;
            CALL PROCESS__TABLE__FUNCTION;
            ARG__FOUND = YES;
        END;
END;
IF ¬ARG__FOUND THEN
    CALL ARG__NOT__FOUND;
```

[3]Ibid., p. 292.

To use the indicator ARG_FOUND as shown in this solution, the variables YES and NO would have been set to "1" and "0", respectively.

The SEARCH structure may also be used for a *binary search*. In a binary search, table arguments must be in ascending (or descending) sequence. The search technique involves comparing the search argument with the middle table argument. For example, if there are 500 table arguments, the search argument is first compared with the 250th table argument. If the search argument is greater than the table argument, the matching code for the search argument should lie within the second half of the table, because the table is sorted. This method allows us to eliminate searching half of the table with just one compare.

The binary search is so named because the technique is to divide each remaining portion of the table in half and compare the search argument with the table argument until an equal compare occurs or the last compare has been made. What is so striking about this method is that after two compares, three-fourths of the table has been eliminated from the search. Here is a binary-search solution using the SEARCH structure:

```
LOW = 1;
HIGH = LIMIT;          /* LIMIT = TABLE SIZE */
SEARCH_AGAIN;
    MID = (LOW + HIGH)/ 2;
    IF HIGH < LOW THEN
        CALL ARG_NOT_FOUND;
    ELSE
        IF SEARCH_ARG = TABLE(MID) THEN
            CALL PROCESS_TABLE_FUNCTION;
        ELSE
            DO;
                IF SEARCH_ARG > TABLE(MID) THEN
                    LOW = MID + 1;
                ELSE
                    HIGH = MID - 1;
                GO TO SEARCH_AGAIN;
            END;
```

To implement a binary search without the SEARCH structure, a DOWHILE is used. In addition, an indicator must be set to control the loop operation through the table search. For example:

```
LOW = 1;
HIGH = LIMIT;
OK_TO_SEARCH = YES;
DO WHILE (OK_TO_SEARCH);
    MID = (LOW + HIGH) / 2;
```

```
                IF HIGH < LOW THEN
                    DO;
                        OK_TO_SEARCH = NO;
                        CALL ARG_NOT_FOUND;
                    END;
                ELSE
                    IF SEARCH_ARG = TABLE(MID) THEN
                        DO;
                            OK_TO SEARCH = NO;
                            CALL PROCESS_TABLE_FUNCTION;
                        END;
                    ELSE
                        IF SEARCH_ARG > TABLE(MID) THEN
                            LOW = MID + 1;
                        ELSE
                            HIGH = MID - 1;
        END;
```

SOME PL/I PROGRAMMING CONSIDERATIONS

With a structured approach to programming, some of the *typical* ways in which PL/I has been implemented must be reevaluated. One specific area is in the use of on-units. The use of an on-unit can violate the constraints of structured programming. For example:

```
                ON ENDFILE(MASTER)BEGIN;
            /*      •
                    •
                    •               */
                GO TO EOJ;
                END;
```

In this unstructured example the GOTO statement was used because an end-of-file condition is raised *after* a READ or GET operation. Had the GOTO statement been eliminated, the END statement in this begin block would have acted as a RETURN, returning to the statement immediately following the READ or GET. Typically, the statements following a READ or GET process the record just read; but this should not be done when an end-of-file occurs.

You may wish to use a GOTO in an on-unit if the branch is to the end of the procedure or to an error routine. Whether or not this rule should be applied to the ENDFILE on-unit is an installation decision. Generally, the principle of returning to the point of invocation must not be violated, even in the handling of on-units. Here, then, is one structured approach to the handling of the end-of-file condition:

```
ON ENDFILE(TAPE)
    MORE_TRANSACTIONS = NO;
MORE_TRANSACTIONS = YES;
DO WHILE (MORE_TRANSACTIONS);
    READ FILE(TAPE)INTO(TAPE_AREA);
    IF MORE_TRANSACTIONS THEN
        DO;

            /* PROCESS RECORD */

        END;
    ELSE
        DO;

            /* HANDLE END OF FILE */

        END;
END;
```

The following example is similar to the previous example. However, the true/false conditions tested are reversed and the end-of-file processing is handled *outside* the range of the DO:

```
ON ENDFILE(TAPE)
    TAPE_EOF = YES;
TAPE_EOF = NO;
DO WHILE(TAPE_EOF = NO);
    READ FILE(TAPE)INTO(TAPE_AREA);
        /* EOF TURNS INDICATOR ON */
    IF TAPE_EOF = YES THEN
        DO;

            /* PROCESS RECORD */

        END;
END;
/* HANDLE END OF FILE */
```

Here is one final example in which there are two READ statements—one to read the first record in a file and one to read all subsequent records in the file:

```
ON ENDFILE(ONHAND)
    MORE_ONHAND_RECS = NO;
MORE_ONHAND_RECS = YES;
READ FILE(ONHAND) INTO(STOCK_RECORD);
DO WHILE(MORE_ONHAND_RECS);

    /* PROCESS RECORD */
```

```
                    READ FILE(ONHAND)INTO(STOCK__RECORD);
          END;
                /* HANDLE END OF FILE */
```

The following PL/I statements should be avoided or used in a limited way:

1. *ENTRY:* This statement defines alternate entry points in a subprogram. It should not be used if the rule of a proper program (one entry, one exit) is to be observed.

2. *STOP and EXIT:* These statements should be avoided lest more than one exit be specified. Because STOP and EXIT terminate execution of the entire program, they should not appear in any but the top segment; otherwise, the rule of returning to the caller is violated.

3. *RETURN:* This statement generally isn't needed since the END statement that matches a PROCEDURE or BEGIN statement accomplishes the same function. A module that has a small block of code (i.e., the top segment) followed by pages of internal procedures might end with a RETURN so that a reader will be sure that the module or segment ends on that page. What is important, however, is that a module has only *one* exit.

4. *GOTO:* Structured programming virtually eliminates the need for GOTO. It might be used *within* a structure, as, for example, CASE.

IMPROVING READABILITY

A pictorial representation of a program's logic is provided by indenting the source code. Readability is improved when the structures are formatted so that logical relationships in coding correspond to physical position on the source listing.

There are no absolute rules on how PL/I code should be formatted. Some PL/I compilers provide a *formatted* source listing along structured programming lines, given any type of source input; others do not. Following are a few general guidelines for formatting a source listing. These are only guidelines, and variations of them exist in the installations using structured programming today.

An *indentation unit* is a standard amount of indentation that corresponds to the number of spaces that a typewriter moves when the tab or skip key is pressed. In this text the indentation unit is 2, although a three-character indentation also gives a good blocking effect.

The *primary origin* is the left-most column in which characters may be printed. Typically, this would be print position 2 or column 2. (Some installations alter the default source margins by specifying that PL/I statements may start in column 1.) For readability, statements should generally be aligned with the one above. Statements such as IF, DO, and BEGIN the alignment position should move one or two indentation units to the right. The END statement, or the end of the IF should revert back one or two indentation units to the left.

Structured programming should reduce the need for extensive comments. If comments appear on a separate line, they should start at the left-most column in which source characters may be printed. A comment that appears on the same line as a PL/I statement should begin at whatever column has been designated as standard.

Because of the reduced need for GOTO statements in structured programming, labels are not often used. In PL/I they may be used to identify a segment or name a procedure. In addition, they are used in the simulation of the CASE and SEARCH structures. Place labels on a separate line, starting in the column of the first primary origin.

Guidelines

Here are some general guidelines for coding PL/I statements that could serve as a base from which to develop personal conventions or installation standards.

1. Code one statement per line. Should a statement require more than one line, continue it on the next line indented *two* or more indentation units.
2. The first statement in a block, do-group, on-unit, or IF is indented from the keyword. For example:

```
ON ENDFILE(CARD)            ON CONVERSION              DO;
    CARD_EOF = NO;            BEGIN;                       X = 1;
                                ONCHAR = "0";              Y = 2;
                                ERR_CT = ERR_CT + 1;     END;
                              END;
```

3. Unless subject to indentation rules, each statement starts in the same column as the statement above it:

```
TOTAL = SUM(PRICE_TABLE);
AVERAGE = TOTAL / NO_ELEMENTS;
```

4. The external PROCEDURE statement is indented from the primary origin. For example:

```
SALES:
    PROCEDURE OPTIONS(MAIN);
```

5. Internal procedures are further indented within the containing procedure.
6. The END statement should be aligned with its corresponding keyword. Do not use a single END statement to terminate multiple blocks or do-groups. Each PROCEDURE, BEGIN, and DO should have its explicitly coded END statement.

7. In an IF statement, the THEN clause (but not the word THEN) is coded on a separate line. The keyword ELSE is written on a separate line, aligned directly under its matching IF. The ELSE clause is then coded on the next line:

```
IF MATCHING__RECORD THEN
    CALL UPDATE__MASTER;
ELSE
    CALL READ__TRANSACTION;
```

If a do-group is to be specified for either the THEN or ELSE clauses, for readability the DO and END appear on separate lines.

8. Declare all data items explicitly. Even though the defaulting of data attributes is a PL/I feature, these defaults seem to be a problem area for PL/I programs. Thus, to avoid potential data-error problems, some installations require that all data items be explicitly declared.

9. Open files explicitly. In most implementations of PL/I, files are *automatically* opened when the first READ or GET is issued to that file. However, when files are *explicitly* opened and closed, it can be an aid to the *reader* of a program.

```
OPEN
    FILE (INFILE),
    FILE (SYSPRINT),
    FILE (MASTER);
```

Whether or not all files are opened with *one* OPEN statement is dictated by each program's requirements and the operating system being used. For example, *exception* files probably should not be opened until the need for them arises in a program.

10. Spell out keywords in the source listing that become part of the final program documentation. If you do abbreviate, perhaps the most commonly used abbreviations—PIC, DEC, CHAR—would be acceptable, but abbreviations that are infrequently used and not obvious to the reader—such as STRZ—should be spelled out. One technique is to abbreviate keywords as is typically done in PL/I programs. Then specify preprocessor code to accomplish the printing of keywords in their entirety. For example:

```
%DECLARE (CHAR,DEC,DCL,PIC,PROC,VAR)CHARACTER;
%CHAR = 'CHARACTER';
%DEC = 'DECIMAL';
%DCL = 'DECLARE';
/* ETC */
```

PROGRAMMING EXAMPLE

The PL/I programming example presented here centers around the inventory update problem that was first introduced in Chapter 2 dealing with top-down program design.

The program code in Figure 8-9 should be consciously examined, noting the solution on several levels. How readable is the code? Does the top segment give a summary of the entire module? Are the data names meaningful to the reader of this program? Does the formatting highlight the logic? Would a maintenance programmer be able to answer this question: Does the UPDATE program allow an ADDITION transaction to be followed immediately by UPDATE transactions for the newly added record?

What about maintainability and modifiability? For example, could a programmer easily modify the module to handle sequence checking and data validation? If so, how long would it take to produce a correct updated version of the program?

```
/*   MATCH - MATCH/MERGE PROGRAM WITH DIFFERENT TRANSACTION TYPES   */
/*******************************************************************/
/*   PROGRAM  NAME:   MATCH                                        */
/*      DESCRIPTION:  THIS PROGRAM MATCHES TRANSACTIONS TO A MASTER */
/*                    FILE.  TO DO THIS, BOTH FILES MUST BE IN     */
/*                    ASCENDING KEY SEQUENCE.                      */
/*                    THE TRANSACTIONS CAN BE ADDS, DELETES OR     */
/*                    UPDATES.  APPROPRIATE ERROR MESSAGES ARE     */
/*                    PRINTED FOR INVALID FIELDS, WHEN A DELETE OR */
/*                    UPDATE TRANSACTION DOES NOT HAVE A MATCHING  */
/*                    MASTER RECORD OR WHEN A MASTER ALREADY EXISTS */
/*                    FOR AN ADD TRANSACTION.                      */
/*                                                                 */
/*        INPUTS:    OLDINV  -  MASTER FILE BEFORE TRANSACTIONS    */
/*                   TRANS   -  TRANSACTION FILE                   */
/*                                                                 */
/*        OUTPUTS:   EXCPTN  -  EXCEPTION REPORT                   */
/*                   NEWINV  -  NEW MASTER FILE AFTER TRANSACTIONS */
/*******************************************************************/
```

Figure 8-9(a). Sample PL/I program (Parts b-g follow.)

Some installations have discouraged the use of the LIKE attribute on the basis that it detracts from the readability of a program. For example, to specify the LIKE attribute at an intermediate level of a structure and reference an intermediate level of another structure is difficult to follow:

```
DCL 1 MASTER_REC,
      2 KEY_FLD CHAR(16),
      2 BASIC_REC LIKE TAPE_REC.EXT1,
      2 REST CHAR(8);
```

Figure 8-9d shows the nucleus. The next level of segments follows in Figures 8-9e through 8-9g. Each subsequent page of the listing reveals more details about the program. The arrangement or order of segments on the source listing generally allows study of the program in a top-to-bottom fashion.

```
1    MATCH:  PROC OPTIONS(MAIN);
     /******************************************************************/
     /*    FILE DECLARATIONS                                           */
     /******************************************************************/
2    DCL EXCPTN                  FILE PRINT STREAM OUTPUT ENV(V BLKSIZE(141));
3    DCL NEWINV                  FILE RECORD OUTPUT SEQUENTIAL;
4    DCL OLDINV                  FILE RECORD INPUT  SEQUENTIAL;
5    DCL TRANS                   FILE RECORD INPUT  SEQUENTIAL;
     /******************************************************************/
     /*    RECORD LAYOUTS                                              */
     /******************************************************************/
6    DCL 1 NEW_MASTER_REC,
           2 NMAST_ACTIVITY_CODE         PIC '9',
           2 NMAST_KEY                    CHAR (6),
           2 NMAST_DESCRIPTION            CHAR (20),
           2 NMAST_QTY_ON_HAND            FIXED DEC(5),
           2 NMAST_TOTAL_ISSUES           FIXED DEC(5),
           2 NMAST_TOTAL_RECEIPTS         FIXED DEC(5),
           2 NMAST_QTY_ON_ORDER           FIXED DEC(5),
           2 NMAST_ORDER_POINT            FIXED DEC(3),
           2 NMAST_REORDER_QTY            FIXED DEC(5),
           2 NMAST_TOTAL_COST             FIXED DEC(7,2),
           2 NMAST_AVERAGE_UNIT_COST      FIXED DEC(7,3),
           2 NMAST_DATE_OF_LAST_ISSUE     CHAR(6);

7    DCL 1 OLD_MASTER_REC,
           2 OMAST_ACTIVITY_CODE          PIC '9',
           2 OMAST_DESCRIPTION            CHAR (20),
           2 OMAST_QTY_ON_HAND            FIXED DEC(5),
           2 OMAST_TOTAL_ISSUES           FIXED DEC(5),
           2 OMAST_TOTAL_RECEIPTS         FIXED DEC(5),
           2 OMAST_QTY_ON_ORDER           FIXED DEC(5),
           2 OMAST_ORDER_POINT            FIXED DEC(3),
           2 OMAST_REORDER_QTY            FIXED DEC(5),
           2 OMAST_TOTAL_COST             FIXED DEC(7,2),
           2 OMAST_AVERAGE_UNIT_COST      FIXED DEC(7,3),
           2 OMAST_DATE_OF_LAST_ISSUE     CHAR (6);

8    DCL 1 TRANSACTION_RECORD             CHAR (80);

9    DCL 1 TRANSACTION_REC       DEFINED TRANSACTION_RECORD,
           2 TRANS_CODE                   CHAR (1),
           2 TRANS_KEY                    CHAR (6),
           2 TRANSACTION                  CHAR (73);

10   DCL 1 RECEIPTS             DEFINED TRANSACTION_RECORD,
           2 RCPTS_CODE                   CHAR (1),
           2 RCPTS_KEY                    CHAR (6),
           2 RCPTS_QTY_RECEIVED           PIC '(5)9',
           2 RCPTS_TOTAL_COST             PIC '(5)9V99';

11   DCL 1 ISSUES              DEFINED TRANSACTION_RECORD,
           2 ISSUE_CODE                   CHAR (1),
           2 ISSUE_KEY                    CHAR (6),
           2 ISSUE_QTY_ISSUED             PIC '(5)9',
           2 ISSUE_CUSTOMER_NUMBER        CHAR (6),
           2 ISSUE_DATE_ISSUED            CHAR (6);

12   DCL 1 ADDITION            DEFINED TRANSACTION_RECORD,
           2 ADD_CODE                     CHAR (1),
           2 ADD_KEY                      CHAR (6),
           2 ADD_DESCRIPTION              CHAR (20),
           2 ADD_QTY_ON_HAND              PIC '(5)9',
           2 ADD_TOTAL_ISSUES             PIC '(5)9',
           2 ADD_TOTAL_RECEIPTS           PIC '(5)9',
           2 ADD_QTY_ON_ORDER             PIC '(5)9',
           2 ADD_ORDER_POINT              PIC '(5)9',
           2 ADD_REORDER_QTY              PIC '(5)9',
           2 ADD_TOTAL_COST               PIC '(5)9V99',
           2 ADD_AVERAGE_UNIT_COST        PIC '(4)9V99',
           2 ADD_DATE_OF_LAST_ISSUE       CHAR (6);
```

169

Figure 8-9(b). Sample PL/I Program

```
        /*****************************************************************/
        /*   CONSTANTS AND VARIABLES                                    */
        /*****************************************************************/
14      DCL HIGH                            BUILTIN;
15      DCL MASTERS_ADDED                   FIXED DEC (3) INIT (0);
16      DCL MASTERS_DELETED                 FIXED DEC (3) INIT (0);
17      DCL MASTERS_IN                      FIXED DEC (3) INIT (0);
18      DCL MASTERS_OUT                     FIXED DEC (3) INIT (0);
19      DCL MORE_TRANSACTIONS               BIT (1)       INIT ('1'B);
20      DCL NO                              BIT (1)       INIT ('0'B);
21      DCL NO_MASTER_RECS                  BIT (1)       INIT ('0'B);
22      DCL TRANSACTIONS_PROCESSED          FIXED DEC (3) INIT (0);
23      DCL 1 TRANSACTIONS,
              2 ADD                         CHAR (1)      INIT ('1'),
              2 RECEIPT                     CHAR (1)      INIT ('2'),
              2 ISSUE                       CHAR (1)      INIT ('3'),
              2 DELETE                      CHAR (1)      INIT ('4');
24      DCL USE_OLD_MASTER                  BIT (1);
25      DCL YES                             BIT (1)       INIT ('1'B);

        /*****************************************************************/
        /*   ON CONDITIONS                                              */
        /*****************************************************************/
26      ON ENDFILE (OLDINV)
           BEGIN;
27             NO_MASTER_RECS     = YES;
28             NMAST_KEY          = HIGH(6);
29             OMAST_KEY          = HIGH(6);
30         END;

31      ON ENDFILE (TRANS)
           BEGIN;
32         MORE_TRANSACTIONS = NO;
33         TRANS_KEY         = HIGH(6);
34         END;
```

Figure 8-9(c).

```
     /**********************************************************************/
     /*   PROGRAM MAIN LOGIC                                               */
     /**********************************************************************/
35   OPEN FILE (EXCPTN),
          FILE (NEWINV),
          FILE (OLDINV),
          FILE (TRANS);

36   DELETE_MASTER  = NO;
37   USE_OLD_MASTER = NO;

38   READ FILE (OLDINV) INTO (OLD_MASTER_REC);
39   IF  NO_MASTER_RECS THEN
          PUT FILE (EXCPTN) SKIP LIST ('MASTER FILE HAS NO RECORDS');
40   ELSE

41   READ FILE (TRANS) INTO (TRANSACTION_RECORD);
42   DO WHILE (TRANS_KEY < HIGH(6) | NMAST_KEY < HIGH(6));
43      SELECT;
44         WHEN(NMAST_KEY < TRANS_KEY)
                CALL PROCESS_MASTER;
45         OTHERWISE
              DO;
46              CALL PROCESS_TRANSACTION;
47              READ FILE (TRANS) INTO (TRANSACTION_RECORD);
48              TRANSACTIONS_PROCESSED =  TRANSACTIONS_PROCESSED + 1;
49           END;
50      END;
51   END;

52   PUT FILE (EXCPTN) SKIP (3) LIST ('****** FILE COUNTS ******');
53   PUT FILE (EXCPTN) SKIP (2) LIST
        ('NUMBER OF TRANSACTIONS PROCESSED:  ' || TRANSACTIONS_PROCESSED);
54   PUT FILE (EXCPTN) SKIP LIST
        ('     NUMBER OF MASTER RECORDS IN:  ' || MASTERS_IN);
55   PUT FILE (EXCPTN) SKIP LIST
        (' NUMBER OF MASTER RECORDS ADDED:  ' || MASTERS_ADDED);
56   PUT FILE (EXCPTN) SKIP LIST
        ('NUMBER OF MASTER RECORDS DELETED:  ' || MASTERS_DELETED);
57   PUT FILE (EXCPTN) SKIP LIST
        ('     NUMBER OF MASTER RECORDS OUT:  ' || MASTERS_OUT);

58   CLOSE FILE (EXCPTN),
           FILE (NEWINV),
           FILE (OLDINV),
           FILE (TRANS);
```

Figure 8-9(d). Sample PL/I Program

```
/***********************************************************************/
/*   PROCESS MASTER RECORD                                             */
/***********************************************************************/
59   PROCESS_MASTER:   PROC;

60      IF   DELETE_MASTER THEN
             MASTERS_DELETED = MASTERS_DELETED + 1;
61      ELSE
             DO;
62              WRITE FILE (NEWINV) FROM (NEW_MASTER_REC);
63              MASTERS_OUT = MASTERS_OUT + 1;
64           END;

65      IF   USE_OLD_MASTER THEN
             USE_OLD_MASTER = NO;
66      ELSE
67              READ FILE (OLDINV) INTO (OLD_MASTER_REC);
68              MASTERS_IN = MASTERS_IN + 1;
69           END;

70      NEW_MASTER_REC          = OLD_MASTER_REC;

71   END PROCESS_MASTER;
```

Figure 8-9(e).

```
/***********************************************************************/
/*   PROCESS TRANSACTION RECORD                                        */
/***********************************************************************/
72  PROCESS_TRANSACTION:  PROC;

73      IF   NMAST_KEY > TRANS_KEY THEN
             SELECT(TRANS_CODE);
74               WHEN(ADD)
                     DO;
75                       USE_OLD_MASTER = YES;
76                       NEW_MASTER_REC = ADDITION;
77                       MASTERS_ADDED  = MASTERS_ADDED + 1;
78                   END;
79               WHEN(DELETE)
                     PUT FILE (EXCPTN) SKIP LIST
                         ('ATTEMPT TO DELETE RECORD NOT IN FILE ',
                         TRANSACTION_RECORD);
80               WHEN(RECEIPT,ISSUE)
                     PUT FILE (EXCPTN) SKIP LIST
                         ('ATTEMPT TO UPDATE RECORD NOT IN FILE ',
                         TRANSACTION_RECORD);
81               OTHERWISE
                     PUT FILE (EXCPTN) SKIP LIST
                         ('INVALID TRANSACTION CODE ', TRANSACTION_RECORD);
82          END;

83      ELSE
             SELECT(TRANS_CODE);
84               WHEN(ADD)
                     PUT FILE (EXCPTN) SKIP LIST
                         ('ATTEMPT TO ADD DUPLICATE RECORD',
                         TRANSACTION_RECORD);
85               WHEN(RECEIPT)
                     CALL PROCESS_RECEIPTS;
86               WHEN(ISSUE)
                     CALL PROCESS_ISSUES;
87               WHEN(DELETE)
                     DO;
88                       DELETE_MASTER = YES;
89                       CALL PROCESS_MASTER;
91                   END;
92               OTHERWISE
                     PUT FILE (EXCPTN) SKIP LIST
                         ('INVALID TRANSACTION CODE ', TRANSACTION_RECORD);
93          END;

94  END PROCESS_TRANSACTION;
```

Figure 8-9(f). Sample PL/I Program

```
      /*************************************************************************/
      /*    PROCESS RECEIPTS                                                   */
      /*************************************************************************/
95    PROCESS_RECEIPTS:   PROC;

96      NMAST_QTY_ON_HAND         = NMAST_QTY_ON_HAND       + RCPTS_QTY_RECEIVED;
97      NMAST_TOTAL_RECEIPTS      = NMAST_TOTAL_RECEIPTS    + RCPTS_QTY_RECEIVED;
98      NMAST_QTY_ON_ORDER        = NMAST_QTY_ON_ORDER      - RCPTS_QTY_RECEIVED;
99      NMAST_TOTAL_COST          = NMAST_TOTAL_COST        + RCPTS_TOTAL_COST;
100     NMAST_AVERAGE_UNIT_COST   = NMAST_TOTAL_COST        / NMAST_QTY_ON_HAND;

101   END PROCESS_RECEIPTS;

      /*************************************************************************/
      /*    PROCESS ISSUES                                                     */
      /*************************************************************************/
102   PROCESS_ISSUES:   PROC;

103     NMAST_QTY_ON_HAND         = NMAST_QTY_ON_HAND      - ISSUE_QTY_ISSUED;
104     NMAST_TOTAL_ISSUES        = NMAST_TOTAL_ISSUES     + ISSUE_QTY_ISSUED;
105     NMAST_TOTAL_COST          = NMAST_TOTAL_COST       -
                              (ISSUE_QTY_ISSUED * NMAST_AVERAGE_UNIT_COST);
106     NMAST_DATE_OF_LAST_ISSUE = ISSUE_DATE_ISSUED;

107   END PROCESS_ISSUES;

108   END MATCH;
```

Figure 8-9(g).

SUMMARY

Modules should be separately compiled subroutines. Segments should take no more than a listing page of code (DECLAREs excluded). Each segment should be a proper program. Comments should precede segments whose logic is complex. Generally, control should be passed to a segment by a CALL (or function reference) or by means of the preprocessor's facility for in-line text inclusion.

With Nested IFs, the depth of nesting should be limited: the entire nest on one page. Repetition structures are implemented by using the DO with or without the WHILE. CASE structure would typically be expressed by SELECT or nested IFs. It can also be done by a GOTO label array or by CALLING an entry array. Here are some other useful procedures for writing clear programs:

1. Use blank lines to separate logical groups of code.
2. Use embedded comments only when necessary.
3. Use self-defining data names.
4. Indent statements within procedures, begin-blocks, and do-groups to highlight the logic and simplify changes.
5. Explicitly code an END statement for each PROCEDURE, BEGIN, or DO.

6. Good programming techniques also dictate using an indicator for a single purpose only, as well as using names for constants and initializing them in the DECLARE statement. Variables and indicators should be initialized in the executable code section of the PROCEDURE.

REVIEW QUESTIONS AND EXERCISES

1. Would you use a GOTO to transfer control to and from a segment? Why or why not?

2. What guidelines should you follow in the use of indicators? Comment on purpose, name, and initialization of indicators.

3. Write a set of standards that you think would make nested IF statements readable and acceptable.

4. What PL/I statements and keywords should be used with caution?

5. Write a set of standards for the programming of modules.

6. Modify the program in figure 8-9 to handle sequence checking on the transaction file.

7. Modify the program in Figure 8-9 to handle *two* input transaction files. One file contains additions and deletions; the other file contains the update records (issues and receipts). Both files are sorted into ascending sequence.

8. Assume the installation in which you are working has indicated that no module should exceed 50 PL/I statements (DECLAREs excluded). Recode the problem in Figure 8-10 to conform to this standard.

9

Structured Programming Using ANS COBOL

Earlier versions of COBOL lacked some of the features necessary to follow all the rules of structured programming in a simple, readable way. In recent years, many features have been added to remove these deficiencies. However, not all compilers provide all the features. Therefore, you will need to know what your compiler offers, and select and adapt accordingly. Throughout the chapter we will present alternate approaches to allow for the variations in compilers.

All compilers permit the basic three structures, and CASE is either directly available or easily simulated. Most compilers allow separate compilations of modules, with data being passed as arguments. A module can be subdivided into parts for clarity and separation of functions.

When COBOL was first introduced in the early 1960s, the compilers did not produce particularly efficient code. This gave rise to a *folklore* about some features that should be avoided, such as PERFORMS and nested IFs. Also, at that time, there was a greater emphasis on machine efficiency instead of people efficiency. As a result, various items in the language were either used or prohibited, in order to achieve maximum execution speed or minimum main storage space. Today the emphasis is on the productivity of people writing and maintaining programs. The new goals (readability, maintainability) now determine which features of a language should or should not be used.

This chapter will discuss some COBOL structured programming techniques and recommend a set of coding standards that could serve as a base or guide for standards developed by an installation. Numerous programming examples throughout the chapter are followed by a complete structured COBOL program.

MODULARITY

Module Organization

Figure 9-1 shows a hierarchy chart of a number of modules in a customer billing application. Each box in this chart represents a module in the application. Ideally, each module in a COBOL program should be a separate compilation. The main module

177

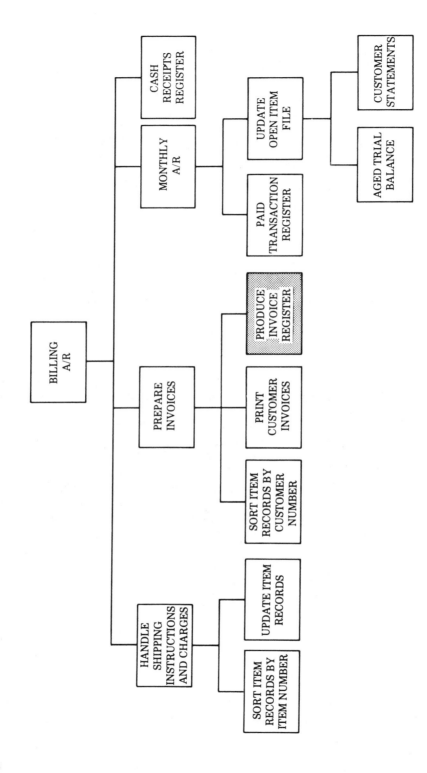

Figure 9-1. Modules in a billing/accounts receivable application

passes control to lower level modules (subprograms) with the CALL statement. Data is passed to the subprogram with USING, thereby identifying the data items used by the called subprogram.[1]

You may be concerned about the additional overhead needed to code, compile, and execute the linkage statements. However, the advantages of separate compilations outweigh the disadvantages. Testing and maintenance are easier, and the necessary framework has been established to develop a library of reusable modules.

The modules in Figure 9-1 are developed from the top down, where *one leg* of the chart probably would be fully developed before the next leg is designed, coded, and tested. Assume that the left-most leg in the hierarchy chart has been completed, and we are now down to the coding stages of the module (shaded box in Figure 9-1) that generates an invoice register (Figure 9-2). This module, like all modules, should be limited to the number of executable source statements that can be managed easily.

Some COBOL installations using structured programming techniques have found it desirable to limit a module to the number of *executable* source statements that can be contained on one printer page of output. Other installations have decided to allow larger modules and subdivide them into segments of 50 to 60 lines of code. The segmenting discussed in this chapter is not the same as the COBOL *Segmentation Feature* provided in some compilers—a feature which allows the dynamic overlay of user-specified subroutines during execution.

How to Segment a Module

Assume that the logic for the PRODUCE INVOICE REGISTER module has already been written in pseudo code. By examining this code, it is determined that the module will require more than 60 lines of source code. Thus, the module needs to be segmented. The *item records* to be processed by this module include, among other things, these fields:

Customer number	Sales rep number	Invoice number	Item number	Quantity purchased	Price	Description

Segmenting is best handled at the stepwise refinement stage. After several iterations it will be apparent whether or not the module will require more than a page of code. In the invoice register example, assume that the logic produced through stepwise refinement is as follows:

---

[1]Although this is the preferred approach, you may find a compiler that does not contain the necessary facility to link to subprograms.

INVOICE REGISTER

INVOICE NUMBER	CUST NO	CUSTOMER NAME	MERCHANDISE AMOUNT	TAX	TOTAL AMOUNT
16799	14753	HOBBYRAMA	52.50	2.61	54.81
16800	14758	HOFF ELEC CO	86.12	4.30	90.42
16801	14764	HOLBRO PAINT CO	92.20	4.61	96.81
16802	14770	HOLLAND CO	80.15	4.01	84.16
16803	14775	HOVER CO	912.12	45.61	957.73
16804	14780	HOWELL CO	200.10	10.00	210.10
16805	14787	HOWKEN UTILITIES	315.00	15.75	330.75
16806	14790	HUGEL MOTORS	930.30	46.50	
16807	14792	IRVING TIRE CO.	1,950.00		
16808	14795	IVY BARN INC.			
16809	14800	JACKSON SALES	.00	2.02	672.42
			1,050.10	40.00	840.10
			280.50	92.51	1,142.61
			555.10	14.03	294.53
			106.66	27.76	582.86
16843	15970	ZACHARY BROS.	1,133.00	5.33	111.99
16844	15972	ZEPHYR ELEC CO		56.65	1,189.65
		TOTALS	61,564.67	3,078.23	64,642.90

Figure 9-2. Invoice-register layout

```
Initialize variables
EOJ = no
DOWHILE more item records
    Read an item record
        At end EOJ = yes
    IF more item records
        Validate data
        IF data ok
            PERFORM process item
        ELSE
            PERFORM data error
        ENDIF
    ELSE
        PERFORM final totals
    ENDIF
ENDDO
```

This pseudo code solution is slightly different from the way in which pseudo code was presented earlier in this book. There is no formal definition of the form that pseudo code should take; simply write it in a way that closely approximates the language in which you will be programming. This pseudo code could now be translated into COBOL source statements and form the *top segment* in this module. The top segment is a synopsis of the entire module. A module, then, is segmented in the same hierarchical fashion that a system or program is developed.

Figure 9-3 shows a hierarchy chart for the segments in the module that will generate the invoice register. The lower level segments could be paragraphs that are executed via a PERFORM. In addition, segments could be subprograms or other code that resides in the COBOL source statement library. In this case the segment is included via the COPY verb. Using the library facility has the advantages of reducing redundant coding effort and facilitating segmenting.

The mechanics of developing segments that reside in the source statement library are these: We assume a segment has been written that requires a lower segment. The lower segment could be initially coded as a stub (containing only the statements needed for the higher segment to execute properly) and placed in the source statement library. After the surrounding code has been tested, the source statement stub is developed into its expanded version. The COPY must immediately follow the procedure name. In addition, some compilers do not allow copied code to contain a COPY statement.

At the point of beginning to code this module, test data should already have been prepared as well as the job control language. The top segment should be coded first. Of course, any segments needed to test the higher level segments would be either coded as stubs or as complete segments. In the invoice register example all of the segments (other than the top segment) could be coded initially as stubs. The top segment would then be tested, followed by the coding and testing of the other segments. A combination of the hierarchical and execution-order approaches is the best method of planning the sequence in which the lower level segments are coded and tested. Thus, the sequence of coding and testing might be: (1) Top segment, (2) Process item, (3) Final totals, (4) Validate data and (5) Data error.

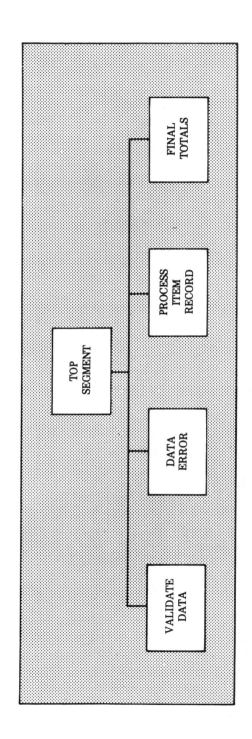

Figure 9-3. Segments in the invoice-register module

However, this development order may not be the best order for the arrangement of paragraphs in the final source listing. Execution order is the most readable; therefore, at the end of module development, you may need to rearrange the paragraphs to reflect the general execution order.

While segments are usually paragraphs, not every paragraph is a segment; that is, you may define paragraphs for reasons other than segmenting a module. Reasons for creating paragraphs include:

- Requirements of COBOL syntax (some compilers require that code that is repetitively executed via a PERFORM needs to be a separate paragraph)
- Improved readability
- Need for reusable code

Paragraphs would normally appear on the same page as the rest of the segment of which they are a part. They would become a separate segment when there are enough statements to require a page of their own.

Figure 9-4 shows how the invoice register COBOL module might be organized in its segmented format in the source listing output. As previously mentioned, the process of segmenting is essentially the same as designing from the top down. First, there is the *main line* or *top segment* which summarizes the processing steps in the module. In this segment these steps would probably be specified:

- *Initialization:* open files, initialize variables
- *Main loop:* usually invoked repetitively because it is controlled by an end-of-file condition for the primary input file
- *Termination:* final totals, completion message, close files

For example, the top segment in the invoice register module might contain the following code:

```
PROCEDURE DIVISION.
    MAIN-PROGRAM.
        PERFORM INITIALIZATION.
        PERFORM MAIN-LOOP UNTIL EOJ-YES.
        PERFORM FINAL-TOTALS.
        STOP RUN.

    MAIN-LOOP.
        READ ITEM INTO ITEM-REC
                AT END MOVE 'YES' TO EOJ.
        IF EOJ-NO
            PERFORM VALIDATE-DATA
            IF DATA-OK
                PERFORM PROCESS-ITEM
            ELSE
                PERFORM DATA-ERROR.
```

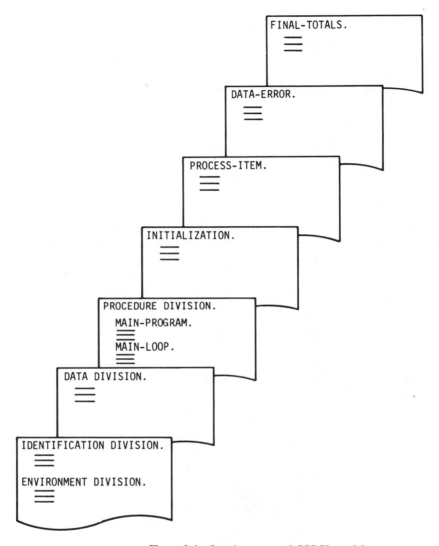

Figure 9-4. Sample segmented COBOL module

Should a segment be a section? Specifying a segment as a section and PERFORMing that section has the advantages of grouping related paragraphs and reinforcing the top-down-development approach. However, it has the disadvantages of limiting readability and hindering maintainability. It is desirable for all readers of any COBOL program to know that every paragraph encountered will be PERFORMed from some higher segment, will never be "fallen into" or "out of," and will always return control to its invoker at the end of its execution. Then when a portion of code is examined, it is not necessary to search through the program to find where the paragraph was invoked or if it will be fallen into. If a paragraph is sometimes PERFORMed alone and sometimes PERFORMed as part of a section, the logic of successive paragraphs is difficult to follow. Furthermore, if a paragraph is added between others or moved out of sequence, results may occur that are difficult to debug.

If a paragraph in a section PERFORMs a lower paragraph, there is another problem. When the section is PERFORMed, the second paragraph will be executed an extra time. For example:

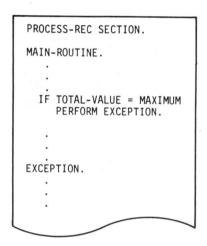

```
PROCESS-REC SECTION.

MAIN-ROUTINE.
    .
    .
    .
    IF TOTAL-VALUE = MAXIMUM
        PERFORM EXCEPTION.

    .
    .
    .
EXCEPTION.
    .
    .
    .
```

When PROCESS-REC is PERFORMed, EXCEPTION will be executed at the conclusion of the MAIN-ROUTINE paragraph.

To avoid these problems, do not PERFORM a section. However, you may use a section name to group paragraphs for the purpose of documenting them, or for using the segmentation feature, or because some statements, such as SORT, require a section name.

A similar rule is made about PERFORM THRU. If it is used to allow various sequences of paragraphs to be executed, then the problems previously stated will occur. Consider, for example, this page of a source listing:

```
WRITE-MASTER.
    ═══

READ-MASTER.
    ═══

READ-TRANS.
    ═══

UPDATE-MASTER.
    ═══
```

When PERFORM THRU is used, you must read another page or more of the source listing to determine how the paragraphs are invoked. Here are some ways in which the paragraphs might have been invoked:

```
PERFORM READ-MASTER THRU
     UPDATE-MASTER.
.
.
.
```

```
PERFORM WRITE-MASTER THRU
     UPDATE-MASTER.
.
.
.
```

```
PERFORM WRITE-MASTER
   THRU READ-MASTER.
.
.
.
```

A maintenance programmer who has to modify the code within the paragraph READ-MASTER must also consider the impact of those changes on the rest of the program. In other words, changes could have unexpected effects on the other paragraphs.

There are two situations where PERFORM THRU is acceptable. One is to PERFORM THRU an EXIT paragraph. This is desirable to ensure the explicit finishing of a paragraph, but there should be no intervening paragraphs between the one being PERFORMed and the EXIT paragraph. The second exception is for those whose compilers do not have the EVALUATE statement. Then the CASE statement needs to be simulated, and a PERFORM THRU is required. This will be described in the section on implementing the structures in COBOL.

An advantage of having every paragraph explicitly invoked is that it facilitates the rearrangement of paragraphs for readability as suggested earlier. Also, you may wish to group exception-handling paragraphs separate from main-line paragraphs, not only to improve readability but also to take advantage of a virtual storage environment. Thus, more readable code requires that all paragraphs be PERFORMed, none are fallen into, no sections are PERFORMed, and with the two exceptions previously noted, no PER-FORM THRUs are used.

Each segment and module should be a *proper program*. As applied to COBOL, segments and modules should have these characteristics:

1. *There is one entry point and it is at the top of the page.* Thus, if the COBOL compiler you are using has the ENTRY statement, it should not be used to define multiple entries.
2. *There is one exit point and it is typically the last statement of the first paragraph on a page.* The EXIT PROGRAM statement should occur only once for each module that is called. If a segment has been PERFORMed, the exit is simply the end of the paragraph. Or, optionally, you may wish to indicate an EXIT paragraph.
3. *The return (exit) is to the invoker.*

Thus, to summarize the subdividing of a COBOL program: (1) the program is designed into modules; (2) each module is compiled as a subprogram (with the exception of the *top module* which is compiled as a main program); (3) if the module's executable code is more than 50–60 lines long, it should be divided into page-long segments; and (4) within the segments some paragraphs may be needed.

STRUCTURING COBOL PROGRAMS

Structuring involves taking the three basic structures as well as any additional structures and combining them to accomplish a given function or subfunction. These are briefly reviewed here with COBOL examples.

Sequence Structure

The sequence structure consists of two process blocks in which control flows from one box to the next in sequence. A box could represent any COBOL statement that does not prevent the flow of control from proceeding sequentially.

The PERFORM and CALL statements are valid in this context because each can be thought of as shorthand for the code it is invoking. If, for example, the paragraph were to replace the PERFORM, the sequential order is obvious. If, for convenience or repetition, it is placed out-of-line, the flow of logic is not altered. As long as the invoked portion returns control to the subsequent statement, the top-to-bottom flow is preserved.

Choice Structure

The choice structure

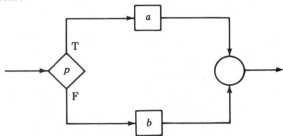

is implemented by using the IF statement. It includes the ELSE clause when there are different actions to be performed—one for the true situation and one for the false.

```
IF STOCK-ON-HAND EQUAL ZERO
        PERFORM STOCK-BALANCE-ZERO
ELSE
        MOVE STOCK-ON-HAND TO QUANTITY-WORK.
```

When no action is to be performed for the false predicate, the ELSE clause can be eliminated. For example:

```
IF STOCK-ON-HAND LESS THAN REORDER-QUANTITY
    PERFORM PURCHASE-ORDER.
```

Some compilers allow END-IF to explicitly end an IF statement. Even when not necessary it provides extra readability.

```
IF AUTHORIZATION-CODE NOT NUMERIC
        PERFORM AUTHORIZATION-ERROR-ROUTINE
        MOVE 'NO' TO PROCESS-RECORD
END-IF
```

If your compiler doesn't permit it, you may wish to use ENDIF pseudo code as a *comment* to indicate the end of the IF. By placing an asterisk in column 7, the ENDIF can be inserted as a comment to improve readability. For example:

```
IF AUTHORIZATION-CODE NOT NUMERIC
        PERFORM AUTHORIZATION-ERROR-ROUTINE
        MOVE 'NO' TO PROCESS-RECORD.
*    ENDIF
```

When used this way, ENDIF is not interpreted by the compiler, and therefore, cannot be used to convey to the compiler that an IF statement is ended. Ending an IF is done by the final period.

Sometimes a programmer finds it convenient to express program logic by using a series of nested IF statements. To many programmers the idea of nesting IFs conjures up an image of code that might look something like this:

IF NOT A OR B IF C THEN GO TO Q ELSE IF D GO TO R ELSE GO TO S ELSE GO TO T.

If this same logic were written, using the rules for structuring and some formatting conventions, the following might be coded:

```
1        IF PAYMENT-LATE OR NOT COMPLETE
2           IF FIRST-TIME
3              PERFORM GENTLE-REMINDER
4           ELSE
5              IF PREVIOUS-LETTER-SENT
6                 PERFORM THREATENING-LETTER
7              ELSE
8                 PERFORM SECOND-REMINDER
9        ELSE
10          PERFORM THANK-YOU.
```

The formatting guidelines of structured programming prevent the *run-on-sentence* type of coding shown in the first nested IF example. Each new statement begins a new line and each level of nesting is indented from the previous one. This highlights the logic of the IF and shows which code is associated with which set of conditions. The ELSEs are aligned with their corresponding IFs. To pair the IFs and the ELSEs, the rule is as follows: pair the innermost ELSE with the immediately preceding unpaired IF. Work backwards until all preceding ELSEs are paired, then go forward to the next innermost ELSE and repeat. Thus, in the preceding example, the ELSE on line 7 is paired with the IF on line 5, the ELSE on line 4 with the IF on line 2, and the ELSE on line 9 cannot be paired with the IFs on line 2 or 5 since they have already been paired. The ELSE on line 9 is therefore paired with the IF on line 1.

Here are a few conventions that simplify the use of nested IFs:

1. *The condition name(s) being tested should be self-explanatory.* Names such as MATCHING-MASTER-FOUND or VALID-AUTHORIZATION convey more meaning than a name such as SWITCH-1. If PERFORMs are used, they should reference paragraph names that are also meaningful.

2. *Compound tests should be kept to a minimum.* A single AND or OR is easy to follow, but combinations of them become increasingly difficult to read. If a statement reads IF A OR B AND C (incidentally violating rule 1 above), then a reader has to figure out whether it means A OR (B AND C) or (A

OR B) AND C. If you need to write a condition like this, use parentheses to indicate the order of operations, even if they are not required.

3. *The use of NOT makes conditions, especially compounds, difficult to interpret.* NOT should be eliminated whenever possible. If you must use NOT with a compound condition, help the reader of your program by using parentheses or reversing the order of terms. Thus,

IF NOT A OR B

should be written as

IF B OR NOT A

4. *Implied subjects and operators should be avoided.* For example, it is difficult to remember that in

A NOT < B AND > C

The NOT is implied after the AND. However, in

A NOT < B AND C

it is *not implied.* Be explicit in your coding. For example:

A NOT < B AND A NOT > C

5. *The depth of nesting in an IF should be limited.* While one or two levels is easy to follow, more than four levels become difficult to read. Indenting each successive IF will help to limit the depth because after several levels of nests, you will be at the right-most edge of the coding sheet.

6. *Keep the nest on one page.* If necessary, use PERFORMs to accomplish this. This allows the reader to see the complete logic on one page. In addition, it keeps the ELSEs close to their matching IFs.

In the past nested IFs have been avoided by some COBOL users because the IFs were hard to read and debug. However, if the previous six conventions are followed, nested IFs are frequently preferred to other methods of achieving the required logic. If you are still concerned about whether or not to use nested IFs, try coding the logic two ways—one without nested IFs and one with nested IFs. The two solutions could then be evaluated for readability and clarity. For example, Figure 9-5 shows the logic flow for calculating a bowling score. One solution, using nested IFs, might be:

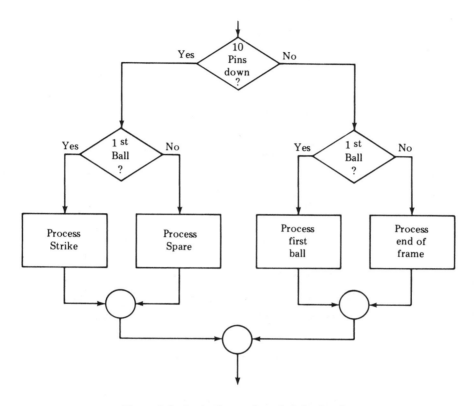

Figure 9-5. Logic diagram for calculating bowling score

```
IF TOTAL-PINS-DOWN = 10
    IF BALL-NUMBER = 1
        ` PERFORM PROCESS-STRIKE
    ELSE
        PERFORM PROCESS-SPARE
ELSE
    IF BALL-NUMBER = 1
        PERFORM PROCESS-FIRST-BALL
    ELSE
        PERFORM PROCESS-END-OF-FRAME.
```

In the following solution the nested IFs are PERFORMed out of line:

```
            IF TOTAL-PINS-DOWN = 10
                PERFORM TEST-FIRST-BALL-1
            ELSE
                PERFORM PERFORM TEST-FIRST-BALL-2.
    *                •
    *                •
    *                •

        TEST-FIRST-BALL-1.
        IF BALL-NUMBER = 1
            PERFORM PROCESS-STRIKE
        ELSE
            PERFORM PROCESS-SPARE.

        TEST-FIRST-BALL-2.
        IF BALL-NUMBER = 1
            PERFORM PROCESS-FIRST-BALL
        ELSE
            PERFORM PROCESS-END-OF-FRAME.
```

Finally, here is a solution without nested IFs:

```
    IF TOTAL-PINS-DOWN = 10 AND BALL-NUMBER = 1
        PERFORM PROCESS-STRIKE.
    IF TOTAL-PINS-DOWN = 10 AND BALL-NUMBER NOT = 1
        PERFORM PROCESS-SPARE.
    IF TOTAL-PINS-DOWN NOT = 10 AND BALL-NUMBER = 1
        PERFORM PROCESS-FIRST-BALL.
    IF TOTAL-PINS-DOWN NOT = 10 AND BALL-NUMBER NOT = 1
        PERFORM PROCESS-END-OF-FRAME.
```

If a branch on the nested IF tree has no action to be performed, then it can be eliminated. However, COBOL syntax requires that something be included at that point. If your compiler allows END-IF, that would end the IF; if not, use NEXT SENTENCE.

```
    IF DATA-FIELD NUMERIC
        IF DATE-FIELD < 89001
            MOVE 'DATE TOO EARLY' TO ERROR-MESSAGE
            WRITE PRINT-LINE
        ELSE
            END-IF
    ELSE
        MOVE 'DATE NOT NUMERIC' TO ERROR-MESSAGE
        WRITE PRINT-LINE
    END-IF.
```

In this example we do not want to test for the range of the DATEFIELD until it has been determined to be numeric. We cannot omit the first ELSE since that will pair the second ELSE with the first IF and print the message for valid dates. Thus we insert the END-IF, or NEXT SENTENCE, at that point. Avoid using NEXT SENTENCE on the true branch of the IF. It is better to change the test so that the action is performed on the true branch and the NEXT SENTENCE is in the ELSE.

For certain logic, programming a nested IF in COBOL can require some care. For example, for the logic shown in Figure 9-6, if you don't have an END-IF statement, the following code might be attempted:

```
1        IF VALID-TRANSACTION = 'Y'
2              PERFORM PROCESS-TRANSACTION
3        ELSE
4              IF ERROR-COUNT = 1
5                    MOVE ' ERROR IN TRANSACTION ' TO ERROR-MESSAGE
6              ELSE
7                    MOVE ' MULTIPLE ERRORS ' TO ERROR-MESSAGE
8              WRITE PRINT-LINE.
```

However, this solution is not correct because the statement on line 8 will be executed only for the false branch of the preceding IF, but the logic requires it to be executed on the true branch as well.

```
IF Valid

    Process transaction

ELSE

    IF one error

        Set up one-error message

    ELSE

        Set up multiple-error message

    ENDIF

    Print message

ENDIF
```

Figure 9-6. Nested IF problem

It might appear that what is required is a period at the end of line 7 to indicate that the IF statement on line 4 is ended. However, since there can be only a single period in an IF statement, that would have the effect of ending the IF on line 1 as well. The WRITE statement would be out of the IF statement entirely and would be executed in all cases including valid transactions. (This error is particularly dangerous and hard to debug since the result is valid COBOL.)

The problem can be solved with END-IF, or by either repeating the WRITE statement on both branches or PERFORMing the second IF test. These three solutions are shown in Figure 9-7. In some cases the problem may also be solved by placing the statement in question *before* the second IF statement. It is not possible in this case since the WRITE statement needs to be performed *after* the second IF test.

```
IF VALID-TRANSACTION = 'Y'
        PERFORM PROCESS-TRANSACTION
ELSE
        IF ERROR-COUNT = 1
            MOVE ' ERROR IN TRANSACTION ' TO ERROR-MESSAGE
        ELSE
            MOVE ' MULTIPLE ERRORS ' TO ERROR-MESSAGE
        END-IF
        WRITE PRINT-LINE
END-IF.
```

```
IF VALID-TRANSACTION = 'Y'
        PERFORM PROCESS-TRANSACTION
ELSE
        IF ERROR-COUNT = 1
            MOVE ' ERROR IN TRANSACTION ' TO ERROR-MESSAGE
            WRITE PRINT-LINE
        ELSE
            MOVE ' MULTIPLE ERRORS ' TO ERROR-MESSAGE
            WRITE PRINT-LINE.
```

```
IF VALID-TRANSACTION = 'Y'
        PERFORM PROCESS-TRANSACTION
ELSE
        PERFORM MULTIPLE-ERROR-TEST
        WRITE PRINT-LINE.
*       •
*       •
*       •
    MULTIPLE-ERROR-TEST.
        IF ERROR-COUNT = 1
            MOVE ' ERROR IN TRANSACTION ' TO ERROR-MESSAGE
        ELSE
            MOVE ' MULTIPLE ERRORS ' TO ERROR-MESSAGE
```

Figure 9-7. Three COBOL solutions for the pseudo-code in Figure 9-6

This problem of intermediate periods is not limited to IF statements but applies to other conditionals as well. Thus, the READ statement is a conditional statement, since the AT END or INVALID KEY options precede statements that are executed only under certain circumstances. Similarly, other options such as ON SIZE ERROR create conditional statements. Here is a list of ANS COBOL conditionals:

Statement	Option
READ, SEARCH, RETURN	AT END
GO TO	DEPENDING ON
ADD, SUBTRACT, MULTIPLY, DIVIDE,	
COMPUTE	ON SIZE ERROR
READ, WRITE, REWRITE, DELETE, START	INVALID KEY
SEARCH	WHEN
WRITE	AT END-OF-PAGE
IF	
PERFORM	UNTIL
EVALUATE	
CALL	ON OVERFLOW

For example, consider the following COBOL code:[2]

```
READ MASTER-FILE
      INVALID KEY MULTIPLY OLD-KEY BY PRIME GIVING NEW-KEY
            ON SIZE ERROR
                  DIVIDE NEW-KEY BY 2 GIVING NEW-KEY
      MOVE 'Y' TO BAD-KEY.
```

If you wish to make the MOVE statement part of INVALID KEY and not part of ON SIZE ERROR, END-MULTIPLY can be used. It would end the MULTIPLY statement with the ON SIZE ERROR and allow the MOVE statement to belong to the INVALID KEY. If your compiler doesn't have the END-MULTIPLY, then, as with the nested IF problem previously shown, one of the alternative solutions presented must be used.

Repetition Structures

Repeated execution of a process block is accomplished in COBOL by use of the PERFORM statement. This powerful statement allows out-of-line executions as well as looping control. For many years the COBOL language required that PERFORM specify a paragraph name. Thus for a block of code to be repetitively executed it needed to be out of line. Current language extensions now permit a PERFORM without a paragraph name. This specifies that the code immediately following the PERFORM, and up to END-PERFORM, is to be repetitively executed. If your compiler does not have this extension, then you will need to create out-of-line paragraphs to be PERFORMed in order to achieve the repetition structures.

---

[2]This is actually not valid COBOL since INVALID KEY must be followed by an imperative statement, but MULTIPLY with ON SIZE ERROR is a conditional. However, many compilers accept these statements as written.

DOWHILE Structure   The DOWHILE figure provides the basic loop capability by specifying that a function is repeated while a specified condition is true. The condition is tested *before* the execution of the statements in the structure; hence, the statements may never be executed if the condition tested initially is false. To review, here is the basic structure for a DOWHILE:

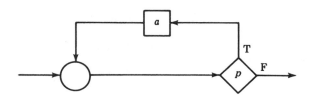

To implement this repetition structure in COBOL, the PERFORM statement with the WHILE option is used. The VARYING option may or may not be specified.

You may want to include WITH TEST BEFORE for clarity, even though it is assumed. Thus to process repeatedly while an end-of-file condition has not been met, the following could be written:

```
PERFORM PROCESS-ROUTINE WITH TEST BEFORE
    WHILE MASTER-FILE-EOF-NO.
```

To implement this structure with a compiler without WHILE you would need to use a PERFORM UNTIL. It will also test the condition first, as the structure requires. However, it will have the reverse logic for the test; that is, instead of repeating the process block as long as the predicate is true, the PERFORM UNTIL will execute it as long as it is false, and terminate when it becomes true. In the previous example, the logic calls for a process to be executed repetitively while an end-of-file indicator is off. You would need to reverse the test as follows:

```
PERFORM PROCESS-ROUTINE UNTIL MASTER-FILE-EOF-YES.
```

As another example, for the pseudo code statement,

```
LOOP 24 TIMES
```

the COBOL statement accomplishing this repetition could be coded:

```
PERFORM CALCULATION-ROUTINE VARYING COUNTER FROM 1 BY 1
    UNTIL COUNTER GREATER THAN 24.
```

The logic of the pseudo code implies that the repetition will be done while a counter is less than or equal to 24, but the COBOL version must state that it is done until the counter is greater than 24.

If it is known, as it frequently is, what language the program will be written in, then the flowchart or pseudo code can be created accordingly. Thus, some installations have adopted a version of pseudo code that matches their COBOL compiler. It might, for example, show repetition using a PERFORM UNTIL structure rather than a DOWHILE.

DOUNTIL Structure   If it is desired that the loop always be executed at least once, then the DOUNTIL logic is needed. Here is the basic structure.

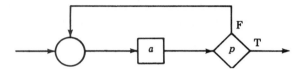

The PERFORM UNTIL statement normally makes the test before the first execution of the process block. This logic, applicable to the DOWHILE, needs to be modified for the DOUNTIL. If your compiler allows the WITH TEST AFTER option on PERFORM, it matches the DOUNTIL logic exactly. Thus you could write:

PERFORM EDIT-ROUTINE WITH TEST AFTER
UNTIL EDIT-ERROR-NO.

This would ensure that the EDIT-ROUTINE would be executed at least once, since the test is not instituted until after the first time.

If you do not have the WITH TEST AFTER option, then the DOUNTIL logic is accomplished in COBOL by one of two methods:

1. Explicitly invoke the paragraph by a PERFORM without repetition before invoking it with the UNTIL clause. For example:

   PERFORM EDIT-ROUTINE.
   PERFORM EDIT-ROUTINE UNTIL EDIT-ERROR-NO.

2. Set the indicator that controls the PERFORM immediately before the PERFORM. Then the indicator in the paragraph that is invoked must be appropriately set to control further repetitions.

   MOVE 'N' TO TRANSACTION-FILE-EOF.
   PERFORM MAIN-ROUTINE UNTIL TRANSACTION-FILE-EOF-YES.

This method is convenient where a routine containing a READ must be executed at least once.

It is common for PERFORM statements to be nested. That is, the paragraph being PERFORMed also contains a PERFORM statement of a lower level paragraph. This might also include repetition under the control of some test and would constitute nested repetition structures. As in the case of nested IF statements, as the level of nested PERFORMS increases, readability decreases. In-line PERFORMS, if your compiler allows them, can help reduce this readability problem.

Optional Structures

CASE Structure   The choice structure provides for a selection between two alternatives based on the results of a test. Frequently, however, a choice must be made from more than two possible alternatives. For this a generalization of the choice structure, known as the CASE structure, is used.

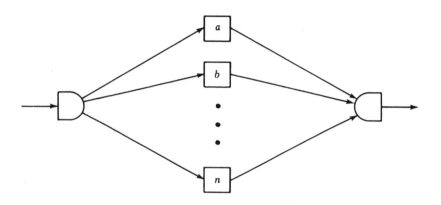

Compilers that support the EVALUATE statement match the CASE logic directly. A test is made for the value of an expression, and various paragraphs are invoked based on the results. For example, consider a program which processes billing transactions for customers based on the type of account a customer has. To select the proper routine to process a given account, the following statement could be written:

```
EVALUATE CUSTOMER-TYPE
    WHEN 'C' PERFORM CASH-ACCOUNT,
    WHEN 'T' PERFORM THIRTY-DAY-ACCOUNT,
    WHEN 'R' PERFORM REVOLVING-ACCOUNT,
    WHEN 'S' PERFORM SPECIAL-ACCOUNT,
    WHEN OTHER PERFORM INVALID-CODE,
END-EVALUATE.
```

For compilers that do not have the EVALUATE statement, there are two other ways to code the CASE structure. One way is to use repetitive IF statements to indicate the various paths for each of the results specified. These may or may not be nested. Thus for the customer billing example above, the following could be written:

```
IF CUSTOMER-TYPE EQUAL TO 'C'
    PERFORM CASH-ACCOUNT
ELSE IF CUSTOMER-TYPE EQUAL TO 'T'
    PERFORM THIRTY-DAY-ACCOUNT
ELSE IF CUSTOMER-TYPE EQUAL TO 'R'
    PERFORM REVOLVING-ACCOUNT
ELSE IF CUSTOMER-TYPE EQUAL TO 'S'
    PERFORM SPECIAL-ACCOUNT.
```

The flow enters the first IF and proceeds to one of the paragraphs indicated. At the conclusion of the execution of that paragraph the program continues with the statement following the period which terminates the IF. The formatting used in these nested IFs differs from the indentation of nested IFs shown earlier. Since all the ELSEs are alternatives to the first IF, the indentation pictured here shows that logic. This formatting also allows you to code a larger number of alternatives without having the indented statements run off the right-hand edge of your coding sheet. You might also eliminate the ELSEs and merely have a series of IFs testing each of the alternatives.

Another way of implementing the CASE structure is to simulate it by using the GOTO DEPENDING ON statement. In this simulation, at the point where the CASE is required, a PERFORM THRU is used. (The CASE structure is an exception to the rule against PERFORM THRUs.) The first paragraph being PERFORMed starts with a GOTO DEPENDING ON. This transfers control to one of a series of paragraphs that immediately follows. Each of these paragraphs ends with a GOTO to the EXIT paragraph at the end of the series of alternative paragraphs. Flow proceeds from the initial GOTO to the final EXIT paragraph, making the logic easy to follow. The EXIT paragraph is the paragraph named in the PERFORM THRU.

The preceding example, assuming the conversion of CUSTOMER-TYPE to another variable called CUSTOMER-CODE, is shown in Figure 9-8. The CASE structure is PERFORMed out of line so that the readability and the one-paragraph-name characteristic of the invoking routine is maintained. All paths merge to the EXIT paragraph, including the situation in which the variable did not have a proper value and dropped through to the error routine.

It is often helpful if a comment describes what the PERFORMed paragraphs are to do, since they will usually be on a separate page. The entire series of paragraphs should appear continuously on one page. If necessary, the alternate paragraphs may need to PERFORM some code out of line to keep within the one-page limit. Because the GOTO DEPENDING ON needs consecutive values for the variable, it can be used only if the codes are in order or if a conversion is made to obtain consecutive values.

Which method—nested IFs or GOTO DEPENDING ON—should you use? The advantages of nested IFs are that the values to be tested need not be consecutive, the source code is usually shorter, and the GOTO statement is not used. If there are a large number of alternatives and the values to be tested are consecutive, the GOTO DEPENDING ON would probably be used. In this case there is probably less source code, which improves readability, because only a single statement is needed to invoke the

```
***         BASED  ON THE TYPE OF ACCOUNT, THE FOLLOWING PERFORM
***         WILL CAUSE THE TRANSACTION TO BE PROCESSED
***           BY THE APPROPRIATE ROUTINE.
       PERFORM ACCOUNT-PROCESSING THRU ACCOUNT-PROCESSING-EXIT.
```

```
      ACCOUNT-PROCESSING.
         GO TO CASH-ACCOUNT
               THIRTY-DAY-ACCOUNT
               REVOLVING-ACCOUNT
               SPECIAL-ACCOUNT
                    DEPENDING ON CUSTOMER-CODE.
         PERFORM INVALID-CODE-ROUTINE.
         GO TO ACCOUNT-PROCESSING-EXIT.


      CASH-ACCOUNT.
*          .
*          .
*          .
         GO TO ACCOUNT-PROCESSING-EXIT.


      REVOLVING-ACCOUNT.
*          .
*          .
*          .
         GO TO ACCOUNT-PROCESSING-EXIT.


      SPECIAL-ACCOUNT.
*          .
*          .
*          .
         GO TO ACCOUNT-PROCESSING-EXIT.


      THIRTY-DAY-ACCOUNT.
*          .
*          .
*          .
         GO TO ACCOUNT-PROCESSING-EXIT.


      ACCOUNT-PROCESSING-EXIT.
         EXIT.
```

Figure 9-8. Example of CASE structure using GOTO DEPENDING ON

appropriate routine. Of course, GOTO DEPENDING ON must be selected if the compiler limits nested IFs to less than the number you need.

SEARCH Structure   Because table look-up or table searching is a common occurrence in programming, a SEARCH structure has been defined. In table searching a *search argument* is compared with a *table argument*. (Usually, an equal compare is being sought but not required. You might be looking for the first entry greater than the search argument.) The *table function* is the actual processing of a record or other data once a *match* is found. An error condition occurs if there is no matching table argument for the search argument being used. Thus, there are two ways to process the search operation: a *normal process* when a matching element is found and an *error process* when no matching item is found. A SEARCH structure, which will handle *serial* or *binary search* operations, is shown in Figure 9-9. In this structure the flow begins at the top. Then the table entry to be compared with the search argument is determined. This would involve incrementing an index value for a serial search or averaging the high and low bounds for a binary search. Next a test is made to determine if there are more table elements to be compared. If not, the table argument was not found—hence an error exit is required. The second test compares the table argument with the search argument. If the condition tested (e.g., table argument = search argument) *is met*, the process block handles the operations needed (i.e., PROCESS TABLE FUNCTION). If the condition tested *is not met*, the loop operation continues. The structure has one entry and one exit. The flow continues to a common point in a forward direction. The comparison loop may be executed many times, but only one of the two process blocks will be executed.

The SEARCH structure is implemented by using COBOL's SEARCH verb. This verb can be specified either with the ALL option for a binary search or without it for a serial search. In either case there are separate actions specified for the *found* and *not*

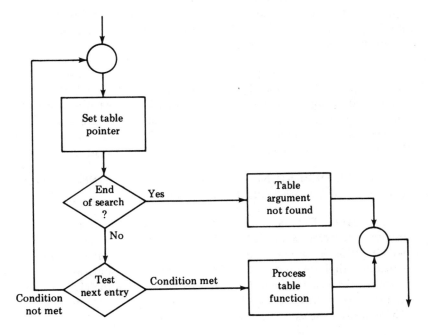

Figure 9-9. SEARCH structure

found conditions. These actions can be a single statement or, more likely, a PERFORM of an out-of-line paragraph. An example of the SEARCH structure follows:

```
SET DEPT-INDEX TO 1.
SEARCH DEPT-NO-TABLE
    AT END
        PERFORM DEPT-NOT-FOUND
    WHEN DEPT-NO-TABLE (DEPT-INDEX) = INPUT-DEPT-NO
        MOVE 'Y' TO DEPT-VALID.
```

PROGRAMMING CONSIDERATIONS

COBOL Statements

The following statements should be avoided because their use generally violates the constraints of structured programming.

ENTRY   The ENTRY statement establishes an entry point in a COBOL subprogram. It should appear only once at most and not be used to define alternate entry points.

STOP RUN   Because the STOP RUN statement stops the program, it should appear only once at the logical end of the program. The exception, noted previously, might be that of allowing a STOP RUN for abnormal termination (in a low level segment or module) of a program.

ALTER   Armstrong states that the ALTER verb is one of those language facilities that should be dropped from the production COBOL repertory.[3] Not only is it more difficult to debug a program that contains ALTERs, but it is also more difficult to read such a program. In fact, you cannot accept such a program at face value. Armstrong suggests that alternatives to the use of ALTER be used: (1) rearrange the code, (2) use PERFORM, or (3) create a flag and use an IF statement test.

GOTO DEPENDING ON   A GOTO DEPENDING ON statement may be used only in the simulation of the CASE structure.

GOTO   The uncontrolled use of the GOTO must be avoided. A GOTO is usually considered controlled if it is *part* of a structure. Thus, implementing the CASE with GOTOs is still structured since they all meet at the merge point of the one structure. Similarly, NEXT SENTENCE is seen by some as a thinly disguised GOTO since it does transfer control. However, here again it merely moves forward to the end of the current structure and does not require any tracing of logic or turning of pages. Therefore, its use is acceptable if the IF statement cannot be rewritten to eliminate it.

[3]Russell M. Armstrong, *Modular Programming in COBOL*, (New York: John Wiley & Sons, 1973), p. 121.

More controversial is a GOTO to the EXIT of a paragraph. This is seen by some as easy to follow and desirable in the following situation: During the execution of a paragraph, a condition is detected which requires that the rest of the paragraph be skipped. This can be coded by testing for that condition and, only if it has not occurred, continuing execution. Thus, the remainder of the paragraph is part of the IF. This can cause problems because of the limitations of the nested IF and might make the program less readable. A simple

```
IF ERRORS GO TO P-EXIT.
```

should not cause confusion and could be considered "controlled." The argument against using it states that if there are several of these in a paragraph, readability *will* be affected. Also, it opens the door to further exceptions. The approach we recommend is as follows:

1. First code *without* the GOTO. It may turn out better than expected. If so, leave it.
2. If not, code it *with* the GOTO. It may turn out to be no better than the first solution. If so, drop it.
3. If not, and you are convinced that it is a significant improvement with the GOTO, leave it that way. Approval should be obtained to do this in an environment where normal standards disallow it.

Indicators

Structured programming tends to increase the use of *indicators* or *switches*. Here are some guidelines for the use of indicators.

1. *Use as few indicators as possible.* One way to do this is to have the *invoked* paragraph take actions for the various situations that arise rather than report back to the *invoker* what has occurred. For example, in the following code, an indicator is used to show the occurrence of an error detected in the exit routine. Upon completion of the routine, the indicator is tested and the error-processing routine conditionally invoked.

```
MOVE 'N' TO EDIT-ERROR.
PERFORM EDIT-ROUTINE.
IF EDIT-ERROR-YES
    PERFORM ERROR-ROUTINE.

*       .
*       .
*       .

EDIT-ROUTINE.
    IF CUSTOMER-CODE NOT NUMERIC
        MOVE 'Y' TO EDIT-ERROR.
```

Here's another way in which the edit routine might have been coded:

```
            PERFORM EDIT-ROUTINE.
   *     •
   *     •
   *     •

            EDIT-ROUTINE.
                IF CUSTOMER-CODE NOT NUMERIC
                PERFORM ERROR-ROUTINE.
```

Here, when the error is detected, the error routine is invoked immediately, eliminating the need for the indicator. Thus, built into the flow of code is the handling of the exception condition. If the code processing the exception is too lengthy to place in line, a PERFORM or CALL may be used instead. This makes it easier to follow the normal sequence of processing. In addition, if the program is to be run in a virtual storage environment, it allows code used less frequently to be executed in a separate page frame.

2. *Use an indicator for one purpose only.* Using the same indicator for more than one purpose makes it difficult for the reader to follow and creates many possibilities for errors. This is particularly true when the program is modified and the use of the indicator is altered either intentionally or inadvertently. This rule of *single use* should be adhered to even in such cases as one indicator being used one time at the beginning of the program and the other near the end. Even here, the possibility of confusion or introducing an error is sufficient reason to avoid this practice.

3. *Use a name which describes the indicator's function.* (This is another reason for using an indicator for only one purpose). Thus, indicators' names are typically long. It may seem tedious to have to write out a long name, but it involves only a few seconds. Compare this with perhaps many minutes on the part of the reader to figure out what an acronym might stand for (and then perhaps guessing incorrectly).

In addition to the indicator name being readable, the value assigned to it should connote something to the reader. The values of *zero* and *one* are not always meaningful. It is better to use an alphabetic character or two so that the reader understands what is being done. Thus, some people use "Y" and "N" for YES and NO or "OK" and "NG" for Okay and No Good. Consistency in the use of a character is important. For example, using "N" to indicate NO in one place and ON in another would be confusing.

Some people use level 88s to enhance the readability of indicators. If you use them, do so sparingly and carefully so that they increase rather than detract from readability. Use meaningful names and adopt standards for how you assign values. For example you might append the suffix "YES" to the level 77 name and use the value "Y" as shown below.

```
77  MASTER-FILE-EOF        PIC X.
    88  MASTER-FILE-EOF-YES                    VALUE 'Y'.
    88  MASTER-FILE-EOF-NO                     VALUE 'N'.
```

Another method would be to use named constants to set the indicator. For example:

```
77  MASTER-FILE-EOF-YES       PIC X       VALUE 'Y'.
```

Then, in the procedure division,

```
MOVE MASTER-FILE-EOF-YES  TO  MASTER-FILE-EOF.
```

Or, if your compiler has the SET statement, you could write:

```
SET MASTER-FILE-EOF  TO  TRUE.
```

This would be the clearest and simplest approach.

Using the Structures

Now let's look at some examples of how these structures can be used in typical situations. First, let's consider the handling of an end-of-file. Without structured programming this was handled by the AT END clause of the READ statement having a GOTO that sent control to an end-of-job routine. In structured programming this should be rewritten so the flow of control is always in a forward direction, and the paragraph that contains the READ has only one exit. Thus, execution continues at the subsequent statement even when end-of-file is reached. This introduces the need for an end-of-file indicator to control the processing.

In addition, the READ statement itself is probably in a loop that needs to be repeated for every record in the file. Without structured programming the iterative operation is typically controlled by a GOTO. Placed at the end of a processing loop, the GOTO sends control back to the beginning. In structured programming the needed repetition is accomplished by a PERFORM of the processing paragraph. The PERFORM shows the loop. For example:

```
MOVE 'N' TO MASTER-FILE-EOF.
PERFORM MAIN-PROCESS-ROUTINE UNTIL MASTER-FILE-EOF-YES.
*     •
*     •
*     •
MAIN-PROCESS-ROUTINE.
    READ MASTER-FILE AT END MOVE 'Y' TO MASTER-FILE-EOF.
    IF MASTER-FILE-EOF-NO
        PERFORM PROCESS-ROUTINE.
```

Loop control is handled by specifying an indicator for the end-of-file and initializing it to 'N'. The main loop is PERFORMed UNTIL the indicator is changed to 'Y', by the AT END clause of the READ. However, even though the indicator is changed to 'Y', control still passes to the statement following the READ, even when the READ encounters the end-of-file. Logically, the processing should not be executed if end-of-file has been reached so it is necessary to prevent processing by testing the status of the end-of-file indicator.

Note that MAIN-PROCESS-ROUTINE is invoked repetitively as long as the indicator is 'N'. When the READ statement encounters the end-of-file, it will change MASTER-FILE-EOF to 'Y'. The IF statement is needed to test the indicator, so that PERFORM PROCESS-ROUTINE is not executed after the end-of-file has been reached. The MAIN-PROCESS-ROUTINE is not executed again because the indicator is 'Y'. The end-of-job coding follows the PERFORM MAIN-PROCESS-ROUTINE statement. Thus, the reader is shown the flow explicitly and under what conditions specific statements are executed. All that needs to be executed for each record processed is an extra IF statement.

There is another way to handle the end-of-file situation in which the extra IF can be avoided. It involves reading one record in the initialization portion. Then the main processing loop consists of processing *that* record folllowed by the code for reading the next record. The loop is still controlled by the end-of-file indicator. Because the READ statement is at the end of the loop and the AT END turns the indicator on, the PERFORM UNTIL will test it before the record processing statements are again executed. For example:

```
          MOVE 'N' TO MASTER-FILE-EOF.
          PERFORM READ-MASTER.
          PERFORM MAIN-PROCESS-ROUTINE UNTIL MASTER-FILE-EOF-YES.
    *         .
    *         .
    *         .
          MAIN-PROCESS-ROUTINE.
    *         .
    *         .
    *         .
          PERFORM READ-MASTER.

      READ-MASTER.
          READ MASTER-FILE AT END MOVE 'Y' TO MASTER-FILE-EOF.
```

This solution is structured, but the fact that the main loop shows processing *before* the READ for subsequent records may be confusing to the reader. This solution will work even if there are no records in the file. If the first READ causes an end-of-file, because the test of the PERFORM UNTIL is made *before* the paragraph is executed the first time, the MAIN-PROCESS-ROUTINE will never be entered.

Another common situation is that some processing depends upon the results of a prior operation and an indicator controls whether or not code is executed. In these cases the indicator is set when the situation arises (e.g., an error detected which prevents output from being produced). Later, when the output routine is written, a test must be included to determine if output is to be produced. For example:

```
MOVE 'OK' TO RECORD-STATUS.
PERFORM VALIDATION-ROUTINE.

OUTPUT-ROUTINE.
    IF RECORD-STATUS-OK
        PERFORM WRITE-ROUTINE.
```

Here if an error is detected in VALIDATION-ROUTINE it will change the value of RECORD-STATUS which is then tested in OUTPUT-ROUTINE. This type of coding is common in structured programming.

Initializing Data Items

Indicators and other variables should be initialized in the PROCEDURE DIVISION rather than via VALUE clauses in the DATA DIVISION. The advantages of improved readability (i.e., the reader of the PROCEDURE DIVISION won't have to refer to the DATA DIVISION to determine initial values of variables) and program reexecution without program reload outweigh the disadvantage of the extra machine instructions required for initialization in the PROCEDURE DIVISION. If your compiler has the INITIALIZE statement, use it. It is a readable, concise way to set variables to initial values. If you don't have INITIALIZE, use MOVE, and perhaps add a comment.

Constants, on the other hand, should be declared in the DATA DIVISION with a VALUE clause. This is better than using actual values in computational statements. By using the name of a constant value, the intent of the statement is stated more precisely. It also is easier to change the value later on, if necessary. This is especially true where the constant appears several times in the routine. Thus, instead of writing

```
MULTIPLY SALARY BY .14 GIVING TAX.
```

we define an item such as MINIMUM-TAX-RATE, give it a VALUE of .14, and write the procedure statement as

```
MULTIPLY SALARY BY MINIMUM-TAX-RATE GIVING TAX.
```

Thus, should the tax rate go down (ha!), only the DATA DIVISION entry needs to be changed.

IMPROVING READABILITY

Another aspect of structured programming is the readability of the program listing. Programs that are formatted in a standard way are easier to read and modify.

Page Layout

EJECT, if available, should be used to provide new pages for segments and divisions. In the DATA DIVISION, record descriptions requiring more than one page of source listing should begin on a new page. Several record descriptions may appear on one page providing they fit completely on that page.

Because paragraphs are invoked rather than fallen into, each paragraph becomes a separate entity, and the termination needs to be more obvious. The SKIP command or blank lines can be used to separate paragraphs on the same page. Two or three blank lines between paragraphs make the listing easier to read.

Although there may be times when the order of execution of paragraphs is variable or unknown, where possible, paragraphs should appear in the order in which they will execute. It is the best order for reading as well as for operating in a virtual-storage environment. Extra paragraph names should not be used.

Comments

In recent years there has been a growing disillusionment with comments and their value to the reader, especially in COBOL programs. In many cases comments simply repeat what the code says. For example, in the following code

```
COMPUTE TOTAL = ON-HAND + RECEIPTS.
***         RECEIPTS ARE ADDED TO AMOUNT ON HAND.
```

the comment adds nothing to the readability of the program. In fact, in some ways it detracts from readability because it tends to break the flow of the eye and the mind as the reader peruses the listing. Comments that contradict the code cause confusion and waste the reader's time trying to determine which is wrong—the comment or the code. Inconsistent comments typically occur because the source code was changed during the debugging phase or subsequent program modification but the comment was not correspondingly altered.

Sometimes comments are vague because little thought was given to how an annotation should be expressed. Another problem with comments is that there may be a tendency to justify tricky code on the basis that there are comments to explain what is happening. This could make unreadable code more likely.

A better approach is to make the code so apparent and unambiguous that there is little need for explanation. Structured programming *reduces* the need for comments. When comments are included, they should add information that cannot be obtained by the code itself. These comments should be reviewed later to ensure that they are still

applicable if the program has been altered. A REMARKS entry in the IDENTIFICA-
TION DIVISION should be included to acquaint the reader with the overall purpose of
the module and its method of solution. These remarks could be several pages long.
Introductory comments should also be included at the beginning of significant segments. If they are general in nature, they should remain valid and consistent with the
code, even if that code is subsequently modified.

Data Names

Because COBOL data names may be up to 30 characters long, select names that convey
as much information about that data item as possible. Arbitrarily selected acronyms and
abbreviations should be avoided. Some acronyms, such as EOF for end-of-file or YTD
for year-to-date, are commonly used and typically unambiguous. An acronym such as
INV-NO is ambiguous. (Is it *invoice number* or *inventory number*?) An abbreviation
such as OVTM for *overtime* should be avoided because even the programmer who
selected the abbreviation might later forget what it stood for. Anyone else seeing this
type of abbreviation for the first time would not immediately infer its meaning. One
approach is for an installation to create a list of allowable acronyms and abbreviations.
    Another idea is to use similar data names for items that are logically related.
Prefixes or suffixes can be appended to indicate not only the *connection* but also the
purpose of similar data items. For example, if you have a computational data item, say

DEPARTMENT-SALES-COMP

and it is to be totaled, then a prefix could be added. For example:

TOTAL-DEPARTMENT-SALES-COMP

If the previous data items are also to appear in an edited format, then suffixes might be
changed as follows:

DEPARTMENT-SALES-PRINT
TOTAL-DEPARTMENT-SALES-PRINT

(Or, assuming that abbreviations of DEPT for DEPARTMENT and P as a suffix for
PRINT are allowed, the last entry could be written TOTAL-DEPT-SALES-P.)
    The same approach of adding prefixes and suffixes could be applied to paragraph
names. In addition they should be the only entry on the line to make them stand out and
separate them from preceding paragraphs. A technique making paragraph names easier
to find is to prefix them with a number. This could be a sequence number or it could be
a number that indicates the page on which the paragraph appears. This is particularly
useful for PERFORMs which refer to paragraphs on other pages. Numbers can be
assigned in multiples of ten or one hundred to allow for future paragraph additions. The
first two digits could represent the page on which the paragraph appears and the

remaining digit(s) the location on the page. Of course, if paragraphs are moved, then the names as well as the number references must be changed to preserve the usefulness of the numbering system.

Indentation

Indentation and alignment of code highlight program logic. In the PROCEDURE DIVISION it is an aid to following logic. Statements which are logically related should be physically grouped by a given amount of indentation. Some formatting suggestions are made here. What is important is not that these conventions be followed, but that a *set of conventions be established* for all programmers in an installation.

A standard *indentation unit* should be defined so that conventions can be expressed in terms of one or more of these units. Two to four columns is a convenient size for an indentation unit.

The various columns in the A margin should be used to distinguish between different types of entries. Thus, division names should begin in column 8, section names in column 9, and paragraph names in column 10.

Identification Division   The IDENTIFICATION DIVISION should contain a descriptive name for the program. Also, as previously mentioned, it should contain a REMARKS section describing the module.

Environment Division   The FILE-CONTROL paragraph, as other paragraphs, should begin in column 10. Each SELECT statement should appear on a separate line and should be aligned in column 12. The ASSIGN clause should be on the same line as the SELECT. If other clauses are to be used, such as ACCESS or RESERVE, they should begin on a new line; thus, they will be aligned in column 16. Similarly, the I-O-CONTROL paragraph should begin in column 10. The clauses pertaining to it should start on a new line and begin in column 12.

Data Division   File Description entries should begin with FD in column 10. This is followed by two blanks and then the file name (column 14). Each clause pertaining to the file should be on a separate line, aligned one indentation unit to the right of the file name. Thus, with an indentation unit of four columns, they would begin in column 18. If any clauses are too long to fit on one line, the continuation should be two indentation units to the right of the start of the clause.

Level 01 and level 77 items should start with the level number in column 10, followed by two blanks and then the data name (column 14). Lower level numbers should be one indentation unit to the right of the one above. If four is used as the unit, each new level number will be aligned with the name of the higher level element.

It is an aid to the reader if all PICTURE clauses are aligned. Thus, place them further to the right, say column 40, so that even the lower level data names will not overlap the PICTURE clause. Thus, elementary items at whatever level will have the

PICTURE clauses aligned. If the level is so deep or the name is so long that the PICTURE cannot begin in column 40, then the clause should be placed in column 40 of the subsequent line. Other clauses, such as USAGE or VALUE, should all be aligned starting in column 52. If a continuation is needed, it should start in column 44.

Procedure Division   Each statement should start a new line. To enhance readability and modifiability, some statements should be continued on one or more lines even though their length may not require it. If a statement requires continuation, then the continuation should be two indentation units to the right of the start of the statement. Break the statement at a logical point rather than crowd a line. For example:

```
IF MASTER-FILE-EOF = 'Y'
      OR TRANSACTION-CUSTOMER-NUMBER = HIGH-VALUES
```

is easier to read and change than

```
IF MASTER-FILE-EOF = 'Y' OR TRANSACTION-CUSTOMER-NUMBER =
      HIGH-VALUES
```

The statements on the true branch of the IF will be offset one indentation unit.

```
IF LINE-COUNT = 50
      PERFORM HEADING-ROUTINE
      MOVE 0 TO LINE-COUNT.
```

For a nested IF, statements pertaining to it will be indented a further indentation unit. The ELSE is aligned with its IF, and the statements under it are also indented, thereby aligning them with the statements of the IF.

Statements which refer to several data names or file names should have each item on a new line with the names aligned. Thus, MOVE, OPEN, and CLOSE, when used with a list should appear as follows:

```
OPEN   INPUT MASTER-FILE-CUSTOMER
             TRANSACTION-FILE
      OUTPUT UPDATED-REPORT.

MOVE ZERO TO TRANSACTIONS-PROCESSED
             INVALID-TRANSACTION
             TOTAL-TRANSACTION-RECORDS.

CLOSE MASTER-FILE-CUSTOMER
      TRANSACTION-FILE.
```

Similarly, when a GO TO DEPENDING ON is used in a CASE structure, the paragraph names should be on separate lines aligned as follows:

```
            GO TO NORMAL-PROCESSING-ROUTINE
                  EXCEPTION-PROCESSING-ROUTINE
                  ERROR-PROCESSING-ROUTINE
               DEPENDING ON EDIT-CODE.
```

The AT END or INVALID KEY portion of the READ statement should be two indentation units from the READ. Similarly, the ADVANCING, END-OF-PAGE, or INVALID KEY options are indented two indentation units from a WRITE.

CASE STUDY

To illustrate some of the principles covered in this chapter, we will show a COBOL version of the program described in Chapter 2. This program updates a sequential file that contains inventory status records. The hierarchy chart for this program is shown in Figure 9-10. The program is in Figure 9-11 on pages 214–219.

Four types of transactions are processed against the inventory file:

- Add a new record to the master file
- Delete a record from the master file
- Update an existing record for *issues*
- Update an existing record for *receipts*

It is possible to update a record just added or to delete a record just updated. Master records not matched by a transaction record are copied to the new file.

Although the example is realistic, several intentional omissions have been made so that it would fit within this text. No data editing or sequence checking, for example, has been included. Usually a program would check to see that the transactions were in sequential order and that additions preceded updates. These and other tests might enlarge many of the routines so that what appears as relatively small paragraphs in the example would probably be full-page segments. Or some of the routines might even be large and complex enough to warrant compilation as separate modules (e.g., data validation).

Function and control flow are depicted in the hierarchy chart in Figure 9-10. Its organization made it easy to debug and modify. For example, the program was originally written without the delete capability. Later, when it was added, all that was needed, in addition to the paragraph to process deletes, was the test in the main processing paragraph for a delete code and a PERFORM of that paragraph. Also, consider the changes required to process the file randomly instead of sequentially. All that is needed, in addition to the paragraph to read the master file, is a change to the paragraph to test for a matching record.

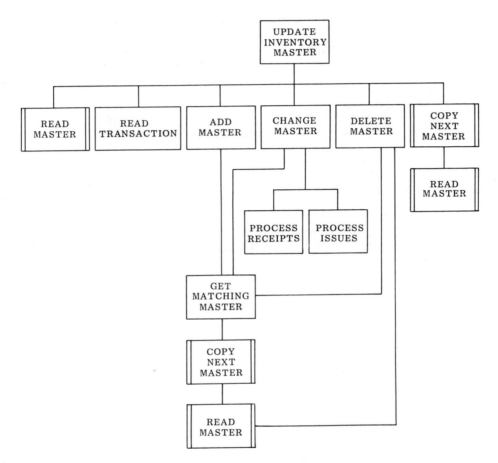

Figure 9-10. Hierarchy chart for inventory update example

```
IDENTIFICATION DIVISION.
 PROGRAM-ID. INVENTRY.

ENVIRONMENT DIVISION.
 INPUT-OUTPUT SECTION.
  FILE-CONTROL.
        SELECT EXCEPTIONS     ASSIGN TO UT-S-OUT.
        SELECT NEWINV         ASSIGN TO DA-3330-S-NEWMAS.
        SELECT OLDINV         ASSIGN TO DA-3330-S-OLDMAS.
        SELECT TRANS          ASSIGN TO UT-S-TRANS.

DATA DIVISION.
 FILE SECTION.
  FD  EXCEPTIONS
        RECORD CONTAINS 80 CHARACTERS
        RECORDING MODE IS F
        LABEL RECORD IS OMITTED
        DATA RECORD IS PRINT-LINE.
  01  PRINT-LINE               PIC X(80).

  FD  NEWINV
        BLOCK CONTAINS 0 RECORDS
        RECORD CONTAINS 63 CHARACTERS
        RECORDING MODE IS F
        LABEL RECORD IS STANDARD
        DATA RECORD IS NEW-MASTER.
  01  NEW-MASTER               PIC X(63).

  FD  OLDINV
        BLOCK CONTAINS 0 RECORDS
        RECORD CONTAINS 63 CHARACTERS
        RECORDING MODE IS F
        LABEL RECORD IS STANDARD
        DATA RECORD IS OLD-MASTER.
  01  OLD-MASTER               PIC X(63).

  FD  TRANS
        BLOCK CONTAINS 0 RECORDS
        RECORD CONTAINS 80 CHARACTERS
        RECORDING MODE IS F
        LABEL RECORD IS STANDARD
        DATA RECORD IS TRANSACT.
  01  TRANSACT                 PIC X(80).

 WORKING-STORAGE SECTION.

  77  NEW-RECORD-ADDED         PIC X.
  77  OLD-MASTER-EOF           PIC X.
```

```
77  TRANS-EOF                       PIC X.
77  TRANS-MASTER-MATCH              PIC X.
77  DUPLICATE-RECORD                PIC X(80)      VALUE
        "ATTEMPT TO ADD DUPLICATE RECORD.".
77  INVALID-CODE                    PIC X(80)      VALUE
        "INVALID CODE.".
77  NO-MASTER                       PIC X(80)      VALUE
        "NO MASTER RECORD FOUND FOR".
77  TRANS-EOF-MESSAGE               PIC X(80)      VALUE
        "END OF FILE ON TRANSACTION FILE.".
77  EMPTY-MASTER-FILE               PIC X(80)      VALUE
        "MASTER FILE CONTAINS NO RECORDS.".
77  TRANSACTIONS-PROCESSED          PIC 999.

01  FINAL-MESSAGE.
    05  TOTAL                       PIC ZZZZ9.
    05  FILLER                      PIC X(75)      VALUE
        "RECORDS PROCESSED.".

01  NEW-MASTER-REC.
    02  ACTIVITY-CODE               PIC 9.
    02  NEW-MASTER-KEY              PIC X(6).
    02  DESCRIPTION                 PIC X(20).
    02  QTY-ON-HAND                 PIC 99999      COMP.
    02  TOTAL-ISSUES                PIC 99999      COMP.
    02  TOTAL-RECEIPTS              PIC 99999      COMP.
    02  QTY-ON-ORDER                PIC 99999      COMP.
    02  ORDER-POINT                 PIC 999        COMP.
    02  REORDER-QTY                 PIC 99999      COMP.
    02  TOTAL-COST                  PIC 9(5)V99    COMP.
    02  AVERAGE-UNIT-COST           PIC 9999V999   COMP.
    02  DATE-OF-LAST-ISSUE          PIC X(6).
01  OLD-MASTER-REC                  PIC X(63).

01  TRANSACTION.
    05  TRANS-CODE                  PIC 9.
        88  ADD-TRANS                              VALUE 1.
        88  RECEIPT-TRANS                          VALUE 2.
        88  ISSUES-TRANS                           VALUE 3.
        88  DELETE-TRANS                           VALUE 4.
    05  TRANS-KEY                   PIC X(6).
    05  FILLER                      PIC X(73).

01  ADDITION REDEFINES TRANSACTION.
    05  FILLER                      PIC X(7).
    05  DESCRIPTION                 PIC X(20).
    05  QTY-ON-HAND                 PIC 99999.
    05  TOTAL-ISSUES                PIC 99999.
```

```
        05   TOTAL-RECEIPTS              PIC 99999.
        05   QTY-ON-ORDER                PIC 99999.
        05   ORDER-POINT                 PIC 999.
        05   REORDER-QTY                 PIC 99999.
        05   TOTAL-COST                  PIC 99999V99.
        05   AVERAGE-UNIT-COST           PIC 9999V999.
        05   DATE-OF-LAST-ISSUE          PIC X(6).
        05   FILLER                      PIC X(5).

    01  RECEIPTS REDEFINES TRANSACTION.
        05   FILLER                      PIC X(7).
        05   QTY-RECEIVED                PIC 99999.
        05   TOTAL-COST                  PIC 99999V99.
        05   FILLER                      PIC X(61).

    01  ISSUES REDEFINES TRANSACTION.
        05   FILLER                      PIC X(7).
        05   QTY-ISSUED                  PIC 99999.
        05   CUSTOMER-NUMBER             PIC X(6).
        05   DATE-ISSUED                 PIC X(6).
        05   FILLER                      PIC X(56).

PROCEDURE DIVISION.

    10-INVENTORY-UPDATE.
        OPEN INPUT      OLDINV
                        TRANS
             OUTPUT NEWINV
                        EXCEPTIONS.
        MOVE "N" TO OLD-MASTER-EOF
                    TRANS-EOF
                    NEW-RECORD-ADDED.
        MOVE LOW-VALUES TO NEW-MASTER-KEY
                           TRANS-KEY.
        MOVE 0 TO TRANSACTIONS-PROCESSED.

        PERFORM 20-READ-MASTER
        IF OLD-MASTER-EOF = "Y"
            MOVE EMPTY-MASTER-FILE TO PRINT-LINE.
            PERFORM 36-MESSAGE-WRITE.

        PERFORM UNTIL TRANS-EOF = "Y"
            PERFORM 21-READ-TRANS
            IF TRANS-EOF = "N"
                EVALUATE TRANS-CODE
                    WHEN 1 PERFORM 22-ADD-MASTER,
                    WHEN 2 PERFORM 24-CHANGE-MASTER,
                    WHEN 3 PERFORM 24-CHANGE-MASTER,
```

```
            WHEN 4 PERFORM 26-DELETE-MASTER.
            WHEN OTHER PERFORM 29-BAD-CODE,
        END-EVALUATE
    ELSE
        IF NEW-RECORD-ADDED = "Y" AND OLD-MASTER-EOF = "Y"
            WRITE NEW-MASTER FROM NEW-MASTER-REC
            MOVE "N" TO NEW-RECORD-ADDED
        END-IF
    END-IF
END-PERFORM.

PERFORM 28-COPY-NEXT-MASTER UNTIL OLD-MASTER-EOF = "Y".
MOVE TRANSACTIONS-PROCESSED TO TOTAL.
WRITE PRINT-LINE FROM FINAL-MESSAGE AFTER ADVANCING 3.
CLOSE TRANS
        OLDINV
        NEWINV
        EXCEPTIONS.

STOP RUN.


20-READ-MASTER.
  READ OLDINV INTO OLD-MASTER-REC
        AT END MOVE "Y" TO OLD-MASTER-EOF
                MOVE LOW-VALUES TO NEW-MASTER-KEY.
  IF OLD-MASTER-EOF = "N"
        MOVE OLD-MASTER-REC TO NEW-MASTER-REC
  ELSE
        MOVE HIGH-VALUES TO NEW-MASTER-KEY.


21-READ-TRANS.
  READ TRANS INTO TRANSACTION
        AT END WRITE PRINT-LINE FROM TRANS-EOF-MESSAGE
                AFTER ADVANCING 2
                MOVE "Y" TO TRANS-EOF
        END-READ.


22-ADD-MASTER.
  MOVE " " TO TRANS-MASTER-MATCH.
    PERFORM 30-GET-MATCHING-MASTER UNTIL TRANS-MASTER-MATCH = "Y"
                                    OR TRANS-MASTER-MATCH = "N"
  IF TRANS-MASTER-MATCH = "N"
        MOVE CORRESPONDING ADDITION TO NEW-MASTER-REC
        MOVE TRANS-KEY TO NEW-MASTER-KEY
        MOVE "Y" TO NEW-RECORD-ADDED
  ELSE
        MOVE DUPLICATE-RECORD TO PRINT-LINE
        PERFORM 36-MESSAGE-WRITE.
```

```
24-CHANGE-MASTER.
    MOVE " " TO TRANS-MASTER-MATCH.
    PERFORM 30-GET-MATCHING-MASTER UNTIL TRANS-MASTER-MATCH = "Y"
                                      OR TRANS-MASTER-MATCH = "N"
    IF TRANS-MASTER-MATCH = "N"
        MOVE NO-MASTER TO PRINT-LINE
        PERFORM 36-MESSAGE-WRITE
    ELSE
        IF RECEIPT-TRANS
            PERFORM 32-PROCESS-RECEIPTS
        ELSE IF ISSUES-TRANS
            PERFORM 34-PROCESS-ISSUES.

26-DELETE-MASTER.
    MOVE " " TO TRANS-MASTER-MATCH.
    PERFORM 30-GET-MATCHING-MASTER UNTIL TRANS-MASTER-MATCH = "Y"
                                      OR TRANS-MASTER-MATCH = "N"
    IF TRANS-MASTER-MATCH = "N"
        MOVE NO-MASTER TO PRINT-LINE
        PERFORM 36-MESSAGE-WRITE
    ELSE
        IF NEW-RECORD-ADDED = "Y"
            MOVE "N" TO NEW-RECORD-ADDED
            MOVE OLD-MASTER-REC TO NEW-MASTER-REC
        ELSE
            PERFORM 20-READ-MASTER.

28-COPY-NEXT-MASTER.
    WRITE NEW-MASTER FROM NEW-MASTER-REC.
    IF NEW-RECORD-ADDED = "Y"
        MOVE "N" TO NEW-RECORD-ADDED
        MOVE OLD-MASTER-REC TO NEW-MASTER-REC
    ELSE
        PERFORM 20-READ-MASTER.

29-BAD-CODE.
    MOVE INVALID-CODE TO PRINT-LINE
    PERFORM 36-MESSAGE-WRITE.
```

```
30-GET-MATCHING-MASTER.
    IF TRANS-KEY LESS NEW-MASTER-KEY
        MOVE "N" TO TRANS-MASTER-MATCH
    ELSE IF TRANS-KEY EQUAL NEW-MASTER-KEY
        MOVE "Y" TO TRANS-MASTER-MATCH
    ELSE IF TRANS-KEY GREATER NEW-MASTER-KEY
        IF OLD-MASTER-EOF = "Y"
            MOVE "N" TO TRANS-MASTER-MATCH
            IF NEW-RECORD-ADDED = "Y"
                WRITE NEW-MASTER FROM NEW-MASTER-REC
                MOVE "N" TO NEW-RECORD-ADDED
            ELSE
                NEXT SENTENCE
        ELSE
            PERFORM 28-COPY-NEXT-MASTER.

32-PROCESS-RECEIPTS.
    ADD QTY-RECEIVED TO QTY-ON-HAND IN NEW-MASTER-REC.
    ADD QTY-RECEIVED TO TOTAL-RECEIPTS IN NEW-MASTER-REC.
    SUBTRACT QTY-RECEIVED FROM QTY-ON-ORDER IN NEW-MASTER-REC.
    ADD TOTAL-COST IN RECEIPTS TO TOTAL-COST IN NEW-MASTER-REC.
    DIVIDE TOTAL-COST IN NEW-MASTER-REC
            BY QTY-ON-HAND IN NEW-MASTER-REC
            GIVING AVERAGE-UNIT-COST IN NEW-MASTER-REC.

34-PROCESS-ISSUES.
    SUBTRACT QTY-ISSUED FROM QTY-ON-HAND IN NEW-MASTER-REC.
    ADD QTY-ISSUED TO TOTAL-ISSUES IN NEW-MASTER-REC.
    COMPUTE TOTAL-COST IN NEW-MASTER-REC =
            TOTAL-COST IN NEW-MASTER-REC −
            (QTY-ISSUED * AVERAGE-UNIT-COST IN NEW-MASTER-REC).
    MOVE DATE-ISSUED TO DATE-OF-LAST-ISSUE IN NEW-MASTER-REC.

36-MESSAGE-WRITE.
    WRITE PRINT-LINE AFTER ADVANCING 2.
    WRITE PRINT-LINE FROM TRANSACTION AFTER ADVANCING 1.
```

Figure 9-11. Sample COBOL Program

SUMMARY

Segmenting

1. Modules should be separately compiled subprograms and pass data with USING.
2. Each segment is no more than a listing page of code.
3. The segments should be coded and tested in a top-down manner. That is, the top segment is coded first and tested with stubs for the other segments.
4. All paragraphs should be invoked explicitly—no falling into or out of paragraphs.
5. Avoid PERFORM THRU and PERFORM of sections, except where necessary (e.g., when using GO TO DEPENDING ON for CASE).
6. All paragraphs should return control to the invoker.

Structuring

The forward flow of the logic should be maintained. The IF statement is used for the choice structure, with or without the ELSE. When using nested IFs the following should be observed: The depth of nesting should be limited; NOTs, compounds, and implied subjects and operators should be avoided wherever possible and limited elsewhere; the entire nest should be on one page; use PERFORM instead of GOTO; and meaningful names should be used for items tested.

Repetition is done by PERFORM UNTIL (or WHILE, if your compiler has it). CASE structure is best with EVALUATE; if not available, use IFs or GO TO DEPENDING ON.

Programming Considerations

Avoid or severely restrict the use of the following statements: ENTRY, STOP RUN, ALTER, GO TO DEPENDING ON, GOTO. Careful consideration should be given to indicators: Use one indicator for only one purpose; use meaningful names and meaningful values; and use only as many as necessary in a program.

Initialize data variables and indicators in the PROCEDURE DIVISION. Use names for constants and initialize in the DATA DIVISION.

Improving Readability

Start divisions and segments on new pages. Use blank lines to separate paragraphs. Use comments at the beginning of a module and when necessary for segments or paragraphs. Use self-defining data names. Indent statements within the PROCEDURE DIVISION to highlight the logic. Avoid literals.

REVIEW QUESTIONS AND EXERCISES

1. What are some arguments in favor of dividing a module into one-page segments? Arguments against?

2. What problems are created in a paragraph that is sometimes PER-FORMed and sometimes *fallen into*?

3. In which situations is PERFORM THRU acceptable?

4. The following pseudo code handles inquiries into a personnel file. The inquiries ask for date of hire and/or current position. Translate this pseudo code into COBOL code.

```
Read inquiry
IF valid inquiry
    IF hire request
        process date of hire response
    ENDIF
    IF job request
        process position request
    ENDIF
ENDIF
```

5. Write a set of restrictions you think will make a nested conditional readable and acceptable.

6. If you don't have EVALUATE, would you use GO TO DEPENDING ON or IFs to implement the CASE structure? Why?

7. Modify the sample program in Figure 9-11 to process the master file randomly.

8. Modily the program in Figure 9-11 to handle sequence checking on the transaction file.

9. Modify the program in Figure 9-11 to handle *two* input transaction files. One file contains additions and deletions; the other file contains the update records (issues and receipts). Both files are sorted into ascending sequence.

10

Structured Programming Using Pascal

"A basic structural design underlies every kind of writing."

William Strunk, Jr.[1]

In 1971, Nicklaus Wirth published "The Programming Language Pascal,"[2] which served as the definition of Pascal. The intent was to create a language which would be useful for teaching "programming as a systematic discipline based on certain fundamental concepts clearly and naturally reflected by the language."[3] Given this goal, Pascal was designed to be simple but reasonably powerful, with clear and understandable constructs.

To ensure that the language did not get out of control, certain restrictions in capability were made. Some features were expressly excluded to avoid inconsistencies, while others were included to enhance clarity and flexibility. It was intended that students using Pascal while initially learning programming would go on to utilize many of the good programming practices which are suggested, if not demanded, by various Pascal features. For these reasons, Pascal has turned out to be almost the quintessential structured programming language.

Not only has Pascal's popularity grown in academia, but its elegance has won it many proponents within the industry. Moving the language out of the classroom has, of course, spawned many different "dialects." Most of these include various extensions—some very useful, others not. Recognizing the need to preserve the good features of Pascal and, at the same time, provide reasonable, consistent extensions to Wirth's original language, the International Standards Organization (ISO) defined a "Standard Pascal."[4]

We will use the ISO Standard as a guideline, occasionally referring to various common extensions where appropriate. One exception is the use of an underscore (_)

---

[1]From *The Elements of Style*, 3rd ed., by William Strunk, Jr., and E. B. White. Copyright © 1979 by Macmillan Publishing Company. Reprinted by permission of the publisher.
[2]N. Wirth, "The Programming Language Pascal," *Acta Informatica*, 1, 35-63, 1971.
[3]K. Jensen, N. Wirth, "Pascal User Manual and Report," 3rd ed., Springer-Verlag, New York, 1985.
[4]Ibid.

as a legal character in identifier names (in examples). Although this is not standard, many compilers provide it (or similar special characters) as an extension to enhance name readability.

It is assumed that the reader has a general understanding of the language so that no additional detailed descriptions will be provided.

While Pascal has many useful features, the following can be considered the most important and those by which the language is generally characterized:

- strongly typed
- user-defined types
- logical constructs
- block-structured
- readable

The last four are discussed in more detail later in this chapter. The first item, strong typing, is perhaps Pascal's most notorious feature. It provides programs with great logical consistency, while occasionally requiring a little more coding than one might like. However, it is a concept which fits in very well with structured programming.

Pascal is a strongly typed language. By that we mean that when data values (variables, functions and constants) are compared, assigned, operated upon, passed as parameters, or otherwise referenced type compatibility must always be preserved. A data value's type is therefore a significant attribute which determines the ways in which that value may be used. By contrast, in the C language the concept of types either does not exist or is not significant, with the compatibility issue easily circumvented.

For example, if you declare one variable to be a character and another to be an integer, you cannot directly add the two. To do so, you would first have to change the type of the character to an integer. The effort to do so may indicate that this is not really what you want to do. The importance of strong typing is that the compiler can help find errors in your program (both logical and typographical) where data is being misused that might otherwise be difficult to locate.

PROGRAM LAYOUT

Modularity

As discussed in Chapter 3, decomposing your programming task into small pieces can help organize your thinking and provide you with a clear overall design.

In Pascal, a module corresponds to a procedure or function. The former is used to carry out a specific task, while the latter is used to calculate some value (not necessarily arithmetic) and return it. (Throughout this chapter we refer to both procedures and functions as *modules*. Where a distinction is needed, the appropriate form is specified.)

The format of procedures and functions is identical to that of the program as a whole. That is, they may contain constant and type definitions, label and variable declarations, as well as other procedures and functions. In addition, they may make use of parameters which may be passed in one of two ways—by value or by reference.

If only the value of the parameter is needed (i.e., the module uses it but does not change it), then you can pass it by value. When this is done, a copy of the evaluated actual parameter is made available to the module. Even if the module modifies this copy, it has no effect on the original value of the actual parameter. This is the default and should be used unless the procedure explicitly needs to alter the actual parameter's value. In that case, it should be passed by reference (by prefixing the formal parameter name in the procedure declaration with the keyword **var**).

Note that we referred only to the use of **var** parameters in procedures, specifically excluding them in functions. Functions should only be used to return a single value—all of their parameters should be passed by value. If a module returns more than one result or updates any actual parameters, then that module should be coded as a procedure. This helps to preserve the distinction between the two different forms of modules.

It may be tempting to code a module which should be a procedure as a function which returns an error flag—TRUE if the module completed successfully and FALSE if there was an error. This allows you to call the routine and check the error return value in one statement, for example:

```
if get_data (data_file, record, sequence_num) then
    process_data (record, sequence_num)
else
    error (BAD_DATA);
```

However, the code size savings (if any) over separate call and error-check statements is small and the error information returned is limited. It is better to return the error status as a parameter. Then it can take on any of several values, including, for instance, NO_ERROR. Also, you might want to call this routine when there is no chance of an error. As a function, you would be forced to use it in an otherwise meaningless expression. As a procedure, you can choose whether or not to check the error status.

Functions should not modify global variables. To do so creates "side effects" and is bad programming practice. Functions are assumed to accept data and return a result. This model is violated if the function changes the state of the program.

Information Hiding

It is often desirable to prevent general access to modules which carry out a specific action or set of actions. Generally these private modules' local data should be kept hidden, too. This concept is called information hiding and was discussed in Chapter 2. The private modules are called *producers* and those that use them are called *consumers* or *clients*.

Information hiding is accomplished in Pascal by nesting these modules, and their data, inside other modules—that is, declaring them within another procedure or function. In this manner, only the parent module, or other modules nested within the same parent at the same level, can access these "local" modules and data.

Use of this feature is particularly appropriate when a data structure might change after the program is partially, or completely, implemented. Ideally, all operations on this structure would be accomplished through a parent interface module (and its enclosed modules), and the definition of the data structure would be unknown to any outside module. Then all that has to be done is the redesign and recoding of those local routines, with little or no modification to the consumers. In Pascal, the actual definition of the type has to be visible to the consumers, but the interface can be restricted in the described manner.

With module nesting some special formatting must be made so that nested procedures and functions can be distinguished from those that aren't nested. Additional indentation, (commented) special characters separating nested routines, and a comment indicating the routine is nested can all be used to accomplish this.

Figure 10-1 provides an example of the use of local modules for complex number arithmetic. The parent routine, *complex*, takes as parameters an operation and two complex operands. The operation is of an enumerated type. The complex result of that operation on those operands is returned through a **var** parameter.

Module Grouping

Grouping logically associated modules into larger development units can segregate unrelated sections of the program which can then be developed and maintained independently.

Unfortunately, in standard Pascal, there is no easy way to accomplish this goal. One possible extension is to allow a source file inclusion compiler directive (similar to PL/I's %INCLUDE or C's #include preprocessor command) or even to allow separate compilation of modules, or groups of modules. If your compiler doesn't have one of these features, you can simulate it in the following manner: Logically group your procedures and functions into separate source files. Keep a listing of which file each routine is located in. Then, before compiling, combine the files. (Depending on your environment, that may or may not be an easy thing to accomplish.)

Another point is that without separate compilation, or some nonstandard means of accessing externally defined routines, the use of standard or general libraries is rather inconvenient. The only way to do it is to have them available in source form, which then leaves them open to unchecked modification.

If all else fails, you can still logically group routines together in one file, with large comments delimiting the different sections. The intent is to create these large, relatively independent pieces of the program which represent logical and separate parts which can then be thought of, implemented and/or maintained independently.

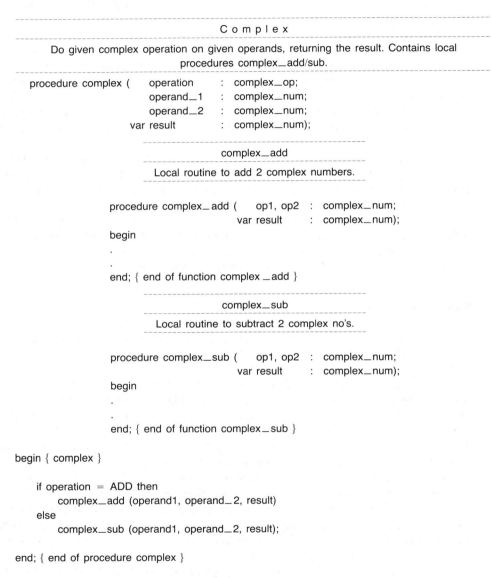

```
                              C o m p l e x
Do given complex operation on given operands, returning the result. Contains local
                      procedures complex_add/sub.

procedure complex (      operation      :  complex_op;
                         operand_1      :  complex_num;
                         operand_2      :  complex_num;
                    var result          :  complex_num);


                            complex_add

                  Local routine to add 2 complex numbers.


            procedure complex_add (    op1, op2  :  complex_num;
                                   var result    :  complex_num);
            begin
            .

            .
            end; { end of function complex _add }

                            complex_sub

                  Local routine to subtract 2 complex no's.


            procedure complex_sub (    op1, op2  :  complex_num;
                                   var result    :  complex_num);
            begin
            .

            .
            end; { end of function complex _sub }

begin { complex }

   if operation = ADD then
       complex_add (operand1, operand_2, result)
   else
       complex_sub (operand1, operand_2, result);

end; { end of procedure complex }
```

Figure 10-1. Example of local modules

Regardless of how you attempt to group modules, Pascal requires that all objects be declared before they are used. Consequently, the order in which modules are declared (i.e., where they appear in your source file) is significant. This makes it difficult to organize your modules in a convenient format for locating them in large listings (e.g., alphabetically). However, Pascal provides an escape in the form of forward declarations. This enables you to declare a module, including its name, formal parameters and, if it is a function, the type of value it returns, without providing the actual body of the module until later. (This was originally included to allow two modules to refer to each other; however, it suits our purpose in this situation as well.) Using the forward declarations, you can declare all your procedures and functions up front (in fact, you can even split them up into the larger sections for easier reference), then list the bodies in alphabetical order.

Readability

Pascal is a free form language; the physical appearance of the program does not affect its content. Statements may be split across lines and multiple statements may be put on one line. This latter feature should be used only when the statements are very simple and similar. An example of this would be initializing indices and counters to zero:

```
count1 := 0; count2 := 0;
```

You are, of course, free to choose your own formatting rules, combining indentation, capitalization and spacing in a consistent manner to make the program easier to read and understand. This is less significant in Pascal than in some other, more cryptic languages because Pascal is generally considered an easy language to read. However, as a general rule, and considering Pascal's verbosity, judicious and consistent use of indentation and blank lines can clarify the nesting of blocks (e.g., in the **if** and **while** statements) and generally make the program easier to read.

It is recommended that any given project adopt a standard set of formatting guidelines to ensure consistent usage in all of its code. A list of sample formatting rules is provided as follows:

1. Begin the program with a comment block listing its name, purpose, author, compiler and system (including version numbers); input and output files; and modification history (including date, what was changed and by whom).

2. Organize the modules within the source file alphabetically. Use forward declarations for all procedures and functions (they, too, should be in alphabetical order). Begin the body of each module with a short comment describing what it does, including input and output formal parameters, and the value returned if it is a function. Make sure each module begins on a separate page (unless there is a series of short and related routines). This can be accomplished by embedding a form feed character in the procedure

heading comment. Follow the closing **end** of a module with a comment containing its name:

```
{ end of procedure/function x }
```

3. Variables should be declared by type and then in alphabetical order, with the colons aligned. A variable's purpose should be clear from its name. If that is not possible its definition should be accompanied by a comment explaining its usage.

4. Put blanks:

- around all binary operators (but not unary), including assignment
- if a module has formal parameters, put a blank between its name and the parameter list
- before and after almost all parenthesized expressions
- on either side of the begin- and end-comment characters
- after every comma in type, set and parameter lists

Put blank lines:

- before and after the module definition heading (i.e., name and parameter list)
- after local variable declarations in modules
- between options in a **case** statement
- before and after multiple-line compound statements (e.g., **if/else** and **for**)
- anywhere else it can provide increased readability

5. Align assignment operators in consecutive statements.

6. Indent a constant amount (e.g., two spaces) at each nested level, such as within a **while** statement. Always align the left-most character of all statements which are at the same nesting level. In many interactive text editors, a TAB can be used for this purpose.

7. Put the opening **begin** of a block on the following line, indented. Then indent the statement group again, beginning on the following line. Finally, align the closing **end** with the **begin**. For example,

```
for count := 1 to max_values do
  begin
    value := get_data ();
    if value in valid_set then
      begin
        display (count, value);
        process (value);
      end; { if }
  end; { for }
```

8. The statements associated with each case constant in a **case** statement should be aligned.

9. When statements are too long, split them at a logical place and align the overlapped portion indented from left-most character.

Comments in Pascal are allowed anywhere a word or symbol may exist, and may be split across lines. Debate exists in the industry as to the preferred manner of comments (e.g., block vs. line); however, block comments at the beginning of any module describing its action, including its parameters, should generally suffice. Individual line comments are sometimes necessary, however, to describe or highlight subtle or machine-dependent code. The most important consideration is that comments be accurate and descriptive, without detracting from the readability of the program.

Note that Pascal defines two different begin-comment and end-comment tokens. They are the left curly bracket { or left-parenthesis and asterisk pair (*, and right curly bracket } or asterisk and right-parenthesis pair *), respectively.[5] The definition states that they are interchangeable, although many compilers do not treat them that way. Even if your compiler considers them interchangeable, it is still a good idea to stick to one form of comment symbol to maintain consistency. You won't have to remember which form of comment you used each time, and it makes it easier to find the matching comment delimiters. If your compiler does not consider both forms identical, consistent use of one form is still a good idea.

Statement Grouping

Pascal is a block-structured language, enabling you to group several statements together (delimited by a **begin/end** pair) and have the compiler consider them as one logical entity. The **for**, **while**, **if** and **with** statements often control the execution of several statements grouped in this manner. Note that the statements inside a **repeat/until** statement are automatically in a block, eliminating the need for a **begin/end** pair.

As with most free-format languages, Pascal requires a semi-colon to know where one statement ends and the next begins. Note that the semi-colon is a statement *separator*, not a statement *terminator*. Consequently, you do not need to put one after the last statement in a block or after an **end** which is followed by another **end**. While these semi-colons are not required, you may want to put them in anyway to prevent surprise errors when later modifying the program (this is what we will do in the examples in this chapter). Be aware, however, that in some compilers this may cause unusual line numbering (because including an unnecessary semi-colon creates a null statement, which may then be given a line number). Note that you may never put a semi-colon immediately preceding the keyword **else** in an **if** statement.

---

[5]This was because many keypunches and keyboards did not have the '{}' characters.

STRUCTURING PASCAL PROGRAMS

Structuring involves taking the three basic programming structures as well as any additional structures and combining them to accomplish a given function or subfunction. These are briefly reviewed here with Pascal examples.

Sequence Structure

The sequence structure consists of two process blocks in which control flows from one box to the next in sequence. A box could represent a single statement, such as assignment, or a group of statements. This group might be a logical block (delimited by a **begin/end** pair) or a procedure call.

Choice Structure

The choice structure specifies a test between two alternatives to determine which of two process blocks to execute.

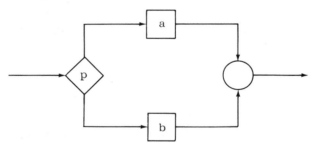

In Pascal, the standard **if/then/else** statement accomplishes this. The format is a single **if/then**, optionally followed by an **else**. The condition must be a Boolean expression. A single statement follows both the **if/then** and **else**, although it could be a block of statements. Here is an example of a simple **if** statement:

```
if value = LAST then
    writeln ('Done.');
```

Note that the condition need not be enclosed in parentheses, although it may be. With complicated conditions, you may find the entire statement easier to read if parentheses are used. For example:

```
if (current_employee^ .manager^ .sal <= get_sal (this_record)) then
    process_mgr (current_employee^ .manager);
```

The statement following the **else** may itself be another **if** statement. Such nesting is often desirable, but it should be handled carefully, with appropriate indentation and meaningful identifier names.

For example:

```
if name = 'George      ' then
       teeth := WOOD

else if name = 'Abe       ' then
       hat := STOVEPIPE

else
       begin
           teeth := NATURAL;
           hat   := NONE
       end;
```

Here is an example of combined sequential and nested **if/then/else's**:

```
(1a)        if (command = ADD) then
                begin
    (2a)            if (rec.kind in employee__set) then
                        begin
                            add__cmd (rec);
                            rec__count [rec.kind] := rec__count [rec.kind] + 1;
                        end
    (2b)            else                                    '
                        error (CANT__ADD__REC)
                end
(1b)        else if (cmd = DELETE) then
                DELETE__CMD (REC)

(1c)        else
                display__help;
```

In this example, note how the nested **if** in (2a) and **else** in (2b) are aligned. In the succeeding sequential statements (1b and 1c), the alignment is different because the second pairing is testing related conditions. This format enhances clarity and eliminates unnecessary indentation. Note that a standard **case** statement could not have been used because there would have been no provision for the last alternative.

Also note that a **begin/end** pair is used around the embedded **if** statement. Syntactically this is not generally necessary, but it can clarify and prevent possible confusion as to which **if** each **else** belongs.

Repetition Structures

Pascal provides both the DOWHILE and DOUNTIL structures. In addition, it provides a simple iteration construct.

DOWHILE Structure   The DOWHILE structure provides basic loop capability by specifying a process that is repeated as long as a given condition is true. The condition is tested before each iteration (including the first one). The diagram is as follows:

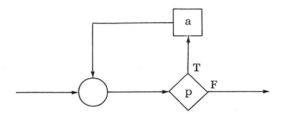

This construct is provided with Pascal's **while** statement. As with the **if** statement, the condition does not need to be enclosed in parentheses, although it is a clarifying option. Here is an example:

```
while lines < page__size do
    begin
        get__line (buffer);
        display__line (buffer);
        lines := lines + 1;
    end;
```

DOUNTIL Structure   The DOUNTIL structure is identical to the DOWHILE, except that the process is continued *until* the given condition is met, and the test is made *after* each execution. The flow diagram for the DOUNTIL is:

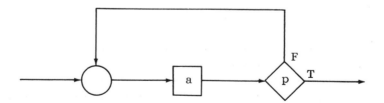

Pascal's **repeat/until** statement handles this. Again, the condition in the **until** part may optionally be enclosed in parentheses. Note that even if the process to be repeated is a block of statements, a **begin/end** pair is NOT required, since the keywords **repeat/until** mark the block already. An example:

```
repeat
    node := node^.next;
    level := level + 1;
until node^.next = nil;
```

ITERATION Structure   Pascal provides a refinement of the DOWHILE structure for general iteration. It is the **for** statement. This gives the programmer an easy method for looping based on a counter, rather than a general condition.

The following is a diagram for a **for** statement, where s is the setting of the index variable i to initial value $v1$, p is the test for $i <= v2$ (**to**) or $i > v2$ (**downto**), a is the process to be repeated and x is the increment (**to**) or decrement (**downto**) of i:

```
for i := v1 to/downto v2 do
    a;
```

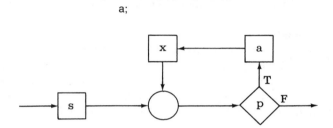

An example of a typical **for** statement is:

```
total_scores := 0;
high_score  := -1;
for i := 1 to class_size do
    begin
        total_scores := total_scores + scores [i];
        if scores [i] > high_score then
            begin
                high_score   := scores [i];
                high_student := i;
            end; {if}
    end; {for}
```

The index variable must be an ordinal type, and the final value must be of a compatible type. The index variable must be declared locally, cannot be altered inside the loop, and has an undefined value upon exiting the loop. In addition, it may only be assigned consecutive values. This is implemented internally with the predefined functions **succ** (successor) and **pred** (predecessor). For example, with integers it increments or decrements by 1. Consequently, to use the **for** statement for looping where the index variable must use something other than consecutive values, either some modifications of the ending value and the index are needed, or you need to use a **repeat** or **while** statement.

In the following example, only the odd-numbered students' scores are accessed:

```
total_scores := 0;
high_score  := -1;
for i := 1 to (class_size + 1)/2 do
    begin
        total_scores := total_scores + scores [i * 2 - 1];
        if scores [i] > high_score then
            begin
                high_score   := scores [i];
                high_student := i;
            end; {if}
    end; {for}
```

Note that this method would not work if the index variable were an enumerated type or a character—a **while** or **repeat** statement would be required.

Premature Loop Exit   Some Pascal extensions define an **exit** statement which can be used to exit a loop (**while**, **repeat** and **for**) before the normal exiting criteria are met. This makes premature exiting easier and is often appropriate for exceptional conditions (such as errors). However, it does not provide any capability not already present in the standard and conflicts with our single entry/single exit concept. Consequently, its use should be limited to those cases where it is specifically called for.

CASE Structure

This structure provides selective execution based on the value of an expression. Although it is just shorthand for a sequence of **if/then/else** statements, it is a clearer construct for cases when a single choice must be made from among several mutually exclusive alternatives. Its diagram is:

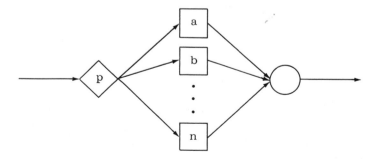

This is implemented with Pascal's **case** statement. Note that each case constant may in fact be a list of constants, which also may include a subrange. The standard does not define a method for dealing with the situation when the case expression is not listed amongst the case constants. Many compilers, however, provide an *otherwise* clause, which acts as a case constant whose value is "anything not covered by the others." If your compiler does not have this extension then you should do one of the following things:

- only use the **case** statement when all possible values can be listed
- test for values out of range before executing the **case** statement
- use a series of **if/then/else** statements instead of the **case**

Whichever you choose, do not use a **case** statement where it is possible for the selector to take on a value which is not explicitly accounted for, even if you are pretty sure it won't occur. If the unexpected happens (and it usually does), any number of undesirable results could occur depending upon your operating system and compiler. You might branch off to some random location, get a run-time error, or just continue to the next statement. You might even find different executions of the program produce different results. In any case, you won't be happy.

Figure 10-2 shows a **case** statement being used to handle command input. Each command is recognized and the appropriate routine is called. To avoid testing for invalid commands, the *get—command* function converts invalid input to the enumeration value *BAD—CMD*.

```
type
    commands = (BAD_CMD, ADD, DELETE, HELP, READ_FILE, WRITE_FILE,
                DISPLAY_LINE, DISPLAY_RECORD, DISPLAY_PAGE);
var
    cmd : commands;

done := FALSE
repeat
        cmd : = get_command;
        case cmd of
            ADD                             :  add_cmd;
            DELETE                          :  delete_cmd;
            EXIT                            :  done := TRUE;
            HELP                            :  help_cmd;
            DISPLAY_LINE . . DISPLAY_PAGE   :  display_cmds (cmd);
            READ_FILE, WRITE_FILE           :  file_io (cmd);
            BAD_CMD                         :  writeln (' ** unknown command');
        end { end of case }
until done;
```

Figure 10-2. Example of **Case** statement

Search Construction (Coded)

While there is no search construct in Pascal, searching algorithms can easily be coded. You may need to write a pattern-matching or string-comparison function if strings of different lengths are to be compared, because there is no function to do this in standard Pascal.

Figure 10-3 contains an example, assuming a pattern-matching function called *match* is available. Note that the pattern searched for is copied into the last element of the array so that the **while** loop is guaranteed to end. This avoids checking the index *i* against the size of the array each time through the loop.

```
const
      max__chars = 25;

type
      text__string = packed array [1 . . max__chars] of char;

var
      strings : array [0 . . max__strings] of text__string;
      .
      .
      strings [max__strings] := pattern;
      i := 0;
      while pattern <> strings [i] do
          i := i + 1;

      if i < max__strings then
          writeln ('pattern found at element #', i:1)
      else
          writeln ('pattern not found');
```

Figure 10-3. Simple string search example

Nonsequential Execution

Pascal has a **goto** statement, provided for those "uncommon situations where the natural structure of an algorithm has to be broken."[6] However, the designer of the language apparently wanted to discourage its use, having placed a number of restrictions upon it. The labels must be declared and are only valid in the scope in which they are declared. In addition, they must be unsigned integers in the range of 0–9999, thus making meaningful label names rather difficult. You may not use a **goto** to jump into the middle of a procedure or compound statement (**if**, **while**, **case**, **for**, **repeat**) from outside of it. In general, it is a good idea to avoid the **goto**.

OTHER FEATURES

This section covers some of the additional Pascal features and how best to use them. The following topics will be discussed.

* data typing
* standard data structures

[6]K. Jensen, N. Wirth, "Pascal User Manual and Report," 3rd ed., Springer-Verlag, New York, 1985.

- sets
- dynamic variables and pointers
- user-defined types and constants

Data Typing

As mentioned in the introduction, Pascal is a strongly typed language. Every data item in the language has a type associated with it. To manipulate the data, you must know its type and what operations are valid with it. Thus, when creating variables, data structures and functions, you should choose the type carefully. Make sure you are able to perform all necessary operations on the data with that type.

Note that files are also typed, allowing you to create a file whose contents are only items of a single type. This feature can be useful when files are used to transfer information from one program to another. As long as both programs use the same file type definition, you are almost assured of accessing the data in the same format in which it was created. Be aware, however, that such files are almost guaranteed to be unusable by other computer systems because of the internal structure of files. Text files should not, in general, have this problem.

Standard Data Structures

Associating data which is logically related is a good way to organize a program and is strongly encouraged. It reduces the number of variables that a programmer has to keep track of and clarifies the relationship of associated items. A typical example of structuring is a list, such as in sorting names or performing several statistical operations on a sequence of numbers. Another example of data structuring is grouping, such as employee data, where there might be fields for name, employee number, department, social security number and salary.

Pascal provides the standard set of data-structuring capabilities found in most high-level languages, in addition to its ordinal data types. These are the **array** (a list, or matrix, structure) and the **record** (a grouping structure). Records provide the capability for an optional variant component, whose type may vary dynamically.

Pascal's **array** type provides the capability of combining data items whose values are all of the same type into a list of a given length. Multiple-dimension arrays may be defined, thereby allowing more complex structures.

You set the size of the array by specifying the lowest and highest index values. Note that the index may be of any ordinal type, including integers, user-defined enumeration types, booleans and characters. The index range is a subrange, with arbitrary endpoint values; that is, if you desire to create an 11-element array of the enumerated type "numbers," you could do it any of the following ways:

```
      type
         numbers = (one, two, three, four, five, six,
                       seven, eight, nine, ten, eleven);
      var
         list1 : array [0 . . 10] of numbers;
         list2 : array [1 . . 11] of numbers;
         list3 : array [-5 . . 5] of numbers;
         list4 : array ['a' . . 'k'] of numbers;
         list5 : array [one . . eleven] of numbers;
```

Note that in each case the array is of the same type (numbers). What is different in each declaration is the type and/or range of the indices.

The **record** is a nestable grouping structure similar to C's **struct** type or PL/I's STRUCTURE. By nestable, we mean that a field in a record may itself be a record. Records may have a single variant component whose type may vary during execution. The current type is determined by a tag field, which may itself be a field of the record. Note that the variant component must be the last field in a Record.

A variant component can be made up of several different variants, each having a different number of fields, whose sizes are independent. An example of a variant component in a record might be family information, based on marital status. Any person is either single (i.e., never married), married, divorced or widowed. If, for the purposes of this example, we make the assumption that single people don't have children, then Figure 10-4 contains a record type which might be defined.

```
    type
       name       = packed array [1 . . 30] of char;
       date       = packed array [1 . . 6] of char;
       family_info = record
                      name       : name;
                      birthdate  : date;
                      case status : marital_status of
                        married  : (spouse_name : name;
                                    kids             : ^ kid_list;
                                    anniversary    : date);
                        divorced : (ex_spouse_ name    : name;
                                    kids_with me             : ^ kid_ list;
                                    kids_with_ex_spouse : ^ kid_list);
                        widowed : (good_kids       : ^ kid_ list;
                                    neglectful_ kids : ^ kid_ list);
                        single   : ();
                      end; {variant part}
                  end; {record}
```

Figure 10-4. A variant record

Note that all fields in all variants within a record must have different names. Also, even though there are no fields for the *single* variant, it is still necessary to include the empty parentheses.

Variant records must be carefully managed by the programmer. Except for standard type-checking, the compiler cannot ensure that you are referencing a field within the correct variant for the current value of the tag field. Variant records are a very powerful tool, but you should be careful using them.

Pascal is one of the few languages with structuring capabilities that allow you to assign an entire record variable in one statement:

```
var
        r1, r2 : employee_record;
        .
        .
        .
    r1 := r2;
        .
        .
```

This avoids assigning each individual field separately, which, for large records, can be quite tedious. Note, however, that you cannot compare entire records directly.

Referencing a record's fields, especially when there are nested records and/or a sequence of pointers, can also be tedious. To help with this, Pascal provides the **with** statement. Using the **with** statement allows you to abbreviate any record field reference to the shortest recognizable portion by leaving off a given prefix. While the **with** allows you to specify several record prefixes at one time, you should be careful doing this. The whole idea of the **with** statement is to clarify the record references. Using several abbreviations at once might defeat the purpose, or worse, make a single reference ambiguous in that the compiler won't know to which record the referenced field belongs. See Figure 10-5 for an example of a **with** statement.

```
var
     i     : integer;
     team : array [1 . . max__teams] of
          record
               name    : packed array [1 . . 15] of char;
               manager : packed array [1 . . 40] of char;
               wins    : integer;
               losses  : integer;
          end;
   .
   .
   .
if result = won then                        { 'with' not used }
     team.wins := team.wins + 1
else
     team.losses := team.losses + 1
   .
   .
for i := 1 to max_teams do
     with team do                           { 'with' used }
          writeln (name, 'managed by ', manager, ' has a record of ',
                    wins, ' wins and ', losses, ' losses ');
```

Figure 10-5. Example of use of With Statement

Sets

Another feature provided by Pascal is the Set type. This enables you to reference a subset of a given base type's values either as a constant or a variable. The basic operations that exist for manipulating sets are summarized in Table 10-1:

Table 10-1. Set operations

Operation	Operator
union	+
intersection	*
difference	−
membership	in
subset inclusion	< = , > =
equality/inequality	= , <>
assignment	: =

Sets can be useful in many ways. One is in checking valid responses from a user:

```
if reply__char in ['n', 'N'] then
    end__process;
```

Another use is to verify a value before using a **case** statement in a compiler that has no "otherwise" option (see the previous discussion, "Choice Structure"):

```
var
    ch     : char;
    vowels : set of char;
    .
    .
vowels := ['a,' 'e', 'i', 'o', 'u', 'y', 'A', 'E', 'I', 'O', 'U', 'Y'];
    .
    .
ch := read__char;
if ch in vowels then
    case ch of
        .
        .
        .
    end {case}
else
    error (invalid__letter, ch);
```

Finally, sets are useful for grouping items that share some attribute:

```
type
      month  =  (January, February, March, April, May, June, July,
                 August, September, October, November, December);
var
      thirty__days            : set of month;
      thirty__one__days   : set of month;
  .
  .
  .
      thirty__days           := [April, June, September, November];
      thirty__one__days   := [January, March, May, July,
                              August, October, December];
```

The implementation of sets varies greatly, affecting (at least) the maximum number of elements a set may contain and the amount of memory it occupies (perhaps as few as 16 elements or as many as 65,536). If you need to create a set larger than your compiler allows, you can use an array of sets instead. It may be a bit awkward but nonetheless allows you to gain the advantages of using sets.

While a set's base type must be an ordinal type, not all ordinal types are allowed. Specifically, a set whose base type is integer is not generally allowed, because its potential size is limited only by the architecture of the machine. Additionally, while a subrange of integer could be used as a set's base type (thereby constraining it to a finite number of values), some compilers may not allow limits whose ordinal value is too large. For example, if the compiler sets a limit of 255 possible values for any set, it would probably not allow the following set type:

```
type
      wwll__years__1  =  set of 1939 . . 1945;
```

while it would probably accept the following:

```
type
      wwll_years_2  =  set of 39 . . 45;
```

Dynamic Variables and Pointers

Allocation of memory for dynamic variables is accomplished with the predefined Pascal procedure **new**. The memory is deallocated with the predefined Pascal procedure **dispose**.[7] The allocated memory is referenced via a pointer variable. Pointers must be declared to point to a specific type of variable, which allows Pascal's type checking to extend to dynamic variables. If this weren't the case, you would be able, for example, to reference an integer as a record, thereby picking up random (and probably wrong) values. Consequently, pointer manipulation in Pascal is relatively safe when compared to similar facilities in other languages. The standard specifies that dereferencing a nil or

[7]Early Pascal compilers may not have the **dispose** procedure. Before standardization, each compiler generally had its own method of dynamic memory allocation and deallocation.

uninitialized pointer is an error. However, whether—and what kind of—run-time errors occur upon assigning a value to an undefined pointer is system-dependent.

Memory allocated via **new** needs to be initialized; otherwise it will contain whatever random values happened to be there before allocation. In particular, when using the variant record form of **new** to specify which variants are allocated (i.e., **new** (ptr, variant1, variant2)), the variant elements are not initialized.

Dynamic variables are useful for creating structures whose size varies during execution. The classic example is a linked list, where you have a "head of list" pointer and a record type containing data fields and a "next item" field. The "next item" field is a pointer from one element of the list to the next; the last element's "next item" field is **nil**, to indicate the end of the list (see Figure 10-6).

```
type
    person_ptr  =  ^ person;
    person      =  record
                       name    : packed array [1 . . 20] of char;
                       ssn     : packed array [1 . . 11] of char;
                       emp_num: integer;
                       next    : person_ptr;
                   end;

var
    list_head : person_ptr;
    .
    .
new (list_head);
with list_head ^ do begin
    name             := 'Sandy Koufax
    ssn              := '123-45-6789';
    emp_num          := 32;
    list_head ^ .next   := Nil;
    end; { with }
    .
    .
```

Figure 10-6. Creation of Dynamic List structure

It is tempting to remove the type *person ptr* and define the field *next* simply as

```
next : ^ person;
```

However, this generally does not work because of Pascal's definition of type compatibility. That is, if you define two different types both to be pointers to the same type:

```
type
    t1 : ^ object;
    t2 : ^ object;
```

you cannot guarantee that types *t1* and *t2* are compatible. If you use the method shown in Figure 10-6, you can guarantee that there will be compatibility and no ambiguity. The fact that the type *person* had not yet been defined does not create a problem for the compiler. Note, however, that if you define something to be a pointer to a type which is never defined, you get a compile-time error.

Pointers can be manipulated with most of the basic operations provided for ordinal types; that is, assignment, comparison and I/O. In general, pointer arithmetic is not allowed (see the following paragraph). Note that the comparison

```
if ptr1 ^ = ptr2 ^ then
      .
      .
```

determines whether the pointers point to objects whose values are equivalent. It does not mean that the pointers have the same value (i.e., you cannot assume *ptr1* = *ptr2*).

Some compilers provide general extensions to pointer variables, allowing them to take on an untyped value (i.e., just a memory location) with no restrictions on the type of value contained therein. This can be useful in the hands of an experienced programmer; it can be deadly if misused. This is because it enables you to reference and modify any memory location (including your program and the operating system). Direct memory address references are generally necessary when doing systems programming but not often needed otherwise. If your compiler provides such features, be sure you know what you are doing before you use them.

User-Defined Types and Constants

In addition to its standard, predefined types, Pascal allows you to define your own types. The most common uses of this feature are in creating enumeration types and subranges, and in naming record structures. The definition of enumeration types enables you to create a new type with its own limited set of named values. This frees you from such archaic practices as using numbers or character strings to signify special values. An example of an enumeration is:

```
type
    cities = (Los_Angeles, New_York, Chicago, Poughkeepsie);
```

Subranges are a type whose values are a subset of their base type, consisting of all consecutive values between the specified endpoints, inclusive. When a variable needs to range over only a portion of a type's values, you should use a subrange as its type. This can be useful in defining an array's index range and the variables that are used to index into it. Note that you cannot define a subrange consisting of nonsequential values, such as all the odd numbers between 1 and 100, or nonordinal values, such as Reals. Some examples of subranges are provided below:

```
type
    positive      = 1 . . maxint;
    month_index   = 1 . . 12;
    day           = (Sun, Mon, Tue, Wed, Thu, Fri, Sat);
    weekday       = Mon . . Fri;
```

Note the difference between this definition and the definition of the sets *thirty_days* and *thirty_one_days* cited earlier. In this case, we have defined a type, of which variables may subsequently be declared. Such variables would only be allowed to take on the limited range of values as defined in the subrange. In the earlier case, we have defined two variables of a set type which actually contain some (or all) of the enumeration type's values.

Once again, the compiler enforces type compatibility. Should an attempt be made at run-time to give the variable a value outside its range, a run-time error will occur.[8] Without this feature, a bug where variables take on illegal values and cause erroneous results might not be detected.

A potential ambiguity arises when two subranges are defined with partially overlapping domains. For example:

```
type
    range1 = 1 . . 10;
    range2 = 7 . . 11;

var
    r1 : range1;
    r2 : range2;
```

The following assignment statement

```
r1 := r2
```

compiles, but could cause a run-time error if *r2* has the value 11 at the time it is executed. To prevent this, we suggest you only use subranges for the following purposes:

- array index range definitions
- array index variables
- restricted use variables

The latter usage serves the purpose of clarifying the intended use of the variable. For example, if a variable is used to designate which of a cat's nine lives is currently in progress, you could declare a variable as follows:

---

[8]Some compilers give you the option of turning this off because extra code is generated for these checks. We recommend that if you have the option, leave the checking on until your program is debugged and then remove it if codesize or performance is to be optimized.

```
                    var
                        cats_life : 1 . . 9;
```

To avoid hiding "magic" values within the program as literals (e.g., numbers) Pascal provides the **const** definition. This enables you to use named values throughout the block in which the constant is defined. This greatly eases understanding of the program at a future reading. Additionally, should that value need to change in a subsequent version of the program, you need only change it in one place. Another advantage of constants defined this way is that they are not variables—they are processed only at compile-time—and consequently should take less space at run-time.[9]

A constant can be an integer (signed or unsigned), a single character, or a character string. Some compilers have extended this to general arrays and other types (although this also requires the extension to change the order of declaration parts so that **type** definitions can come before **const** definitions). Some sample constants are:

```
                const
                    min_score   = 0;
                    max_score   = 100;
                    title       = 'Godel, Escher, Bach';
                    delimiter   = '/';
```

MISSING FEATURES

While Pascal has many strengths and features that contribute to making structured programming easy, it is instructional to look at some of the features Pascal does not have. These features were excluded generally to keep the language compact, to avoid unnecessary complications, and to increase compiler efficiency. The most glaring omissions are:

- automatic initialization
- exponentiation
- flexible string manipulation
- general I/O
- separate compilation

Automatic Initialization

Because Pascal does not provide an automatic variable initialization capability, you must explicitly include statements to set variables to their starting values. The standard does not specify the values of undefined variables so this has become compiler-

---

[9]Depending on the operating system, initialization of constants, particularly strings, may take up some codespace.

dependent. Even if your compiler does provide known values, however, you should not rely on them. Such a practice can prevent your program from being portable and can build in unspecified assumptions which might not be valid after a future modification.

Exponentiation

It is not clear why an exponentiation operator is excluded. However, it is simple to create your own. An example is provided in Figure 10-7. It uses a recursive technique and requires both *number* and *exponent* to be integers, and *exponent* to be positive.

```
function power (number   : integer;
                exponent : integer) : integer;

begin
    if number = 0 then
        power := 1

    else
        power := number * power (number, exponent − 1);

end; { power }
```

Figure 10-7. Integer exponentiation function

Flexible String Manipulation

Character string manipulation in Pascal is rather awkward. A "string" is a **packed array of char** whose index type is integer. This string is then type compatible only with strings of the same length. Note that the length of a string is constant, regardless of what value you assign to the string. There are no string functions or procedures defined in the standard. You may use the relational and the assignment operators on strings of the same length.

Some compilers provide a predefined **string** type, objects of which need not have the same defined length, and whose values' lengths may change dynamically. If you don't have these extensions, you may find yourself having to allocate a maximum length string, all of which may rarely be required (e.g., providing a 30-character array for names when most names will fit into 15–20 characters). In addition, you will need to pad out all string constants with blanks to that maximum string length.

General I/O

Pascal provides relatively straightforward input and output facilities (the procedures **read/readln**, **write/writeln**, **get** and **put**). While many people feel this simplicity is an advantage, some consider it a weakness. For instance, there is no random I/O capability (for accessing specific records in a file) and no equivalent to the FORMAT statements of FORTRAN or PL/I. The latter makes the usage and creation of formatted input and output rather tedious. However, most compilers' run-time libraries do provide a good set of I/O routines, and you can use the built-in left- and right-justification features, along with blanks and tabbing loops to get some quite reasonable output formatting.

Pascal does not provide a means for input and output of enumerated types. To do this, you can create a character array indexed by the enumeration type whose values are the textual representation of each corresponding enumerated value. Then for input you need to read characters and check them against the list for validity. For output, you simply index into the array. Here is an example:

```
type
    sex = (Male, Androgynous, Female);

var
    sex_text : array [Male . . Female] of packed array [1 . . 10] of char;
.
.
.
sex_text [Male]          := 'Male        ';
sex_text [Female]        := 'Female      ';
sex_text [Androgynous]   := 'Boy George';
```

Another I/O problem arises from the fact that Pascal was designed in the era of punched cards. When it is used in an interactive state, the functions **eof** (end-of-file) and **eoln** (end-of-line) will behave differently from one system to another. Some compilers have introduced a new file type (e.g., Terminal) or a file modifier (e.g., Interactive) to handle this problem. Others merely force different semantics on those functions for interactive files. This is one area you will almost certainly have to modify if you need to transport your program from one system to another.

Separate Compilation

As mentioned earlier, standard Pascal does not allow separate compilation. This is because Pascal programs are considered one "block." To allow externally defined procedures and functions violates this format. See the previous section entitled "Module Grouping" for further discussion of separate compilation.

CASE STUDY

The programming example presented here is an implementation of a reverse polish notation calculator. Such a calculator is one in which both operands are entered before the operator. For example, to add 5 to 7, we would enter:

and the result, 12, is displayed. The usual implementation for this (and the one we have chosen here) is a stack, with each number pushed onto the stack as it is entered. Then for each operator entered, the necessary number of operands (usually two) are popped off the stack, the operation is performed, and the result is pushed back onto the stack. The result of the calculation (i.e., the value on top of the stack) is displayed only when requested.

The hierarchy chart for the CALC program is presented in Figure 10-8a. Note that three of the modules—EXECUTE COMMAND, GET COMMAND, and DISPLAY STACK—are not coded as separate Pascal procedures. This was done to avoid having excessive numbers of small functions. In addition, the standard Pascal procedure **readln** may be used for module GET LINE. Also note that the chart does not include the utility routines *error*, *is_digit*, *push* and *pop* which are used in several locations. While these are independent steps, they should be thought of not as logical modules but rather as tools to carry out the steps outlined in the modules.

The flowchart for the CALC program is presented in Figure 10-8b.

An entire line is read in (terminated by a carriage-return/linefeed) before it is analyzed. Input consists of a sequence of numbers and commands. The numbers may be real or integer, and may optionally be preceded by a minus sign. A command is either a simple arithmetic operator (+ , -, *, /) or one of the following:

Clear ('c' or 'C')   : clears the stack
Display ('d' or 'D')   : displays the entire stack
End ('#')   : exits the program
Equals ('=')   : pops the top value off stack and displays it
Top ('$')   : displays the top of the stack

Blanks and tabs are treated as delimiters.

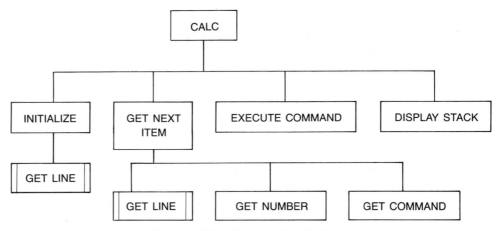

Figure 10-8(a). Hierarchy chart for Calculator

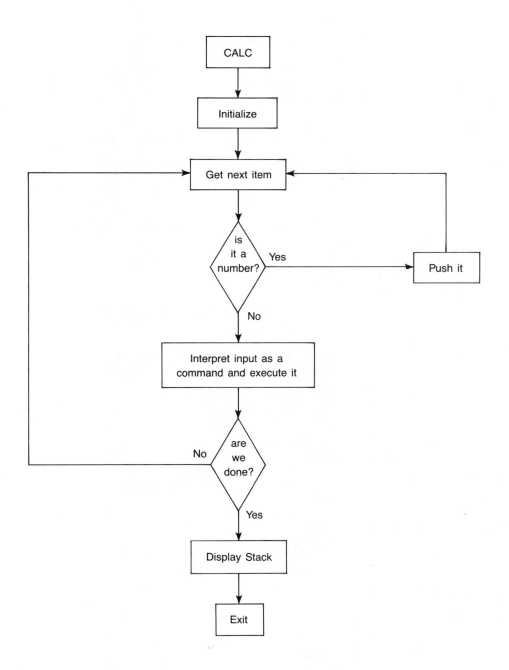

Figure 10-8(b). Flowchart for Calculator

```
{ * --------------------------------------------------------------------- *
  *                    Program:  Calc                                     *
  * --------------------------------------------------------------------- *
  *                    Purpose:  Polish Notation Calculator               *
  *                                                                       *
  *                    Author:   Blaise Pascal                            *
  *                    System:   Escarg OS, V1.0                          *
  *                    Compiler: Triangle's Pascal; V2.31                 *
  *                    History:                                           *
  *                          9/1/88     created                           *
  *                          9/7/88     changed stack size to start at 0, not 1 *
  * --------------------------------------------------------------------- * }

program calc (input, output);

const
    BLANK            = ' ';
    copy_rt          = '(c) Copyright Spiffy Programs, Inc, 1988';
    sign_on          = 'CALC V2.0';
    max_line_length  = 80;
    max_stack        = 50;

type
    commands         = (add, sub, mult, divide, clear, equals, stop,
                          top, display, invalid);
    entry_type       = (number, command);
    errors           = (stack_overflow, stack_underflow, divide_by_zero,
                          illegal_input);

    line_index_range = 0 .. max_line_length;
    text_line        = string [max_line_length];          { an extension of this compiler }

    stack_range      = 0 .. max_stack;
    float_stack      = record
                          tos  : stack_range;             { top of stack }
                          nums : array [stack_range] of real;    { numbers }
                       end;

    variant_element  = record
                          case kind : entry_type of
                          number  : (num : real);
                          command : (cmd : commands)
                       end;

var
    done    : boolean;
    i       : integer;
    item    : variant_element;
    line    : text_line;
```

```
    line_idx      : line_index_range;
    line_length   : line_index_range;
    stack         : float_stack;
    val1,
    val2          : real;
```

{page}
```
{ * ---------------------------------------------------------------- *
  *                  f o r w a r d   d e c l a r a t i o n s         *
  * ---------------------------------------------------------------- *
  *      All the procedures and functions are forward-declared so that they   *
  *               may be listed in alphabetical order.              * }
  * ---------------------------------------------------------------- *
```

```
procedure error          (err      : errors);                              forward;
procedure get_next_item (var item  : variant_element);                     forward;
procedure get_number     (var num  : real;
                          var index : line_index_range);                   forward;
procedure initialize;                                                      forward;
function is_digit         (ch       : char)              : boolean;        forward;
function pop                                             : real;           forward;
procedure push            (value    : real);                               forward;
```

{page}
```
{ * ---------------------------------------------------------------- *
  *                           e r r o r                             *
  * ---------------------------------------------------------------- *
  *    Display error message.                                       * }
  * ---------------------------------------------------------------- *
```

```
procedure error {(err : errors)};

    begin
        writeln;
        write (' *** Error: ');
        case err of
            stack_overflow   : writeln ('Stack Overflow');
            stack_underflow  : writeln ('Stack Underflow');
            divide_by_zero   : writeln ('Divide By Zero');
            illegal_input    : writeln ('Illegal Input');
        end; { end case }

end; { end of error }
```

{page}
```
{ * ----------------------------------------------------------------- *
  *                    g e t _ n e x t _ i t e m                      *
  * ----------------------------------------------------------------- *
  *     Get the next item from the input line. If we reach end of line, *
  *            read another line. Blanks are delimiters.               *
  * ----------------------------------------------------------------- * }

procedure get_next_item {(var item : variant _element)};

    label
        100;

    begin

        100:
            while (line [line_idx] = BLANK) and (line_idx <= line_length) do
                line_idx := line_idx + 1;

            if line_idx > line_length then
                begin
                    write ('=> ');
                    readln (line);
                    line_length := length (line);
                    line_idx := 1;
                    goto 100;
                end { end if }

            else if is_digit (line [line_idx]) or
                    (line [line_idx] = '.') or
                    ((line [line_idx] = '-') and
                    (is_digit (line [line_idx + 1])) ) then
                begin
                    item.kind := number;
                    get_number (item.num, line_idx);
                end { end else if }

            else                 { assume it is a command }
                begin
                    item.kind := COMMAND;
                    case line [line_idx] of
                        '+': item.cmd := add;
                        '-' : item.cmd := sub;
                        '*' : item.cmd := mult;
                        '/' : item.cmd := divide;
                        'c',
                        'C' : item.cmd := clear;
                        '$' : item.cmd := top;
                        '=' : item.cmd := equals;
```

```
                              'd',
                              'D' : item.cmd := display;
                              '#' : item.cmd := stop;

                           else
                                    item.cmd := invalid;
                           end; { end case }
                           line_idx := line_idx + 1;
                      end; { end else }
            end; { end of get _next_item }
```

{page}
```
{ *----------------------------------------------------------------------  *
  *                          g e t _ n u m b e r                           *
  *----------------------------------------------------------------------  *
  *           The given index is at the beginning of a number (digit, minus *
  *           sign or decimal point). Read it, return it and update the index. *}
  *----------------------------------------------------------------------  *}

procedure get_number  {(var num  : real;
                            var index : line_index_range)};

    var
        decimals : real;
        neg      : boolean;

    begin

        if (line [index] = '-') then
            begin
                neg   := TRUE;
                index := index + 1;
            end

        else
            neg := FALSE;

        num := 0;
        while is_digit (line [index]) and (index <= line_length) do
            begin
                num   := num * 10 + (ord (line [index]) - ord ('0'));
                index := index + 1;
            end;

        if index <= line_length then
            if line [index] = '.' then
```

```
                    begin
                        index := index + 1;
                        decimals := 10;
                        while is_digit (line [index]) and (index <= line_length) do
                            begin
                                num      := num + (ord (line [index]) - ord ('0')) / decimals;
                                index    := index + 1;
                                decimals := decimals * 10;
                            end;                { end while }

                end; { end if }

            if neg then
                num := num * -1;

        end; { end of get_number }
```

{page}
```
{ *------------------------------------------------------------------------*
  *                          i n i t i a l i z e                           *
  *------------------------------------------------------------------------*
  *            Initialization. Set top of stack to 0. Read in first line.  * }
```

```
procedure initialize;

    begin
        writeln (sign_on, copy_rt);

        stack.tos := 0;

        write ('=> ');
        readln (line);
        line_length := length (line);
        line_idx    := 1;

    end; { end of initialize }
```

```
{ *------------------------------------------------------------------------*
  *                          i s _ d i g i t                               *
  *------------------------------------------------------------------------*
  *            Return true if the input character is a digit, false otherwise.  * }
```

```
function is_digit {(ch : char) : boolean};

    begin
```

```
            is_digit := (ch >= '0') and (ch <= '9');

    end; { end of is _digit }



{page}
{ *  --------------------------------------------------------------------  *
  *                                                                        *
  *                             p o p                                      *
  *  --------------------------------------------------------------------  *
  *          If stack is not empty, remove top item and return it. Decrement  *
  *                          stack pointer.                                *
  *  --------------------------------------------------------------------  * }

function pop {: real};

    begin
        if stack.tos > 0 then
            begin
                stack.tos := stack.tos − 1;
                pop       := stack.nums [stack.tos];
            end

        else
            begin
                error (stack_underflow);
                pop := 0;
            end

    end; { end of pop }

{ *  --------------------------------------------------------------------  *
  *                                                                        *
  *                            p u s h                                     *
  *  --------------------------------------------------------------------  *
  *          If there is room on the stack, push the given number onto it and  *
  *                     increment the stack pointer.                       *
  *  --------------------------------------------------------------------  * }

procedure push {(value : real)};

    begin
        if stack.tos < MAX_STACK then
            begin
                stack.nums [stack.tos] := value;
                stack.tos              := stack.tos + 1;
            end

        else
            error (stack_overflow);

    end; { end of push }
```

256 Structured Programming Using Pascal

```
{page}
{ * ----------------------------------------------------------------- *
  * -------------------------- m a i n ----------------------------- *
  *                                                                   *
  *    Main program for Calc. Do initialization. Main loop is:        *
  *        —get next entry                                            *
  *        —if it's a number, push it onto stack                      *
  *        —else interpret as a command                               *
  *        —display stack upon exit (if non-empty)                    * }
  * ----------------------------------------------------------------- *

begin

    initialize;

    done := FALSE;
    repeat
        get_next_item (item);
        if item.kind = NUMBER then
            push (item.num)

        else
            case item.cmd of
                add:    begin
                            val1  := pop;
                            val2  := pop;
                            push (val1 + val2);
                        end;

                sub:    begin
                            val1  := pop;
                            val2  := pop;
                            push (val2 − val1);
                        end;

                mult:   begin
                            val1  := pop;
                            val2  := pop;
                            push (val1 * val2);
                        end;

                divide: begin
                            val1  := pop;
                            val2  := pop;
                            if val1 <> 0 then
                                push (val2 / val1)
                            else
                                error (divide_by_zero);
                        end;
```

```
equals:  begin
             val1   := pop;
             writeln (val1:8:4);
         end;

top:     if stack.tos > 0 then
             writeln (stack.nums [stack.tos - 1]:8:4)
         else
             error (stack_underflow);

clear:   stack.tos := 0;                          { clear stack completely }

display: begin
             for i := stack.tos − 1 downto 0 do
                 write (stack.nums [i]:8:4, '   ');
             writeln;
         end;

stop:    done := TRUE;

invalid: error (illegal_input);

     end; { end case }

 until done;

if stack.tos <> 0 then
    begin
        writeln ('Final Stack Contents:');
        for i := stack.tos − 1 downto 0 do
            write (stack.nums [i]:8:4, '   ');
        writeln;
    end; { end if }

end. { end of program calc }
```

Figure 10-8(c). A Pascal programming example

Our stack *stack* consists of an array of real numbers *nums* and a current top of stack index *tos*, combined in a record of type *float_stack*. Note that the maximum size of the stack is determined by the constant *max_stack*, so that it can easily be changed.

Note the use of a variant record for the parameter to procedure *get_next_item*. This enables the routine to return either a real number or an element of the user-defined type *commands* in a single parameter. The selector *entry* indicates which type of value is actually returned, thereby eliminating the need for an additional parameter.

Note the use of the label *100* and the **goto** statement in the procedure *get_next_item*. This is a relatively simple usage of the **goto** statement, and fits in logically with the flow of the program. While we could have coded this routine in such a way as to avoid using the **goto**, that would have resulted in a more complicated and wordy solution with no great benefit.

Regarding the format and layout of the code, you should note the following features:

- The procedures and functions are all forward-declared to enable presenting them in alphabetical order.
- The formal parameters to each routine are included with their contents (they are commented out as they are not required if the routine has been forward-declared).
- Each routine begins on a new page (the '{page}' comment contains a form-feed character which causes the printer to go to the top of the next page).
- Each routine is preceded by a description of its utility.
- Generous use is made of whitespace, indentation and alignment.
- The closing **end** for each routine and compound statement is followed by a comment identifying it.

MANAGEMENT IMPLICATIONS

While Pascal, as defined in the ISO Standard, is a well-designed, relatively consistent and structured language, it may be necessary, or at least helpful, to acquire a compiler with some extensions. The features you will most likely desire are:

- flexible string manipulation
- separate compilation
- a source file inclusion capability
- an "otherwise" clause in the **case** statement

In general, you will probably need to build or acquire an entire I/O library, since Pascal does not provide random access files or a formatted I/O capability. In addition, for systems work, you may need specific machine interface routines and additional display services (e.g., cursor manipulation).

Whenever extensive programming is anticipated, it is advisable not only to adopt standards with regard to naming conventions and formatting style, but also in the definition of types and constants. It is easy to go overboard and create many types and constants; but if all programmers in a group do that, it is likely to create inconsistent overlapping. It is a good idea to define the data types and interfaces before any coding is begun.

Finally, although Pascal is standardized, do not overestimate a Pascal program's portability. There are several implementation-dependent features, and not all versions of Pascal even attempt to conform to the ISO Standard.

SUMMARY

Programming in Pascal can be substantially easier than in some less well-designed languages, although some of its shortcomings do require special attention. The saving grace is that Pascal tends to be a very "safe" language in which to program. Many of the common programming errors (e.g., mismatched parameters, not dereferencing a pointer, invalid array subscripts) are either caught by the compiler or detected automatically at run-time. This means that programmers can concentrate on the design of the program and the logical flow, rather than on whether they have dotted their tees and crossed their eyes. The end result is that a more reliable program can be created in less time.

The down side to this is that Pascal makes the programmer do a lot more "bookkeeping" in creating the program. This can lead to grumbling and the temptation to find shortcuts.

Pascal provides all of the basic programming structures needed for structured programming, rigorously enforces type compatibility, requires all items to be declared before use, and completely defines almost all of its features. Because of these, and notwithstanding its I/O deficiencies, Pascal appears to have been ideally designed for structured programming.

REVIEW QUESTIONS AND EXERCISES

1. What is a subrange and why is it useful?

2. Design a complete and consistent set of formatting, naming and indentation rules for Pascal.

3. Why do you think the designer of the language chose to exclude exponentiation, but not the trigonometric functions?

4. How would you organize a group of seven to ten programmers all working on the same Pascal program? In what manner would you split up the work?

5. Write a **for** statement that accesses every other element of an array indexed by the enumeration type *month* (defined in the section covering Sets), starting with *January*. For each element, display its textual representation.

6. Why would you use a constant rather than a simple variable which is explicitly initialized at the beginning of the program?

7. Modify the program in Figure 10-8 so that it can handle up to 100 values rather than 50. Also, change the characters used for each operator and command. Note how easy these common types of changes are when the program is written with the proper use of constants and information hiding.

8. In the program in Figure 10-8, a fractional value may be entered without a leading 0 (e.g., .201). However, negative fractions currently require the leading 0 (e.g., -0.185). Correct this error.

11

Structured Programming Using C

"With these mechanical details mastered, everything else is comparatively easy."

Kernighan and Ritchie[1]

"Omit needless words!"

Rule 17, *Elements of Style*[2]

Programming language C, as defined by Kernighan and Ritchie, provides all of the necessary capabilities required for structured programming. In addition, several other features are available to enhance readability, simplify programming, enable easy sharing of code, and represent complex algorithms clearly.

C has primarily been designed as a systems programming language and, therefore, contains several features aimed at improving efficiency and allowing direct access to the machine. However, because it provides all of the structured programming facilities, it is also used as a general-purpose language. Its simple data types, flexibility, rich set of operators and preprocessor make C a popular and useful programming language for both systems and general work. As an example, note that almost all of the UNIX operating system is written in C. (UNIX is a Trademark of Bell Laboratories.)

While there is no official standard for the language,[3] the Kernighan and Ritchie text can be considered definitive and the one we shall reference. Compiler- and operating system-dependent features will be so indicated. This chapter assumes familiarity with C and, therefore, no effort is made to instruct you on the syntax or meaning of various C constructs. Instead we will concentrate on how to use the constructs to achieve a clear, understandable and maintainable program. Let's start with a summary of the language constructs and features that directly provide the capabilities for structured programming.

---

[1]Brian W. Kernighan and Dennis M. Ritchie, *The C Programming Language* (Englewood Cliffs, NJ: Prentice-Hall, 1978).

[2]From *The Elements of Style*, 3rd ed., by William Strunk, Jr., and E. B. White. Copyright © 1979 by Macmillan Publishing Company. Reprinted by permission of the publisher.

[3]Work in this area is being conducted by ANSI Standards Committee X3J11.

PHYSICAL PROGRAM LAYOUT

Modularity and Separate Compilation

One of the basic requirements in creating a program in a structured manner is to separate parts of the system in logical, virtually independent pieces. We will refer to these as *units* throughout the text (often each unit would correspond to a physically independent file). Units are made up of logically related single-purpose elements, called *modules*. This may be pictured as follows:

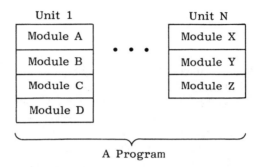

A Program

Units should have a well-defined interface for access by other units, but their internal contents should be essentially unknown to each other. In addition, to avoid putting all of the code into one monolithic source file, you separate these units and compile them independently. This allows the use of general libraries, which in turn enables the sharing of code and minimizes "reinventing the wheel."

All of these facilities are available in C. A module simply translates to a C function. A single C source file is then considered the physical equivalent of a logical unit. This unit contains a series of #defines, type definitions, variable declarations and functions (#defines are discussed in more detail shortly). Note that the manner in which separate compilation is handled is both system- and compiler-dependent.

All functions (modules) are public by default and therefore directly accessible by other units. However, you can hide a function from other units by prefixing its name with the keyword **static**. This makes it inaccessible outside the unit in which it is declared. To clarify which functions are externally accessible, the following convention is suggested. Create two #defines, PUBLIC and PRIVATE, with the values null and **static**, respectively. Then use these as prefixes for public and private functions. For example:

```
#define PUBLIC
#define PRIVATE static
    .
    .
```

```
                    PUBLIC display (value_ptr)
                        value *value_ptr;
                        {
                          .
                          .
                          .
                        }
                  .
                  .
                  .
                    PRIVATE display_int (int_ptr)
                        int *int_ptr;
                        {
                          .
                          .
                          .
                        }
```

In addition, to keep track of where a public function is defined, a useful naming convention is to prefix its name with the name (or abbreviation) of the unit in which it resides. Keep in mind that the definition of the C language specifies that only eight characters are significant in identifier names—and possibly fewer for external names (this is compiler-dependent). For example, if the unit that handles a display command is called DISPLAY, its interface routines for displaying records, text, and numbers could be DISP_RECORD, DISP_TEXT and DISP_NUMBER. Note the full name "DIS-PLAY" is not used as a prefix since, with the underscore character, that would be eight characters, making the three names (potentially) indistinguishable. Fortunately, most compilers today no longer enforce this eight-character restriction, and it will probably not be included in the ANSI standard.

All variables declared outside of any function are known to the entirety of the unit and can be made accessible by other units. For another unit to access public variables defined in other units, they must be declared in the accessing unit with the keyword **extern** prefixing the type (see Figure 11-1). The advantage to this is that no reference to external data can be made accidentally by using its name inadvertently. Also, because external data items must be specified before they are used, the overall logical design and unit interfaces can more easily be determined.

Because of this format, you can use common names for different variables in separate units without fear of confusion, either by the compiler or the reader. When a variable is intended to be public, it must be expressly noted by each unit importing it.

Figures 11-1a and 11-1b show an example of the use of **extern**. In this example, we only want to display sensitive information if the user is privileged. Determination of privileged status is made in the unit *sys* by the routine *sys_get_user_priv()* which returns a TRUE or FALSE value. This value is stored in the public variable *privileged* which is then interrogated by *io_display_user()* in the unit *io*. In Figure 11-1a, the variable *privileged* is defined in the main unit and set by a call to function *sys_get_user_priv()*. Figure 11-1b shows the function *io_display_user()* contained in a separate unit, which has an **extern** definition for *privileged*, because that variable is used in one of its routines.

```
#define MAX_USER_ID 100

int privileged, user;

struct {
        char *name;
        float money;
        } users [MAX_USER_ID];
.
.
privileged = sys_get_user_priv ();
.
.
for (user = 0; user < MAX_USER_ID; user++)
        io_display_user (user);
.
.
```

Figure 11-1(a). Main unit contains variable definition

```
extern int privileged;
.    /
.
io_display_user (user_id)
        int user_id;
{

        printf ("User #%d is assigned to %s\n",
            user_id, users [user_id].name);
        if (privileged)
            printf ("Account has $%4.2f left\n", users [user_id].money);

} /* end of function io _display_user */
```

Figure 11-1(b). Unit *IO* uses the public variable via extern

While it might sound tedious to list all public variables used in each source file, a common definition file can be created and included with the preprocessor #include command. This enables you to list all the public variables in one place, and thereby provide a single reference location. An easy way to do this is to prefix all public variables in this file with the word GLOBAL, rather than **extern**. Then, in the unit where you wish them to be defined (probably the main unit), use the preprocessor #define command to set GLOBAL to null:

```
#define GLOBAL
```

Finally, in each unit which references these public variables, define GLOBAL to be equivalant to **extern**:

```
#define GLOBAL extern
```

This avoids having to keep two separate lists of public variables consistent and in synch.

Occasionally, you may need to define a public variable in a different unit due to various initialization requirements. For example, you may create a table of addresses of local variables or functions, or initialize variables to values which are determined by using a local #define. In these cases it makes more sense to put the definition in that unit, but don't forget to include an **extern** declaration in all units that will use such variables.

Another useful idea is to create a file listing all of the functions, declared **extern** (i.e., headings only—not the bodies). Because C assumes a function is of type **int** if it is not told otherwise, a common, and obscure, bug can occur if you reference an external function with the wrong type. Such a header file can eliminate that problem. Note that subsequent redeclarations of each function in its own unit overrides the **extern** definition (provided they are of the same type). See Figure 11-2 for an example.

Unit independence can be obtained, along with some limited information hiding, by decomposition of the program into logical parts. (Information hiding is defined in Chapter 2.) This can be eased by use of a data flow diagram or hierarchy chart discussed in Chapter 2. The interface to a unit consists of its functions and public variables; whatever resources it needs for its own purposes can be kept "secret." Note that limited usage of public variables is advised for the following two reasons:

- Uncontrolled manipulation of global information can lead to a disorganized and error-filled program.
- C allows any function to modify any public variable—without verifying strict type compatibility—thus increasing the potential for errors.

The separate compilation feature not only eases the programming effort by allowing the independent modification of small parts of a system, but it also makes general use of common units easy. A library of C routines (or routines written in assembler, accessible from C) is easy to create, enhance, and then share among programmers by simply linking in those routines needed by any set of units. By definition, C provides no I/O capabilities. Consequently, libraries containing these, along with other standard run-time facilities, are generally provided with the compiler. (These functions are usually a subset of the UNIX I/O and run-time library.)

Statement Grouping and Blocks

C is a block-structured language, enabling you to logically group statements under control of certain conditions. However, C goes one step further by allowing its blocks

```
/* file 'decls.h' containing all functions declared extern */

extern        this_function (x, y, z);
extern        that_function (a, b);
extern char other_function ( );

    ------------------------------

/* file 'funcs1.c' containing actual bodies of functions */

this_function (x, y, z)
        int x;
        char y;
        char *z;
{
.
.
.
}     /* end of function this _function */

that_function (a, b)
        float a, b;
{
.
.
.
}     /* end of function that _function */

char other_function ( )
{
.
.
.
}     /* end of function other _function */

    ------------------------------

/* main source file includes others */

#include "decls.h"
#include "funcs1.c"
#include "funcs2.c"
.
.
.
```

Figure 11-2. Function declarations

to have local variable definitions.[4] Use of this feature can decrease the amount of static memory required by the program, and enhance modularity by declaring variables in the most limited context in which they are used.

Figure 11-3 shows an example of this. Here, employee names are read from the employee file and counted. Each name is then displayed, preceded by its sequence

----

[4]These variables are dynamic, as opposed to static, and are called "automatic" in the Kernighan and Ritchie text. They behave the same as variables defined inside functions.

```
#include "stdio.h"

int    counter;
FILE *emp_file;

counter = 0;

do {
    char employee [15];

    get_employee (emp_file, employee);
    counter++;
    printf ("Employee #%d is %s\n", counter, employee);

    } while (counter < 10);
```

Figure 11-3. An example of local variable declaration within a block

number. The variable *employee*, defined inside the **do/while** loop, is used as a temporary receptacle for a value returned by the function *get_employee*. It is only in existence within that block and therefore may not be referenced outside of that scope. Note that the availability of the standard I/O header file "stdio.h" is assumed.

STRUCTURING C PROGRAMS

Structuring involves taking the three basic structures as well as any additional structures and combining them to accomplish a given function or subfunction. These are briefly reviewed here with C examples.

Sequence Structure

The sequence structure consists of two process blocks in which control flows from one box to the next in sequence. A box could represent a single statement, such as assignment, or a group of statements accessed by a function call.

Choice Structure

The choice structure specifies a test between two alternatives to determine which of two process blocks to execute.

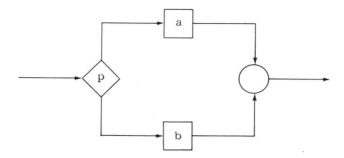

In C, the standard **if/else** statement accomplishes this structure. The format is a single **if**, optionally followed by an **else**. The condition is an arbitrarily complex integer expression, tested for zero (FALSE) or nonzero (TRUE). A single statement follows both the **if** and **else**, although it could be a block of statements. Here is an example of a simple **if** statement:

```
if (end_of_page)
    putchar (CLEAR_SCREEN);
```

The statement following the **else** may itself be another **if** statement. Such nesting is often necessary, but it should be handled carefully, with appropriate indentation and meaningful identifier names.

For example:

```
if (age > 30)
        trust = FALSE;

else if (age < 18)
        can_draft = FALSE;

else {
        trust = TRUE;
        can__draft = TRUE;

    }
```

Note the indentation used. The preceding format is suggested to provide maximum clarity with minimum waste of space. If you are testing a series of mutually exclusive conditions, additional indenting at each level can be troublesome. The examples in Figure 11-4 demonstrate the comparison.

```
            if (cond1)
                stmt1

        else
            if (cond2)
                stmt2

            else
                if (cond3)
                    stmt3

                else
                    if (cond4)
                        stmt4

                    else
                        stmt5
```

```
        if (cond1)
            stmt1

        else if (cond2)
            stmt2

        else if (cond3)
            stmt3

        else if (cond4)
            stmt4

        else
            stmt5
```

Figure 11-4. Excessive vs. minimum indentation of nested If/Elses

Repetition Structures

C provides both the DOWHILE and DOUNTIL structures. In addition, it provides a generalized, flexible iteration construct which can fit into either of those formats.

DOWHILE Structure   The DOWHILE structure provides basic loop capability by specifying a process that is repeated while a given condition is true. The condition is tested before each iteration (including the first one). The diagram is as follows:

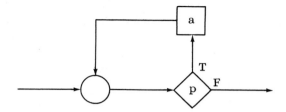

This construct is provided with C's **while** statement. Here is an example:

```
while (lines < page_size) {
    get_line (&buffer);
    display_line (&buffer);
    lines++;
    }
```

DOUNTIL Structure   The DOUNTIL structure is identical to the DOWHILE, except that the process is continued *until* the given condition is met, and the test is made *after* each execution. The flow diagram for the DOUNTIL follows:

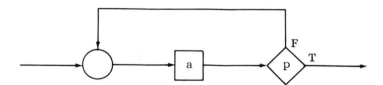

C's **do/while** statement, with a negative condition, can be used here. An example:

```
do {
    get_data (input_file, &data_rec);
    result = process_data (&data_rec);
    } while (result != INVALID);
```

Alternatively, you could define a macro called UNTIL(c) to equate to "while not c", as follows:

```
#define UNTIL(cond) while (!(cond))

do {
    get_data (input_file, &data_rec);
    result = process_data (&data_rec);
    } UNTIL (result = INVALID);
```

ITERATION Structure   C provides a refinement of the DOWHILE structure for general iteration. It is the **for** statement. This gives the programmer the opportunity to create any form of repetition desired, under a set of arbitrarily complex conditions. The following is a diagram for a **for** statement, where i is initialization, p is the tested condition, a is the process to be repeated, and x is the trailing statement to be executed (note that i, p, and x are all optional):

```
for (i; p; x) {
          a
}
```

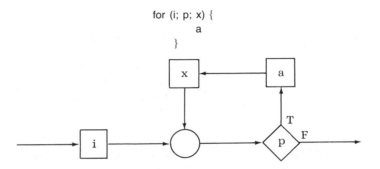

An example of a typical **for** statement is:

```
high_score = -1;
for (i = 0; i < class_size; i++) {
    total_scores += scores [i];
    if (scores [i] > high_score) {
        high_score   = scores [i];
        high_student = i;
    }
}
```

Case Structure

This structure provides selective execution based on the value of an expression. Although this is simply shorthand for a sequence of **if/else**'s, it is a clearer construct for those times when a single choice must be made from among several mutually exclusive alternatives. Its diagram is:

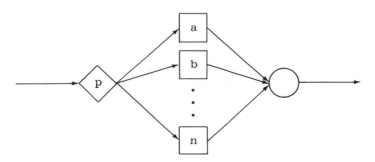

This is implemented with C's **switch** statement. The key to the **switch** statement is that it is actually just a conditional GOTO. The unique case expressions act as labels to which control is transferred. Execution begins with the first statement after the case expression and continues until either the end of the **switch** statement or a **break** statement is encountered. A **break** causes a branch to the end of the **switch** statement.

This setup allows multiple labels to refer to the same sequence of statements, as well as the option of a case "falling through" to the next case. The latter usage is not generally a good programming practice because it detracts from the assumed flow of control. That is, one expects only one of the alternatives to be executed, whereas if one case falls through to the next, then in fact two alternatives will be executed. In addition, the order of cases in a **switch** statement is usually insignificant. This ceases to be true, however, if a case is allowed to fall through. It then makes editing the source file potentially dangerous. In general, if this construct is used, it should be clearly commented as such (you'll be sorry at least once if you don't!).

The label **default** is provided as a destination when the selecting expression doesn't equal any of the case expressions. A very common error in C is neglecting to use the **break** statement, thus causing the above-mentioned problems. Another common error is not using the **default** label. Unlike other languages, if none of the cases match, control just continues to the statement following the **switch** statement without error. Sometimes this is desired, but other times it is not.

Figure 11-5 shows a **switch** statement being used to handle keyboard input. Backspace (BS), Carriage Return (CR), and End of Input (EOI) are handled as expected. Nongraphic ASCII characters (those between 0 and 1F hex (0-31, decimal)) are converted to a question mark before falling through to be processed normally. The default is to process the character by adding it to the input buffer.

Search Construction (Coded)

While there is no search construct in C, searching algorithms can easily be coded. In addition, most C compilers' run-time systems provide pattern-matching functions which facilitate such searching operations. Here is an example of a sequential list search:

```
for (i = 0; !match (pattern, text {i}); i++)
    ;
```

Note that the **for** statement contains everything necessary for the loop, requiring only a null statement as its block.

Miscellaneous Structures

There are a few statements in C 'which do not fit into one of the categories just mentioned, but transfer control in an unusual, although well-defined manner. They are:

- **break**
- **continue**
- **goto**

```
char      ch;
int       done = FALSE;

#include "ascii.h"        /* contains #defines of ascii values */

.
.
.

while (!done) {
        ch = getchar ();
        switch (ch) {
            case BS          : del_prev_char ();
                               break;

            case CR          : process_line ();
                               break;

            case EOI         : done = TRUE;
                               break;

            case ASCII_01H :
            case ASCII_02H :
                    .     :
                    .     :
            case ASCII_1FH : ch = '?';      /* fall through */

            default          : add_to_buf (ch);
                               break;

        }    /* end of switch */
} /* end of while */
```

Figure 11-5. Switch statement example

Each of these can be useful under the right circumstances and are sometimes essential for proper execution (e.g., the **break** in a **switch** statement). However, because they transfer control in a nonsequential manner, you should comment their use and avoid overusing them.

The **return** statement partially belongs in this group. While it does transfer control in a nonsequential manner, it is also required in order for functions to return a value. The main consideration for a **return** statement is that it should be used at the end of the function. You should avoid using several **returns** or putting them inside loops. Otherwise you would violate the rule that a function have only one exit point.

READABILITY

Now let's look at some additional features provided by C which can be used to aid in clarity and programming ease.

Spacing, Formatting, and Comments

C is a free format language; the physical appearance of the program does not affect its content. Statements can be split across lines and multiple statements can be put on one line. This latter feature should be used only when the statements are very simple and similar, such as related increment/decrement operations. For example, it is quite common to advance the argument vector pointer and to decrement its associated counter (e.g., with program invocation arguments) on one line:

```
argv + + ; argc--;
```

If you are working alone, you are, of course, free to choose your own formatting rules, combining indentation, capitalization,[5] and spacing in a consistent manner. This is particularly important in C, because a C program can otherwise become quite unreadable. Judicious use of indentation can clarify the nesting of blocks (e.g., in the **if** and **while** statements).

It is recommended that any given project adopt a standard set of formatting guidelines to ensure consistent usage throughout its code. A list of suggested formatting rules is included at the end of this chapter.

Comments in C are allowed anywhere a word or symbol may exist, and may be split across lines. Debate exists with respect to C as to the preferred manner of comments (block vs. line). Block comments at the beginning of any function, describing its action and including its formal parameters, should generally suffice. Individual line comments are sometimes necessary, however, to describe or highlight subtle or machine-dependent code.

Figures 11-6a and 11-6b present the same function with different formatting, naming and commenting considerations. We expect you will conclude that one is superior in terms of clarity. Again, note the use of values from the standard I/O header file "stdio.h."

Preprocessor

As part of the definition of C, there is a preprocessor which provides several useful commands:

#define, the text replacement command

#include, the file inclusion command

[5]Note that in most C compilers, case of identifiers is significant. See the section that follows entitled "Tips and Traps."

```
get_line(p)
char *p;
{
int n=0;char c1,c2='\0';
while(!n){
*p++ =(c1=get char(f));
if(c1==LF&&c2==CR){
*p=c2='\0';
n=l;}
c2=c1;}
*p='\0';
}
```

Figure 11-6(a). Example of no formatting

```
/ * ----------------------------------------------------------------------- *
  *                          g e t _ l i n e                                *
  * ----------------------------------------------------------------------- *
  *         Get a line of text from keyboard and return it. Append a        *
  *                         '\0' after the CR/LF.                           * /
  * ----------------------------------------------------------------------- *

get_line (buf)
    char *buf;

{
        char        chr;
        BOOLEAN newline = FALSE;
        char        prev_char = '\0';

        while (!newline) {
            chr       = get_char (input_file);
            *buf++    = chr;
            if ((chr == LF) && (prev_char == CR)) {
                *buf        = '\0';
                prev_char = '\0';
                newline    = TRUE;
                }
            prev_char = chr;

            }  /* end while */

        *buf = '\0';

}  /* end of function get_line */
```

Figure 11-6(b). Example of full formatting

One of C's most attractive features is the #define compiler directive. It allows the assignment of any text to a single name and can include parameters to provide a macro facility. Names created with the #define command share the same name space as other objects. This means that their names must be unique not only among each other, but among all other variables, functions and typedefs accessible within that unit. However, they are known only within the unit in which they are created and cannot be made public.

The most common uses of this feature are to:

- provide named constants
- use mnemonic names for common and/or unclear procedures
- hide complicated and ugly operations without requiring a function call

In the second case, one of the main advantages is not having to worry that the same operation is key entered exactly the same each time. Also, modification is limited to one place. Note that the last item on the list requires more code space than a function call, but runs faster. This is a trade-off that you must evaluate on a case-by-case basis.

When the preprocessor encounters an identifier which is a #define, it replaces that identifier with the actual text represented by the #define. The compiler then sees the entire program; it does not distinguish between text brought in by the preprocessor and text originally in the file (indeed it cannot).

This can cause some unexpected compile-time errors, such as lines being too long. In the following examples of #define given in Figure 11-7, note in NEXT _NAME, the variable *cur_id* is assumed to have been defined beforehand, whereas in FAHR, *deg* is a parameter to the macro. In this latter case, *deg* is enclosed in parentheses because it could be replaced by an expression, which might otherwise be evaluated incorrectly when the replacement is done. This is also the reason the entire text of both of these macros is enclosed in parentheses.

```
#define E_BAD_CMD 1
#define E_ILL_NUM 2
#define E_UNK_NAME 3

#define SIGN_ON "Fred's Spreadsheet V1.2\n"
#define COPY_RT "(c) Fred's Software\tMay 2, 1988"

#define SET_FLAG    flag = TRUE
#define RESET_FLAG  flag = FALSE

#define NEXT_NAME  ((cur_id <= 10) ? mgrs [cur_id] : getname (cur_id))

#define FAHR(deg)    (((deg) * 1.8) + 32)
```

Figure 11-7. Sample uses of #define

Another useful feature of C's preprocessor is the #include compiler directive. This allows a separate source file to be brought into a unit for compilation as if it resided there originally. These auxiliary files are often called header files, because they usually are #included at the top, or head, of the unit. As such, their names often have the format "<name>.h" (e.g., "stdio.h", "mydefs.h").

Header files are useful for placing public variable declarations and type definitions, as well as constants and macros created with the #define command. This allows a single reference location for all of these items. It also provides one file which can easily be used by others in the same project to ensure compatibility. This can be useful, too, for unrelated programs. It allows you to define standard constants and use them in all your programs without having to redefine them each time. Finally, when any of these items need to be changed, only the header file needs to be updated, rather than the entire unit. Figure 11-8 contains an example of a general header file.

```
/* some useful standard constants */
#define   TRUE              1
#define   FALSE             0
#define   BLANK             ' '
#define   BS                \b
#define   TAB               \t
#define   LF                \n
#define   CR                \r

/* these are in octal and are ASCII specific */
#define   BEEP              '\007'
#define   ESC               '\033'
#define   DEL               '\177'

/* ANSI standard screen functions - must be preceded by ESC */
#define   SAVE_CURSOR        "[s"
#define   RESTORE_CURSOR     "[u"
#define   ERASE_LINE         "[K"
#define   CLEAR              "[2J"
#define   HIGHLIGHT          "[7m"
#define   ATTR_OFF           "[0m"

/* some useful macros */
#define MAX(a,b)      ((a) > (b) ? (a) : (b))
#define MIN(a,b)      ((a) < (b) ? (a) : (b))
```

Figure 11-8. Sample general include file

SIMPLIFYING FEATURES

There are several features in C which allow code to be written in a straightforward manner. These features include:

- the typedef construct
- the conditional expression
- the operation/assignment operators
- the pre- and post-increment/decrement operators
- the short-circuit logical operators
- initialization of variables

The Typedef Construct

C allows you to create types by assigning a name to a data structure you create. This enables you to use the structure again without reentering it in its long form. Such naming of structures allows meaningful names to be used in place of complicated definitions. It also ensures consistency of definition between different uses. When a type of general use is created with the typedef construct, it should be kept in one of the standard header files just discussed.

The most common usage of this feature is in naming types created with the **struct** construct or renaming standard types. Once defined, these types can be used wherever a predefined typename is expected. For example, it can be used in the definition of a variable or of a formal parameter to a function. See Figure 11-9 for examples of how this is used.

```
typedef struct {
        char     name[40];
        char     ssn[12];
        unsigned emp_num;
        unsigned dept_num;
        } emp_struct;

typedef unsigned char byte;
    .
    .
    .
emp_struct pres = { "Fred T. Boss", "123-45-6789", 1, 100 };
byte       data [10];
    .
    .
    .
get_employee (emp_ptr)
     emp_struct *emp_ptr;
{
    .
    .
    .
}
```

Figure 11-9. Examples of user-defined types

The Conditional Expression

The conditional expression yields a value dependent upon the given condition, without the need of an **if/else** statement (see the MIN and MAX macros defined in Figure 11-8). Because this expression can be placed anywhere a normal expression is expected, codespace can be decreased while flexibility is increased. A shortcoming of this construct is that until you are used to it, it is somewhat cryptic. However, liberal use of white space (blanks and tabs) and parentheses around the symbols, and meaningful variable names, should provide the desired clarity.

A common use of the conditional expression is in output statements, where some, but not all, of what is to be displayed is dependent on a particular value. It is tedious and wasteful to use an **if/else** statement, thereby requiring two output statements. It is also handy when the display of a value is to be in a different format from the value itself. Figure 11-10 shows an example first utilizing the conditional expression, and then what you would do if there were no conditional expressions.

```
#define MALE    0
#define FEMALE 1

struct {
        char *name;
        int   age;
        int   sex;
        } person;

/* one printf statement using a conditional expression to display sex */

printf ("Name: %s\nAge : %d\nSex : %s\n",
        person.name, person.age,
        (person.sex = = MALE ? "Male" : "Female"));

/* two printf statements, in an if/else required */

if (person.sex = = MALE)
    printf ("Name: %s\nAge : %d\nSex : Male\n",
            person.name, person.age);
else
    printf ("Name: %s\nAge : %d\nSex : Female\n",
            person.name, person.age);
```

Figure 11-10. Output with and without conditional expressions

Operation/Assignment Operators

The set of binary operation/assignment operators allows the modification of a variable in almost any manner in a compact but clear way. For example, when you wish to add expression to a variable and retain the result in that variable, the add/assignment operator is used. It eliminates the need to repeat the original variable name on both sides of the assignment operator, thereby replacing the mathematical ambiguity of

total_size = total_size + size (item);

by

total_size += size (item);

Increment and Decrement Operators

The increment and decrement operators provide a shorthand for the most common of these binary operations: adding or subtracting 1 to and from a variable. With them, you can use

a++;

and be clearer, simpler, and mathematically less ambiguous than

a = a + 1;

Another feature of these operators is that they give you the option of referencing the value of the object before (a++) or after (++a) it is modified. Thus code is saved by compressing the use and updating of an object in one place. This is particularly useful in character string manipulation. Be aware that overuse of this feature in expressions can make the statement difficult to interpret (by the reader, not the compiler).

In the example in Figure 11-11, a string is searched for a specific prefix character. The program is passed a pointer to this string. If the prefix is found, a pointer to the following location is returned. If not, a null pointer value is returned.

```
char *find_char (prefix, buf_ptr)
    char prefix;
    char *buf_ptr;

{
    while (*buf_ptr)
        if (*buf_ptr++ == prefix)
            return (buf_ptr);

    return (NULL);

}
```

Figure 11-11. Example of post-increment operator

Short-Circuit Logical Operators

The next feature we will briefly discuss is the existence of the short-circuit logical operators && (AND) and || (OR). By short-circuit, we mean that evaluation proceeds in the specified order until the value of the logical expression is unalterably determined. For &&, this happens as soon as one of the operands evaluates to 0 (FALSE). For ||, it is when one operand evaluates to a nonzero value (TRUE). Of course, should you not want to use the short-circuit operators, the bit-wise comparison operators & (AND) and || (OR) are always available.

The short-circuit operators can be handy when manipulating pointers or indexing into arrays. Because they permit you to test for validity before use, you can prevent an invalid reference (such as an array index out of bounds). In the following example, you wouldn't want to get the object to which *person_ptr* points (called dereferencing the pointer) if the pointer had a NULL value:

```
person_rec *person_ptr;
    .
    .
    .
person_ptr = get_rec ();
if ((person_ptr != NULL) && (person_ptr->salary > 5000))
        compute_tax (person_ptr)
```

While these operators are useful, they do create implicit assumptions about the relationships between various pieces of data which might not be apparent from a cursory reading of the listing. Consequently, usage with subtle assumptions should be documented.

Initialization

The last of the simplifying features we will discuss is the ability to initialize variables at their point of declaration. This includes static arrays and structures as well as both static and automatic scalars (see Figure 11-9 for an example). The value of uninitialized static and external variables is 0, but it is undefined for automatic (local) and register variables. Initializing variables in this manner provides three advantages:

- a single reference point for type and initial value
- a means to initialize constants
- elimination of the need for additional statements, such as a series of **for** loops.

Figure 11-12 is an example of the use of initialization with a counter variable. It is a loop which gets a pointer to an input record and processes it. A check is made to ensure that the data read is actually present. A count of the number of valid records

```
int          count = 0;
unsigned int high_salary = 0;
rec          *index;
NAME         person = EMPTY_STRING;

do {
    index = get_data_record ();
    if (index != NULL) {
        count++;
        display_rec (index);
        if index->salary > high_salary {
            high_salary = index->salary;
            person      = index->name;
        }
    }
} while (count < RECS _TO_ READ);
printf ('\n\nHighest salary of $%u belongs to %s\n');
```

Figure 11-12. Example of initialization

input is kept, and processing stops when a predetermined number of valid records are processed.

OTHER FEATURES

Data Structures

Associating data which is logically related is a good way to organize a program. It reduces the number of variables that you have to keep track of and clarifies the relationship of associated items. A typical use of such data structuring is grouping, such as with employee data, where there might be fields for name, employee number, department, social security number and salary. Another example of structuring is a list, such as might be used in sorting names or performing statistical operations on a sequence of numbers.

C provides the standard set of data structuring capabilities found in most high-level languages, in addition to its basic scalar data types. These are the **struct**, **union**, and array. The **struct** is a nestable grouping structure. Nestable means that members of a **struct** may themselves be **structs**. The **union** is a variable whose type may vary dynamically. C's array is a single dimension list whose values may be of any type, including arrays, thereby allowing multiple dimensions.

The definition of the language specifies that if two structures contain members with the same name, then the offsets within their respective structures must be the same. Many compilers do not enforce this, but you should be aware that such usage may make your program nonportable.

In addition to these relatively standard data structures, C also provides the capability of creating bit-fields, enabling you to pack several pieces of information into one machine word. Note that use of this feature can make your program nonportable because of the direct access to the machine word.

Pointers

One of C's basic types is the pointer. It is a variable whose value is the address of another object. While the pointer has a type (i.e., it is a pointer to an object of a specific type), the compiler does not enforce strict compatibility. (See the discussion of LINT which follows.) This makes pointers a very powerful tool, but also a dangerous one, because it allows unchecked access to any address in the machine.

Pointers have many uses including:

• parameter passing
• dynamic memory allocation
• string manipulation

Because C does not allow entire nonscalar objects (such as an array or **struct**) to be passed as parameters, you must instead pass the address of that object. If you want to modify a parameter (of any type), you must pass the address of that object to the function. The routine then dereferences the pointer to access the object.

Allocating memory dynamically is the ideal method for handling objects of varying size, such as linked lists. Memory allocation routines are generally provided in the compiler's run-time library. They usually return a pointer to the block of memory allocated. You may then consider that storage area to be occupied by a **struct**, an array, or whatever other object you choose. It is up to you to ensure that the memory location pointed to contains the information you expect it to.

Character String Handling

In C, strings are an array of characters, terminated by a null. All string operations are performed by functions (e.g., *strcmp* to compare two strings) supplied in the run-time library. Using a pointer as a "finger" or "placeholder" within the string is a common means of manipulating strings. However, because a string is an array, you may also index into it. Refer to Figures 11-6b and 11-11 for examples of how pointers are used with strings.

Casts

While C does not generally enforce type compatibility (performing type conversions implicitly), it does provide a means for explicit type coercion. This is the Cast operator and it is applied as a prefix, unary operator. When converting various objects from one type to another, especially pointers, it is a good idea to use casts. This clarifies any subtleties at a future reading and can help point out areas which might need to be modified when porting the program to another machine.

The following provides an example of using a Cast. Because the memory allocation routine returns a pointer to a character, it must be converted to a pointer to a *record*, a user-defined structure. The variable *record_ptr* may now be manipulated as a pointer to the *record* structure.

```
typedef struct {
           .
           .
           } record;

record *record_ptr;
           .
           .
record_ptr = (record *)allocate (record);
           .
```

SOME C PROGRAMMING CONSIDERATIONS

Potential Problem Areas

C has many features that contribute to making structured programming easy. However, it also has some attributes which, if you are not aware of them, can make programming in C more difficult than it needs to be. Take special note of the following:

1. Pointer arithmetic is automatic
2. Programs can be cryptic
3. All parameter passing is by value
4. C is not strongly typed

Almost surprisingly, C does just what you would expect with regard to pointer arithmetic. That is, it is based on the size of the object to which the pointer points. For example, if you increment a pointer to an **int**:

```
int *p;
     .
     .
p++;
```

it adds *n* bytes to the current value of *p*, where *n* is the number of bytes used to store an **int** (e.g., 2 on a 16-bit machine and 4 on a 32-bit machine). If you are used to doing this manually and forget that C does it for you, the results will be incorrect. In general, you should restrict the use of pointer arithmetic to traversing an array of a given type, such as characters in a string.

With respect to the second point, many C programmers have a tendency to write undecipherable programs. This is due, in part, to C's reliance on a sequence of symbols for most of its operations and the ability to place expressions, including assignment, almost anywhere. There is sometimes a tendency to make the program more compact than necessary to save both execution speed and typing. An example of this is in pointer dereferencing (getting the value to which the pointer is pointing). While the meaning of

$$x = *p++;$$

is fairly clear (dereference the pointer p and assign it to x, then increment the pointer), the meaning of

$$y = *--*p++;$$

is far less evident (dereference the pointer p, increment it, decrement the dereferenced value which is also a pointer, then dereference that and assign it to y). Use of parentheses can clear up some of the confusion and ambiguity:

$$y = *(--(*p++));$$

Using multiple statements to carry out the operation is another solution:

```
q = *p++;          /* dereference and increment */
y = *--q;          /* decrement and dereference */
```

This may require a few more instructions, but it is far less cryptic.

The opportunity to write tricky code arises often. However, the gain in efficiency is not worth the decreased clarity. A good programmer will generally resist the temptation. When such resistance breaks down, or when an absolute minimum of execution time is required, be sure that the section is clearly commented.

The third area mentioned in the list is that parameter passing is all by value. This means that for a function to modify an actual parameter, a pointer to that variable must be passed in. This opens the door to all sorts of potential problems, since any operations are valid on pointers, no checking for type compatibility is made for pointer dereferencing, and no check for uninitialized pointers is made.

Here is an example of what can happen. When calling a function, you pass in a variable by value, while the function is actually expecting a pointer to that variable. The function happily dereferences what it thinks is a pointer and writes into that memory location. However, because it is only some number, you have just written over a random location in memory—possibly in your program, possibly in the operating system. (Most mainframe systems protect against this, while most personal computer systems don't.) In either case, it is probably not what you wanted and will most certainly yield unexpected results.

The final potential problem area of C, lack of strong typing, is one of degree. While C does have types, most C compilers are lenient in verifying their correct usage and combination. This can be a problem in using global (unit level) and external variables, as well as in passing parameters. (This latter example is especially significant when using library routines, the source of which will probably be inaccessible to you.)

For example, if you define a variable as an **int** (standard size integer), but later pass it to a function expecting a **long int** (double size integer), that function will end up accessing an undefined part of the stack, thereby using an invalid value.

To combat this, and some of the pointer-related problems mentioned earlier, UNIX provides a program verification tool called LINT. Among other things, LINT lists all type inconsistencies in a program. In the absence of such a tool on other systems, the programmer should be careful and be aware of this potential problem. This is one of the first places to look when an otherwise inexplicable bug occurs.

Tips and Traps

Here are some tips for achieving good C program structure, as well as some traps to avoid.

All functions in C return a value (an **int**, by default). However, if the function's value is not referenced, it is discarded. This makes these functions look just like procedures (as in Pascal or PL/I). Note that calls to parameterless functions still require the parentheses. This helps to distinguish them from simple variables or macros. For example, see *sys_get_user_priv()* in Figure 11-1a.

Remember that there is a definite difference between the pre- (prefix) and post- (suffix) increment and decrement operators when used in an expression. While these are all very useful operators, it is a good idea to use only one set or the other (i.e., prefix or suffix) throughout a program. For example, you can set up the program's logic to use the suffix operators exclusively, drawing on the prefix operators only when necessary and documenting those cases. Otherwise, you may find occurrences of the fabled "off by one" error.

Recall that the assignment operator can be placed wherever an expression is expected. This flexibility can be useful in saving steps; however it can also be a problem in **if** statements. If a single equal sign ($=$) is entered instead of the double ($==$), it is interpreted as an assignment and yields the value of the right-hand side.

Figure 11-13 provides an example of this. In (a), x takes the value of y, as does the expression, yielding a condition whose value is y, which will be syntactically acceptable but probably not what was intended. In (b), the value of the condition is either 1 or 0, depending on whether or not x equals y, respectively. This is a common type of mistake for which you should check whenever an inexplicable bug appears.

(a)   (b)

if (x = y) {   if (x = = y) {
.   .
.   .
.   .
}   }

Figure 11-13. Assignment erroneously in condition

Note that a single expression, by itself, is considered a legal C statement. While this is a marginally useful feature, it provides the opportunity for error. For example, if you inadvertently entered

x;

or

x + 5;

when you meant

x++;

or

x += 5;

respectively, the compiler does not detect any error. Chances are, however, that this will provide incorrect results in your program.

Consistent indentation rules can make a program much easier to read. Because C's syntax can be somewhat cryptic, free use of white space is recommended, especially around operators and parameter lists. Alignment of brackets around statement blocks is a common formatting technique.

Figure 11-14 contains a sample set of formatting rules which can be used as a guideline. It is recommended that you devise a set for yourself and that any given project consistently use one set of such rules.

1. Begin each unit with a block of comments listing its name, purpose, contents and modification history (including date, what was changed, and by whom).

2. Begin the main unit with a similar set of comments, but include the programmer's name(s) and the compiler and system (including version numbers of both).

3. Organize the functions within a unit alphabetically. (Note that because C assumes a function returns an **int** by default, and that it does not require

declaration before use, alphabetical organization could cause problems. See the discussion at the beginning of this chapter entitled "Modularity and Separate Compilation" for a solution to this.)

Begin each function with comments describing what it does, including input and output formal parameters, and the value returned by the function, if appropriate. Start each function on a separate page unless several functions are short and related routines. (If you don't have a printing program which provides a 'page' capability, you can accomplish this by embedding a form feed character in a comment at the function heading.) Finally, follow the closing bracket of a function with a comment containing its name:

/* end of function x */

4. Put all #include commands at the beginning of the unit. Then use the following sequence for a unit's local definitions:

- #defines
- typedefs
- externals
- other variables
- functions

5. Variables of like types should be declared together, preferably in alphabetical order. Variable names should be aligned. If a variable's purpose is not clear from its name, its definition should be accompanied by a comment explaining its usage.

6. Put blanks

- around all binary operators (but not unary), including assignment
- between a function's name and its parentheses
- before and after almost all parenthesized expressions, including those in **if**, **switch**, **for**, and **while** statements
- after the beginning comment characters and before the ending comment characters
- after every comma in a parameter list
- after every semi-colon in a **for** statement list

Put blank lines

- before and after the function definition heading (i.e., name and parameter list)

- after local variable declarations in functions
- between cases in a **switch** statement
- before and after multiple-line **if/else**, **for**, and **while** statements
- anywhere else they can provide increased readability

7. Align assignment operators in consecutive statements.
8. Indent consistently (e.g., 3 spaces) at each nested level, such as within a **for** statement. Always align the leftmost character of all statements at the same nesting level. In many interactive text editors, a TAB can be used for this purpose.
9. Put the opening bracket for blocking at the end of the heading for the compound statement, and align the closing bracket with the nested statements. For example,

```
while (cond) {
     .
     .
     .
}
```

10. Align the statements from all cases within a **switch** statement.
11. When statements are too long, split them at a logical place and align the overlapped portion indented from the leftmost character.
12. Put function return values in parentheses.

Figure 11-14. Formatting guidelines

Keywords and variable names in C are case-sensitive; that is, a variable name in all lowercase letters is different from the same name where any character appears in uppercase. This can be both useful and annoying. Create a set of naming conventions regarding capitalization. Figure 11-15 contains a sample. Whether case is significant for external names is system dependent.

- C keywords in lowercase
- Variables and functions in lowercase
- #defines in uppercase
- Hexadecimal constants in uppercase
- Use of underscores for name readablility, rather than capitals

Figure 11-15. Capitalization guidelines

A common trap is forgetting that parameters to #defined macros are evaluated each time they are used. This is because the text of a #define is actually expanded and substituted into the source during the preprocessor pass. This can cause problems if the parameter contains an increment operator, for example, because the increment takes place each time the parameter is referenced. For example,

```
#define MAX(a,b) ((a > b) ? a : b)
     .
     .
top_score = MAX (scores[i++], top_score);
```

will result in incrementing the array index *i* twice.

C generally doesn't require the explicit closing of files, as it will close them automatically when the program exits. However, it is good programming practice to close files as soon as they are no longer going to be used. This way, should the program abnormally terminate after the file's usefulness has ended, its contents will be intact.

Finally, remember that C distinguishes a string constant of length 1 (i.e., only 1 character) from a character constant. Thus

'a'

is a different type of entity from

"a"

The former is a character while the latter is actually a pointer to a character.

Portability

C is generally considered a portable language; however, there are many things you can do to a C program to make it nonportable. Sometimes these are appropriate solutions to a particular problem, in which case they should be clearly marked to ease any future porting effort.

Some of the areas you should be aware of as being potentially nonportable include:

- use of ASCII versus EBCDIC
- word size
- dependency upon byte ordering
- signed and unsigned chars
- order of evaluation of a function's actual parameters

This last point bears additional attention. The order of evaluation of the actual parameters to a function can be significant if evaluation of one parameter can affect another. For example,

func_1 (x, x++, y)

sends different values to func_1() depending on whether the second actual parameter is evaluated before or after the first (since it increments *x*). Another subtle cause of this problem could be if one of the actual parameters is a function call itself, which has the side effect of modifying one of the other parameters:

func___2 (a, func___3 (x));

where *func_3()* changes the value of global variable *a*. In general, this is bad programming practice. No module should ever have side effects—that is, modifying global variables.

CASE STUDY

The programming example presented here is an implementation of a reverse polish notation calculator. (Compare to the Pascal case study in Chapter 10.) Such a calculator is one in which both operands are entered before the operator. For example, to add 5 to 7, you would enter:

5 7 +

and the result, 12, is displayed. The usual implementation for this (and the one we have chosen here) is a stack, with each number pushed onto the stack as it is entered. Then for each operator entered, the necessary number of operands (usually two) are popped off the stack, the operation is performed, and the result is pushed back onto the stack. The result of the calculation (i.e., the value on top of the stack) is displayed only when requested.

The hierarchy chart for this CALC program is presented in Figure 11-16a. The three modules EXECUTE COMMAND, GET COMMAND, and DISPLAY STACK are coded as one C function. This was done to avoid excessive numbers of small functions. Similarly, the chart need not include the utility routines *error, push,* and *pop* which are used in several locations. While these are independent steps, they should be thought of not as logical modules but rather as the tools to carry out the steps outlined in the modules.

The flowchart for the CALC program is presented in Figure 11-16b.

An entire line is read in (terminated by a newline) before it is analyzed. Input consists of a sequence of numbers and commands. The numbers may be real or integer, and may optionally be preceded by a minus sign. A command is either a simple arithmetic operator (+ , -, *, /) or one of the following:

- Clear ('c' or 'C')   : clears the stack
- Display ('d' or 'D')   : displays the entire stack
- End ('#')   : exits the program
- Equals ('=')   : pops the top value off stack and displays it
- Top ('$')   : displays the top of the stack

Blanks and tabs are treated as delimiters.

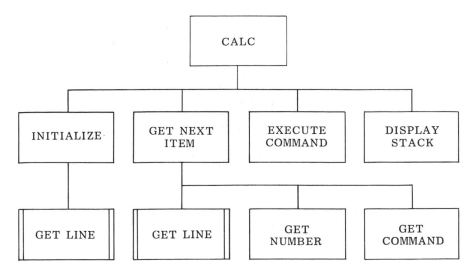

Figure 11-16(a). Hierarchy chart for Calculator

The stack (*stack*) consists of an array of **float** (*nums*) and a current top of stack index (*tos*), combined in a structure of type *float_stack*. Note that the maximum size of the stack is determined by a defined constant *MAX_STACK*, so that it can easily be changed.

Note the use of a **union** structure *variant_element* for the parameter to function *get_next_item*. This enables the routine to return either a real number or a command in a single parameter. The parameter *kind* indicates which type of value is actually returned.

We use the label *top* and the **goto** statement in the function *get_next_item()*. This is a relatively simple use of the **goto** statement and fits in logically with the flow of the program. While we could have coded this routine in such a way as to avoid using the **goto**, that would have resulted in a more complicated and wordy solution with no great benefit.

Regarding the format and layout of the code, note the following features:

- the functions are presented in alphabetical order
- each function begins on a new page (the '/* page */' comment contains a form-feed character which causes the printer to go to the top of the next page)
- each function is preceded by a description of its utility
- all defined constants are in uppercase
- generous use of white space, indentation, and alignment
- the closing brace for each function and compound statement is followed by a comment identifying it

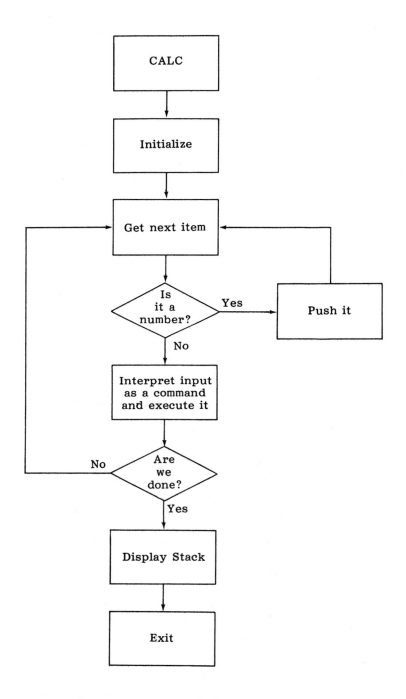

Figure 11-16(b). Flowchart for Calculator

292

```
/* -----------------------------------------------------------
 *    PROGRAM:    calc
 *    -----------------------------------------------------------
 *    PURPOSE:    polish notation calculator
 *
 *
 *    Author:     Ada Lovelace
 *    System:     Mikin OS 1.1
 *    Compiler:   Mediterranean C, v5.4
 *    History:
 *          8/8/88    created
 *          8/23/88   added CLEAR and TOP commands
 *          9/7/88    fixed bug in reading negative numbers
 *    ----------------------------------------------------------- */

#include <stdio.h>              /* standard io package from compiler */
#include <ctype.h>              /* character macros, includes isdigit   */
#include <mydefs.h>

#define SIGN_ON "CALC V1.0\n(c) Copyright Spiffy Programs, Inc., 1988\n\n"

#define MAX_STACK       50
#define NUMBER          0
#define COMMAND         1

#define ADD             0
#define SUB             1
#define MULT            2
#define DIV             3
#define CLEAR           4
#define EQUALS          5
#define END             6
#define TOP             7
#define DISPLAY         8
#define INVALID         255

#define STACK_OVERFLOW    0
#define STACK_UNDERFLOW   1
#define DIVIDE_BY_ZERO    2
#define ILLEGAL_INPUT     3

typedef struct {
            unsigned tos;                   /* top of stack   */
            float nums [MAX_STACK];         /* actual numbers */
            } float _stack;

typedef union {
            float num;
            int   cmd;
            } variant_element;
```

```
char                    line [80];
char                    *line_ptr;
float_stack             stack;
float get_number ( );   /* since these routines return something other than   */
float pop ( );          /* an int, they must be declared before used. they    */
                        /* are put here so the functions can be alphabetical  */
```

/* page */

```
/* -----------------------------------------------------------------------
 *                              e r r o r                                 *
 * -----------------------------------------------------------------------*
 *                       Display error message.                          * /
 * -----------------------------------------------------------------------*/
error (err)
    int err;

{
    printf ("\n *** Error: ");
    switch (err) {

        case STACK_OVERFLOW:     printf ("Stack Overflow");
                                 break;
        case STACK_UNDERFLOW:    printf ("Stack Underflow");
                                 break;
        case DIVIDE_BY_ZERO:     printf ("Divide By Zero");
                                 break;
        case ILLEGAL_INPUT:      printf ("Illegal Input");
                                 break;
        } /* end switch */

    printf ("\n");

    } /* end of error */
```

/* page */

```
/* -----------------------------------------------------------------------
 *                             g e t _ l i n e                            *
 * -----------------------------------------------------------------------*
 *       Get a line of text from keyboard and return it. Append a NULL (\0)*
 *            after the CR/LF. Set line_ptr to beginning of line;         *
 * -----------------------------------------------------------------------*/
get_line (buf_ptr)
    char *buf_ptr;
```

```
{
    BOOLEAN newline = FALSE;
    char      chr;

    printf (" => ");
    while (!newline) {
        chr = getchar ( );
        if (chr == '\n')
            newline = TRUE;
        else
            *buf_ptr++ = chr;

        } /* end while */

    *buf_ptr = '\0';
    line_ptr = &line[0];

} /* end of get _line */



/* page */

/* -------------------------------------------------------------------- *
 *                        g e t _ n e x t _ i t e m                     *
 * -------------------------------------------------------------------- *
 *        Get the next item from the input line. If we reach end of line, *
 *            read another line. Blanks and tabs are delimiters.        *
 * -------------------------------------------------------------------- * /

get_next_item (item_ptr, kind_ptr)
    variant_element   *item_ptr;
    int               *kind_ptr;

{

top:
    while ((*line_ptr == BLANK)    ||    (*line_ptr == TAB))
        line_ptr++;

    if (*line_ptr == '\0') {
        get_line (line);
        goto top;
        } /* end if */

    else if (isdigit (*line_ptr)    ||    (*line_ptr == '.')  ||
        ((*line_ptr == '-') && isdigit (*(line_ptr + 1))) ) {
    *kind_ptr       = NUMBER;
     item_ptr->num = get_number (&line_ptr);
    } /* end else if */
```

```
    else {            /* must be a command */
        *kind_ptr = COMMAND;
        switch (*line_ptr++) {
            case '+': item_ptr->cmd = ADD;
                    break;

            case '-': item_ptr->cmd = SUB;
                    break;

            case '*': item_ptr->cmd = MULT;
                    break;

            case '/': item_ptr->cmd = DIV;
                    break;

            case 'c':
            case 'C': item_ptr->cmd = CLEAR;
                    break;

            case '$': item_ptr->cmd = TOP;
                    break;

            case '=': item_ptr->cmd = EQUALS;
                    break;

            case 'd':
            case 'D': item_ptr->cmd = DISPLAY;
                    break;

            case '#': item_ptr->cmd = END;
                    break;

            default:  item_ptr->cmd = INVALID;
                    break;

        } /* end switch */
    } /* end else */

} /* end of get _next_item */
```

```
/* page */

/     ------------------------------------------------------------------    *
      .                        g e t _ n u m b e r                          *
      . ----------------------------------------------------------------    *
      .       The given pointer is at the beginning of a number (digit, minus    *
      .    sign or decimal point). Read it, return it, and update the pointer.   *
      .    Note that the address of the pointer is passed so it can be updated.  *
      .    Note also that since this function does not return an int, but        *
      .    rather a float, the type must be explicitly specified.               *
      . ----------------------------------------------------------------    * /

float get_ number (ptr_ptr)
    char **ptr_ptr;

{
    BOOLEAN neg = FALSE;
    char    *ptr;
    float   decimals;
    float   val;

    ptr = *ptr_ptr;            /* set local ptr to current value of line pointer */
    if (*ptr == '-') {
    neg = TRUE;
    ptr++;
    }

    val = 0;
    while ((*ptr >= '0') && (*ptr <= '9'))
        val = val * 10 + (*ptr++ - '0');

    if (*ptr == '.') {
        ptr++;
        decimals = 10;
        while ((*ptr >= '0') && (*ptr <= '9')) {
            val += ((*ptr++ - '0') / decimals);
            decimals *= 10;
            } /* end while */

        } /* end if */

    if (neg)
        val *= -1;

    *ptr_ptr = ptr;            /* update line pointer parameter to new value */

    return (val);

    } /* end of get _number */
```

/* page */

```
*  ----------------------------------------------------------------------------  *
*                                                                                *
*                              i n i t i a l i z e                               *
*             Initialization. Set top of stack to 0. Read in first line.         *
*  ----------------------------------------------------------------------------  *
```

initialize ( )

{

    printf (SIGN_ON);

    stack.tos = 0;

    get_line (line);

    } /* end of initialize */

/* page */

```
/  *  --------------------------------------------------------------------------  *
   *                                                                              *
   *                                    p o p                                     *
   *         If stack is not empty, remove top item and return it. Decrement      *
   *         stack pointer. Note that since this function does not return an       *
   *         int, but rather a float, the type must be explicitly specified.      *
   *  --------------------------------------------------------------------------  *  /
```

float pop ( )

{
    if (stack.tos > 0) {
        stack.tos--;
        return (stack.nums [stack.tos]);
        }

    else {
        error (STACK_UNDERFLOW);
        return (0);
        }

    } /* end of pop */

```
/* --------------------------------------------------------------------- *
 * --------------------------------------------------------------------- *
 *                            p u s h                                    *
 * --------------------------------------------------------------------- *
 *      If there is room on the stack push the given number onto it and  *
 *      increment the stack pointer.                                     *
 * --------------------------------------------------------------------- */

push (value)
    float value;

{

    if (stack.tos < MAX_STACK)
        stack.nums [stack.tos++] = value;

    else
        error (STACK_OVERFLOW);

    } /* end of push */




/* page */
/* --------------------------------------------------------------------- *
 * --------------------------------------------------------------------- *
 *                            m a i n                                    *
 * --------------------------------------------------------------------- *
 *      Main program for Calc. Do initialization. Main loop is:          *
 *      - get next entry                                                 *
 *      - if it's a number, push it onto stack                           *
 *      - else interpret as a command                                    *
 *      - display stack upon exit (if nonempty)                          *
 * --------------------------------------------------------------------- */

main ( )

{
    BOOLEAN         done = FALSE;
    int             i, kind;
    float           val1, val2;
    variant_element item;

    initialize ( );

    do {
        get_next_item (&item, &kind);
        if (kind == NUMBER)
            push (item.num);
```

```
else
    switch (item.cmd) {
        case ADD:       val1 = pop ( );
                        val2 = pop ( );
                        push (val1 + val2);
                        break;

        case SUB:       val1 = pop ( );
                        val2 = pop ( );
                        push (val2 - val1);
                        break;

        case MULT:      val1 = pop ( );
                        val2 = pop ( );
                        push (val1 * val2);
                        break;

        case DIV:       val1 = pop ( );
                        val2 = pop ( );
                        if (val1 != 0)
                            push (val2 / val1);
                        else
                            error (DIVIDE_BY_ZERO);
                        break;

        case EQUALS:    val1 = pop ( );
                        printf ("\t%f\n", val1);
                        break;

        case TOP:       if (stack.tos > 0)
                                        printf ("\t%f\n", stack.nums [stack.tos − 1]);
                        else
                                        error (STACK_UNDERFLOW);
                        break;

        case CLEAR:     stack.tos = 0;      /* clear stack completely */
                        break;

        case DISPLAY:   for (i = stack.tos - 1; i >= 0; i--)
                            printf ("%f ", stack.nums [i]);
                        printf ("\n");
                        break;

        case END:       done = TRUE;
                        break;

        case INVALID:   error (ILLEGAL_INPUT);
                        break;
```

```
                } /* end switch */

            } while (!done);

    if (stack.tos != 0) {
        printf ("\nFinal Stack Contents:\n");
        for (i = stack.tos - 1; i > 0; i--)
            printf ("%f", stack.nums [i]);
        printf ("\n");
        } /* end if */

} /* end of main */

/* END OF PROGRAM CALC */
```

Figure 11-16(c). A calculator program using polish notation

MANAGEMENT IMPLICATIONS

In addition to the usual management practices required for overseeing a programming project, C programs raise a number of additional considerations. Since of all the program development phases, maintenance is generally the most costly, any reduction of effort there is desirable. Use of standard formatting and naming techniques can give code written by different programmers a consistent appearance, thereby easing the burden of modification by someone other than the original programmer. Additionally, names that inform the program reader where a function or external variable is defined can be very useful, especially in large projects.

Use of one or more standard header files for interunit communication decreases the concern regarding type incompatibilities of both external variables and parameters, as well as other inconsistencies often not checked by the compiler.

Setting up a standard definitions file containing general-purpose constants and macros to be #included in all units is strongly recommended. It makes it easier for programmers to read each other's code, and to modify it, if necessary. Figure 11-8 contains an example of such a file.

SUMMARY

Programs should be divided into logical units, with each unit being a separately compiled entity. Public variables should be defined in standard files, accessed via the preprocessor's #include command. Additionally, constants and macros should be created with the #define command, and types with the **typedef** construct. Those which are general-purpose should be kept in a standard definitions file, again accessed with the #include command.

Formatting and naming conventions should be adopted and used consistently. Liberal use of white space is needed to compensate for potentially cryptic programs. Meaningful names should be chosen for all named items (functions, variables, constants and macros), and in large projects the external names should indicate in which unit they are defined.

In general, nonsequential statements should not be overused. Specifically, although use of the **break** statement is often the best way to solve a problem, there are times when it adds more confusion than efficiency. Also, use of the **continue** statement should be restricted to those cases where it is absolutely necessary, and then clearly commented. Initialization of variables at their definition should be used for data items whose initial values might be significant.

Use of pointers can often be the best (and only reasonable) method of accomplishing a certain task (e.g., string manipulation or dynamic memory allocation). However, because of the ease with which pointer mistakes can be made without notification, they should be used with caution. Their utility is great but so is their potential for error.

Be aware of potential parameter-passing problems, particularly with external and library routines. Be careful of type inconsistencies and when it's available, use LINT.

REVIEW QUESTIONS AND EXERCISES

1. What problem might arise from a #defined macro that accesses one of its parameters twice?

2. Of what should you be careful in using external functions?

3. The formatting guidelines given are vague about how to handle overlapped lines. Design some formatting rules to handle that situation.

4. Which C statements cause nonsequential flow of control? Which of these are to be approached with caution, and why?

5. What are the advantages of breaking a program into separately compiled units? What problems can arise from this?

6. What's wrong with defining two variables with the names employee_dept and employee_number?

7. Why use #define? Under what circumstances would you not use it?

8. Modify the program in Figure 11-16c so that it can handle up to 100 values rather than 50. Also, change the characters used for each operator and command. Note how easy these common types of changes are when the program is written with the proper use of constants and information hiding.

9. Modify the program in Figure 11-16c to add a memory capability (e.g., S could be store value in memory, R could be recall value from memory, and E could be erase memory).

Glossary

Abstracting. A generalizing process in which one concentrates on similarities between things and gathers them into a group based on those similarities, thus making up the abstraction.

Acceptance phase. The part of a project in which an orderly and user-coordinated installation of the system is completed. The output of this phase is a production program or system.

Actual parameter. The data sent to a subprogram. See *Argument.*

Analysis. The procedure of studying the components of a problem so that a solution can be designed.

Argument. Data sent to a subprogram by an invoking module. Also called actual parameter, since it is the particular value which is being supplied to match the formal parameter with which the subprogram was defined.

Array. An ordered set of data items identified by a single name.

Batch compile. Compiling several procedures in one invocation of the compiler. Although physically together, each procedure is logically separate.

Binary search. A technique for finding a particular item in an ordered set of items by repeatedly dividing in half the portion of the ordered set containing the sought-for item until only that item remains.

Binding. The degree of cohesion of a module; what it is that defines the module.

Block. A group of statements which can be inserted where a single statement is expected. Many languages allow local data declarations within blocks.

Bottom-up approach. Coding and testing by starting with the lowest modules on a hierarchy chart.

BS program. A nonstructured program that has such convoluted logic that it resembles a bowl of spaghetti.

Buffer. See *Data buffer.*

Call by name. A method of parameter passing in which each actual parameter is not evaluated until it is needed. This is as if the subroutine had been substituted for its call (as if it were a macro).

Call by reference or address.   A method of parameter passing wherein the address of the actual parameter is passed to the called routine. Each reference to the formal parameter is then an indirect reference to the actual parameter, allowing modification.

Call by value.   A method of parameter passing wherein the actual parameter (argument) is evaluated and this value passed in for the corresponding formal parameter. This method does not allow the parameter's value to be modified.

Called routine.   A procedure that is activated by another procedure.

Caller.   A module or segment that invokes another module or segment.

Choice structure.   A basic program structure in which a predicate is tested and one of two process blocks is executed, based on the outcome of the test. Also called IFTHENELSE, selection, or alternation.

Collector node.   A circle representing a merge point. One of three fundamental symbols used in the construction of structured flowcharts. Performs no function, serving only as a junction point.

Concatenate.   In DP, to join together or connect data sets, modules, character or bit string data.

Constant.   A fixed or invariable value or data item.

Control break.   A change in the value of a field which indicates the last record in a series. Usually some special action (e.g., summarizing) is performed when this occurs.

Coupling.   The degree with which two modules are tied together, measured by how interdependent they are.

Critical path.   A chain of activities in a project, each of which requires that the previous one complete before it can start. Thus all must be completed on time in order for the entire project to finish on schedule.

Data buffer.   Intermediate storage, used in input/output operations, into which a record is read during input and from which a record is written during output.

Data dependency.   The requirement that a module has for data produced or modified by another module.

Data generator program.   See *Test data generator.*

Data list.   A list of the data items needed by a module along with their attributes. Usually developed during the course of stepwise refinement.

Debugging.   The process of removing errors from a program.

Decision symbol.   A diamond representing a choice between two alternatives; one of the three nodes used in the construction of structured flowcharts, see *Predicate node.*

Decompose.   Subdivide into more detailed components.

Design phase.   That part of a project in which the details of a system to fulfill stated requirements are completed. The output of this phase includes a hierarchy chart, module descriptions, file and record definitions, and so on.

Developer.   A designer, analyst, programmer, tester, documentor, or any other person who is involved in the technical aspects of a project.

Direct access.   Retrieval or storage of data by reference to its location on a volume rather than on the basis of previously retrieved or stored data.

Driver program.   A program specially written to test a module by simulating the environment in which it will run.

Entry point.   A point in a procedure or subroutine at which it may be invoked.

Executable statement.   A statement which specifies action to be taken by the program; for example, calculations to be performed, conditions to be tested, flow of control to be altered.

Execution order.   The order for writing and testing modules of a program based on the sequence in which they are expected to execute in a production run.

Exposure.   An error or omission discovered during a structured walk-through.

Feasibility phase.   The initial part of a project in which the requirements, benefits, and costs are briefly examined to determine if the project is viable.

File (ANS definition).   A collection of related records treated as a unit.

File maintenance (ANS definition).   The activity of keeping a file up to date by adding, changing, or deleting data.

Flow of control.   The invocation and subsequent return of one module by another.

Formal parameter.   The name used in defining a subprogram which specifies what data the procedure expects to be sent. See *Parameter.*

Function.   The transformation of input to output that occurs when a module is invoked.

Function reference.   The invoking of a subprogram by using its name in an executable statement. The value returned by the function is then used in the execution of the statement that invoked it.

Hierarchical development order.   The order for writing and testing modules based on their level in a hierarchy chart. All modules on one level would be completed before those on a lower level.

Hierarchy chart.   A graphic method for describing program design that is used in the top-down design process. A hierarchy chart shows the functions (or modules) in a program and the flow of control.

Implementation phase.   That part of a project in which the modules are designed in detail, coded, tested, and integrated. The output of this phase is a completed, tested system.

Indentation unit.   The number of columns for indenting source statements to improve readability. This is usually standardized for all programs in an installation.

Indicator.   A variable with limited values—usually only two—which is used to record the occurrence of a particular event. For example, an end-of-file indicator would have two values to state whether or not the end-of-file has occurred.

Information hiding.   Keeping local implementation details of a portion of a program inaccessible by external users of that portion. This can be done when such details are unrelated to these external users.

Initialization.   The capability of providing a starting value for a variable when it is declared.

Input/Output list.   A list prepared for each module showing the data items read by it or passed to it, and the data items generated or modified by the module.

Installation.   A particular computing system understood in terms of the work it does and the people who manage it, operate it, apply it to problems, service it, and use the results it produces.

I/O list.   See *Input/Output list.*

Integration.   Combining and testing modules to verify that they work properly with each other.

Interface.   Any connection that exists between modules. It could be data passed in either direction during invocation, data shared in common, or any other assumptions one module makes about the other.

Invoke.   To activate a procedure.

Job control language (JCL).   Statements used in identifying a job or describing its requirements to the operating system.

Linkage (ANS definition).   In programming, coding that connects two separately coded routines.

Logical expression.   A combination of variables, constants, and relational operators that results in a true or false condition.

Loop structure.   See *Repetition structure.*

Maintainability.   The ease with which an existing program can be corrected or modified.

Maintenance.   Any activity intended to remove faults from a program or make minor improvements to it.

Manager.   The person who exercises administrative and personnel authority over others. Concerned with hiring, assigning, and evaluating people.

Master file (ANS definition).   A file that is either relatively permanent, or that is treated as an authority in a particular job.

Merge point.   Any point on a flowchart where two or more flow paths meet to form a single path. In structured flowcharts this is shown by a collector symbol.

Module.   (1) A program unit that is discrete and identifiable with respect to compiling, combining with other units, and loading. (2) A functional unit of code.

Multiprogramming.   Technique for handling two or more programs by overlapping and interleaving their execution.

Nesting.   The inclusion of one programming statement within another of the same type; for example, an IF statement that has another IF statement as one of its alternate actions.

Node.   The representation of a state or an event by means of a symbol on a diagram. In structured programming this refers to one of the three fundamental elements—process node, predicate node (decision symbol) or collector node—used to construct the structured programming flowchart figures.

Nucleus.   The "top" of a program, consisting of the top module on the hierarchy chart plus other stubs or modules necessary to execute correctly.

Null else.   The ELSE process in an IFTHENELSE in which no action is to be performed. Often required to maintain logic in nested IFs.

Object program.   The set of machine language instructions that is the output from the compilation of a source program. The actual processing of data is done by the object program.

Overlay.   See *Program overlay.*

Page.   In virtual storage systems, a fixed-length block of instructions, data, or both, that can be transferred between real storage and external page storage.

Parameter.   A name used in defining a procedure which specifies the data that the procedure expects to be sent. The particular data that is sent is called an argument or an actual parameter to distinguish it from a (formal) parameter.

Partition size.   That portion of main storage which is assigned to one job in a multiprogramming environment. Also called region size.

Phased-development cycle.   The subdivision of a project into several sequential parts, each of which emphasizes a particular aspect of the project.

Pilot project.   A project which is carefully studied and measured for the purpose of evaluating a new technique, but which also produces a usable result.

Planner.   A person responsible for determining how a project will be implemented by establishing the order in which modules will be coded and tested.

Planning phase.   That part of a project in which the details of the implementation phase are determined. The output of this phase is a plan for the order and method in which the modules will be coded and tested.

Pointer.   A data item whose value is the location of another data item.

Portability. A measure of the ease of moving a program from one computer and/or operating system to another.

Predicate node. A diamond representing a test; one of three fundamental nodes used in the construction of structured flowcharts. This node always has one input and two outputs and represents a binary decision such as true/false, yes/no, and go/no go.

Preprocessor. A program which runs before a compiler, taking program source as input and producing modified source as output. This modified source is then used as input to the actual compiler.

Process node. A rectangle representing a function or process. One of three fundamental symbols used in the construction of structured flowcharts.

Production run. The execution of a program in order to use the intended results, as contrasted with execution for the purpose of testing.

Productivity. A measure of the useful output produced, as compared with the expenditure of resources to produce it.

Program. An executable entity that consists of one or more modules.

Program overlay. A program in which certain sections can use the same storage locations at different times during execution.

Program stub. See *Stub*.

Project leader. The person who coordinates the activities of the people working on a project and is the technical authority (contrast with *Manager*).

Proper program. A program with only one entry, one exit, and no unreachable (dead) code or infinite loops.

Pseudo code. A noncompilable quasi-code that requires programmer translation to a compilable language prior to execution.

Recursive program. A program or portion of a program that invokes itself.

Region size. See *Partition size*.

Reliability (ANS definition). The probability that a device or program will function without failure over a specified time period or amount of usage.

Repetition structure. A basic program structure in which iterative execution is controlled by means of a test of a predicate (also called *loop structure*). DOWHILE and DOUNTIL are two types of repetition structures.

Requirements phase. That part of a project in which the needs for the proposed system are defined in detail and whose output is the system specifications.

Search argument. In a search operation, that which is to be compared against the members of a list of values.

Segment. In structured programming, a collection of related source program statements (usually 60 or fewer lines) that perform a part of a module's function. Program segments may be invoked using CALLs, PERFORMs, for example, or they may be included in source text using compiler functions such as COPY (in COBOL) and %INCLUDE (in PL/I).

Selection structure. See *Choice structure*.

Sensor-based computer. A computer designed and programmed to receive data (analog or digital) from transducers, sensors, and other data sources that monitor a physical process.

Separate compilation. Compiling pieces of a program apart from each other, generally at different times. These pieces are then bound (linked) together to form the final program.

Sequence structure.   A basic structured programming figure providing a means for expressing sequential functions or processes.

Sequential access.   An access mode in which logical records are obtained from, or placed into, a file in such a way that each successive access to the file refers to the next subsequent logical record in the file.

Serial search.   A search performed by sequentially comparing each entry in a table of values with the search argument.

Source statement.   A statement written in symbols of a programming language.

Source statement library.   A facility whereby groups of source statements are maintained so as to be easily included into programs and modified. COPY (in COBOL) and %INCLUDE (in PL/I) are used to access the statements.

Specifications.   The details of how a proposed system is to operate.

Stack.   A one-dimensional list data structure with additions and deletions possible only at one end. Generally, only the top item is immediately accessible. The last item added (pushed) is the first item removed (popped).

Stepwise refinement.   An iterative process whereby more details are gradually added until the complete logic of a program has been determined.

Structured programming.   (1) The designing, writing, and testing of a program made up of interdependent parts in a definite pattern of organization. (2) A method of programming according to a set of rules that enhances a program's readability and maintainability.

Structured walk-through.   A formalized review in which technical work is examined in detail by the developer's peers for the purpose of validating its accuracy and completeness.

Stub.   In top-down development, the code necessary for execution testing of higher level modules or segments. Stubs are typically short sections of code that, when invoked, display a message or generate data essential for testing higher level modules or segments.

Switch.   See *Indicator.*

System.   A collection of methods, programs, or techniques united by regulated interaction to form an organized whole.

Table argument.   One item in the list of values that is used in a search operation to compare with the search argument.

Table function.   The programming activity that takes place when the table argument matches the search argument.

Test data generator.   A program whose output is used as input data to test another program.

Testing.   The process of validating a piece of work by demonstrating that it meets its specifications.

Throw-away code.   Any code used during the process of developing a program that does not become part of the finished program.

Top-down design.   Defining the modules of a program and their relationship to each other by starting at the top and proceeding downward, creating a hierarchy chart; a part of top-down development.

Top-down development.   A method of program development, patterned after the natural approach to system design, in which programming originates at the highest level of control logic within the system and proceeds downward through respectively lower level modules. It includes top-down design and top-down implementation.

Top-down implementation.   That part of the top-down development process related to program coding and execution testing.

Type.   An attribute of a data item describing the kind and range of values it may hold. This attribute can generally be checked by the compiler only at run time (e.g., only integer values being assigned to a variable described as integer). Some languages allow programmers to define their own types.

Variable (ANS definition).   (1) A quantity that can assume any of a given set of values. (2) A data item whose value may be changed during execution of the object program.

Virtual storage.   Addressable space that appears to the user as real storage, from which instructions and data are mapped into real storage locations. The size of virtual storage is limited by the addressing scheme of the computing system (or virtual machine) and by the amount of auxiliary storage available, rather than by the actual number of real storage locations.

Volume.   A physical unit of data storage, such as a reel of tape or a disk pack.

Bibliography

Aron, J.D. *The Program Development Process, Part 1*. Addison-Wesley, 1974.

Ashcroft, E., and Z. Manna. "The Translation of GO TO programs to WHILE programs." *Proceedings of IFIP Congress* 1971, Vol I. Amsterdam, The Netherlands: North Holland Publishing Co., 1972, pp. 250–255.

Ashley, Ruth. *Advanced Structured Programming in COBOL*. John Wiley, 1985.

Baker, F.T. "Chief Programmer Team Management of Production Programming." *IBM Systems Journal*, Vol. II, No. 1, 1972, pp. 56–73. Reprinted as G320–5320.

———. "System Quality through Structured Programming." *Fall Joint Computer Conference*, Vol. 41, Part 1, 1972.

———., and H.D. Mills. "Chief Programmer Teams." *Datamation*, December 1973.

Barton, Doreen Schultz. "Quality Control and Systems Development Process." *Journal of Information Management*, Vol. 6, No. 1, Fall 1984, pp. 21–31.

Belford, Geneva G. *Pascal*. McGraw-Hill, Inc., 1984.

Blank, J., et al. *Software Engineering, Methods and Techniques*. John Wiley and Sons, 1983.

Böhm, Corrado, and Guiseppe Jacopini. "Flow Diagrams, Turing Machines, and Languages with Only Two Formation Rules." *Communications of Association for Computing Machinery*, Vol. 9, May 1966, pp. 366–371.

Bolsky, M.I., and P.G. Mathews. *The C Programmer's Handbook*. Prentice-Hall, Inc., 1984.

Booch, Grady. *Software Engineering with Ada*. Benjamin/Cummings Publishing Co., 1983.

Bowles, Kenneth. *Microcomputer Problem Solving using Pascal*. Springer-Verlag, 1977.

Brown, A.R., and W.A. Sampson. *Program Debugging*. MacDonald, 1973.

Campanizzi, J.A. "Structured Software Testing." *Quality Progress*, Vol. 17, No. 5, May 1984, pp. 14–15.

Constantine, L.L. *Concepts in Program Design*. Paragon Press, 1967.

Cooper, D.C. "Böhm and Jacopini's Reduction of Flow Charts." *Communications of Association for Computing Machinery*, Vol. 10, No. 8, August 1967, pp. 463–473.

Dahl, O.J., E.W. Dijkstra, and C.A.R. Hoare. *Structured Programming*. Academic Press, 1972.

Dijkstra, Edsger W. "A Constructive Approach to the Problem of Program Correctness." *BIT*, Vol. 8, No. 3, 1968, pp. 174–186.

―――. "Complexity Controlled by Hierarchical Ordering of Function and Variability." In *Software Engineering, NATO Science Committee Report*, eds. Peter Naur and Brian Randell, January 1969, pp. 181–185.

―――. "GO TO Statement Considered Harmful." *Communications of Association for Computing Machinery*, Vol. 11, No. 3, March 1968, pp. 147–148.

―――. *Notes on Structured Programming, T.H. Report 70–WSK–03.* Eindhoven, Netherlands: Technological University, 1970.

―――. "Structured Programming." In *Software Engineering Techniques, NATO Science Committee*, eds. J.N. Burton and B. Randell, 1969, pp. 88–94.

―――. "The Humble Programmer." *Communications of Association for Computing Machinery*, Vol. 15, No. 10, October 1972, pp. 859–866.

―――. "The Structure of 'THE'—Multiprogramming System." *Communications of Association for Computing Machinery*, Vol. 11, No. 5, May 1968.

Frank, Werner. "Structured vs. Prototyping Methodology." *Computerworld*, Vol. 17, No. 33, August 15, 1984, pp. 51–52.

Freedman, Daniel P., and Gerald M. Weinberg. *Handbook of Walkthroughs, Inspections and Technical Reviews.* Little, Brown and Co., 1982.

Frost, David. "Psychology and Program Design." *Datamation*, May 1975, p. 137.

Gane, Chris, and Trish Sarson. *Structured Systems Analysis: Tools and Techniques.* Prentice-Hall, Inc., 1979.

Garfunkel, Jerome. "In Defense of COBOL." *Computerworld*, Vol. 18, No. 24, June 11, 1984, pp. 19–26.

Gilbert, Philip. *Software Design and Development.* Science Research Associates, 1983.

Gillett, Will D., and Seymour V. Pollack. *An Introduction to Engineered Software.* Holt, Rinehart and Winston, 1982.

Grauer, Robert T. *Structured COBOL Programming.* Prentice-Hall, Inc., 1985.

Haney, F.M. "Module Connection Analysis." *Proceedings of the 1972 FJCC.* AFIPS Press, pp. 173–180.

Harbison, Samuel P., and Guy L. Steele. *C: A Reference Manual.* Prentice-Hall, Inc., 1984.

Higgins, David. *Designing Structured Programs.* Prentice-Hall, Inc., 1983.

"HIPO—A Design Aid and Documentation Technique." Form GC2O–1851, IBM.

Hoare, C.A.R. "Proof for a Program: FIND." *Communications of the Association for Computing Machinery*, Vol. 14, No. 1, January 1971, pp. 39–45.

Hughes, Joan K. *PL/I Structured Programming.* John Wiley & Sons, 3rd edition, 1986.

Improved Programming Technologies, Management Overview. Form GE19–5086, IBM.

An Introduction to Structured Programming in COBOL. Form GC2O–1776, IBM.

Jensen, Kathleen, and Niklaus Wirth. *Pascal User Manual and Report.* Springer-Verlag, 1985.

Johnson, Doug. "Development Tools Move into High Level Programming Environments." *Digital Design*, Vol. 13, No. 7, July 1983, pp. 90–92.

Johnson, S.C., and Dennis M. Ritchie. "Portability of C Programs and the UNIX System." *Bell System Technical Journal*, Vol. 57, No. 6, Part 2, July–August 1978.

Kernighan, Brian W., and P.J. Plaugher. *The Elements of Programming Style*. McGraw-Hill, 1974.

Kernighan, Brian W., and Dennis M. Ritchie. *The C Programming Language*. Prentice-Hall, Inc., 1978.

Knuth, Donald E. *The Art of Computer Programming, Volume 1: Fundamental Algorithms*. Addison-Wesley, 1968.

————. "A Review of 'Structured Programming'." *Stanford Computer Science Department Report STAN–CS–73–371*, Stanford University, June 1973, 25 pp.

————. "Structured Programming with **go to** Statements." *Computing Surveys*, Vol. 6, No. 4, December 1974, p. 292.

————, and R.W. Floyd. *Notes on Avoiding GO TO Statements*. Report No. SC–148, Computer Science Department, Stanford University, 1970.

Koffman, Elliot B. *Problem Solving and Structured Programming in Pascal*. Addison-Wesley, 1985.

Lattice 8086/8088: C Compiler Functional Description Manual. Lifeboat Associates, Version 2.04, 1984.

Lim, P.A. *A Guide to Structured COBOL*. Van Nostrand Reinhold, 1980.

Liskov, Barbara H. "A Design Methodology for Reliable Software Systems." *Proceedings of FJCC*, December 1972.

Maynard, J. *Modular Programming*. Auerbach, 1972.

McCracken, Daniel D. "Revolution in Programming." *Datamation*, December 1973.

McGowan, Clement L., III, and John R. Kelly. *Top-Down Structured Programming Techniques*. Petrocelli, 1975.

Metzger, P.W. *Managing a Programming Project*. Prentice-Hall, 1973.

Mills, Harlan D. "Chief Programmer Teams Principles and Procedures." IBM Federal Systems Division, June 1971.

————. *Mathematical Foundations for Structured Programming*. IBM, Form No. FSC 72–6012, February 1972.

————. "New Discipline Wins Programmer Approval." *THINK*, IBM Corp., March 1973.

————. "On the Psychology of Quality." *IBM Research*, March 1972.

————. "Top-Down Programming in Large Systems." In *Debugging Techniques in Large Systems*, ed. Randall Rustin, Courant Computer Science Symposium 1, NYU, 1971, pp. 41–45.

Morris, John M. "Structured Programming." *Pattern Analysis & Recognition Corp. Tech. Memo No. 73–20*; 1973, p. 2.

Myers, Glenford J. *Reliable Software Through Composite Design*. Petrocelli, 1975.

————. *Composite/Structured Design*. Van Nostrand Reinhold, 1978.

————. *The Art of Software Testing*. John Wiley and Sons, 1979.

Parnas, D.L. "On the Criteria to be Used in Decomposing Systems into Modules." *Communications of Association for Computing Machinery*, Vol. 5, No. 12, December 1972, pp. 1053–1058.

————. "A Technique for Software Module Specifications with Examples." *Communications of Association for Computing Machinery*, Vol. 14, No. 5, May 1972, pp. 330–336.

Parukh, Girish. *How to Measure Programmer Productivity*. Hayden Publishing Co., 1981.

Perry, William E. *A Structured Approach to Systems Testing*. Prentice-Hall, Inc., 1983.

Pressman, Roger S. *Software Engineering: A Practitioner's Approach*. McGraw-Hill, 1981.

Proceedings of the International Conference on Reliable Software, IEEE Cat. No. 75, CHO 940–7CSR, Los Angeles, 1975.

Purdum, Jack J., Timothy C. Leslie, and Alan L. Stegemoller. *C Programmer's Library*. Que Corp., 1984.

Rajaraman, M.K. "Structured Techniques for Software Development." *Journal of Systems Management*, Vol. 34, No. 3, March 1983, pp. 36–39.

Rajlich, Vaclav. "Stepwise Refinement Revisited." *Journal of Systems & Software*, Vol. 5, No. 1, February 1985, pp. 81–88.

Rapps, Sandra, and Elaine J. Weyuker. "Selecting Software Test Data using Data Flow Information." *IEEE Transactions Software Engineering*, April 1985, pp. 367–375.

Rice, J.R. "GO TO Statement Reconsidered." *Communications of Association for Computing Machinery*, Vol. 11, No. 8, Aug. 1968, p. 538.

Richardson, Gary L., Charles W. Butler, and John D. Tomlinson. *A Primer on Structured Program Design*. Petrocelli Books, Inc., 1980.

Springer, Allen. *A Comparison of Language C and Pascal*. Technical Report, IBM Cambridge Scientific Center, Form G320–2128, August 1979.

Stevens, Wayne P. *Using Structured Design*. John Wiley and Sons, 1981.

————. "How Data Flow Can Improve Application Development Productivity." *IBM Systems Journal*, Vol. 21, No. 2, 1982, pp. 162–178.

Stevens, W.P., G.J. Myers, and L.L. Constantine. "Structured Design." *IBM Systems Journal*, Vol. 13, No. 2, 1974.

Stevenson, Henry P., ed. *Proceedings of a Symposium on Structured Programming in COBOL*, Los Angeles, ACM, 1975.

Stewart, S.L., ed. *Concept in Quality Software Design*. U.S. Dept. of Commerce, NBS–TN–842, August 1974.

Thomson, Jeff. "Don't Blame Structured Programming." *Computerworld*, Vol. 18, No. 22, May 28, 1984, p. 39.

Turbo Pascal Version 3 Reference Manual. Borland International, 1985.

Van Duyn, J. *DP Professional's Guide to Writing Effective Technical Documentation*. John Wiley and Sons, 1982.

Van Tassel, D. *Program Style, Design, Efficiency, Debugging, and Testing*. Prentice-Hall, 1974.

Waite, Mitchell, et al. *C Primer Plus*. Howard W. Sams & Co., 1984.

Weinberg, Gerald M. "Primer on Programming." *THINK*, October/November 1974.

————. *The Psychology of Computer Programming*. Van Nostrand Reinhold Company, 1971.

Wirth, Niklaus. "The Programming Language Pascal." *Acta Informatica*, Vol. 1, 1971, pp. 35–63.

————. "Program Development by Stepwise Refinement." *Communications of Association for Computing Machinery*, Vol. 14, No. 4, April 1971, pp. 221–227.

————. *Systematic Programming: An Introduction*. Prentice-Hall, 1973.

————. *Algorithms + Data Structures = Programs*. Prentice-Hall, Inc., 1976.

Wolberg, John R. *Conversion of Computer Software*. Prentice-Hall, Inc., 1983.

Wulf, W.A. "A Case against the GOTO." *Proceedings of the ACM Annual Conference*, Boston, August 1972, pp. 791–797. Association for Computing Machinery, 1972.

Yourdon, Edward. *Techniques of Program Structure and Design*. Prentice-Hall, 1975.

―――, and Larry L. Constantine. *Structured Design*. Prentice-Hall, 1979.

Index

Abbreviation:
  COBOL, 209
  PL/I, 167
Abstraction, 27, 44
Acceptance phase, 120–21, 140
Air pollution case study, 92–108
ALTER, 202
AND in COBOL, 189–90
ANSI Standard (C), 260, 262
Argument, 24, 35
  in SEARCH, 160, 200
  matrix, 137–38
Armstrong, Russel M., 202
Array:
  in C, 281
  in Pascal, 237

B

Bank inquiry program, 27–36, 47–51
BEGIN block, 165, 166, 229, 231
Billing application:
  in COBOL, 177–79
  in PL/I, 146
Binary search:
  in COBOL, 201

  in PL/I, 162–63
Binding, 22–23
Black box, 21
  testing, 133–35, 138, 143
Bohm, Corrado, 63
Bottom-up approach, 5–7, 13, 59

C

C, 260–302
  blocks, 264–66
  data structures, 281–82
  iteration structure, 270
  modularity, 261–64
  programming considerations, 283–86
  structured programming, 266–71
Calculator example:
  in C, 290–301
  in Pascal, 247–58
CALL:
  in COBOL, 187
  by name, 25
  in PL/I, 145
  by reference, 25, 224
  by value, 25, 224, 284
Canning, Richard G., 36